When Eagles Dared

A Whimsical Account from the terraces behind Board 51 (and lurking at tracks elsewhere) of a Triumphant Eastbourne Speedway season with ultimate success missed by a merest Cat's Whisker that features those handlebar heroes: Nicki, Floppy, Mooro, Deano, Watty, Shieldsy plus bosses, Cooky and Geery, and a vital yet innumerable cast of others – the whole experience crowned with the unique aural accompaniment of MC KC, oh, and not forgetting our own inimitable "Arena track specialist" Mr Steen Jensen... but sadly missing a chat with the Dugard's

Jeff Scott

methanol
press

First published in Great Britain by
Methanol Press
2 Tidy Street Brighton East Sussex BN1 4EL

For a complete catalogue of current and forthcoming publications please write to the address above, or visit our website at
www.methanolpress.com

ISBN 0-9553103-1-8
ISBN 978-0-9553103-1-7

A catalogue for this book is available from the British Library

(Long suffering) Editor: Michael Payne
Word Wrangler: Graham Russel
Proof Reader: Caroline Tidmarsh
Design: Rachael Adams <www.scrutineer.co.uk>
Photographs Edited by: Rachael Adams

Cover Design: Rachael Adams
Cover Photograph: Steve Dixon
Back Cover Photograph: Julie Martin

UK Distributor:
Central Books
99 Wallis Road London E9 5LN
020 8986 4854
www.centralbooks.com

Contents

"Ever been tattooed? It takes a whim of iron"
Michael Donaghy

To Luther Ivan

Preface

This book came was conceived and written as a companion to my book *Showered in Shale*. My editor, Michael Payne, realised halfway through *SiS* that I had gone totally bonkers and had begun to write a gargantuan account of all the meetings that I'd attended in 2005, not just the ones necessary to achieve the original book's goal. He sensibly observed that no one would ever want to read a speedway book more than 728 pages long, and one that long would be too difficult to bind anyway. He sought the comfort and counsel of despair, but wisely reasoned that since he couldn't stop me scribbling away like a madman and he had failed to change my more-is-more writing style that so irks him, he suggested that I write this book, *When Eagles Dared*.

Since 1975 I have been by background and inclination a Reading Racers fan and still go very frequently to Smallmead. But I have lived in Brighton for many years and so Eastbourne is now my LOCAL club and I now follow them as well as feel truly at home and welcome there. The racing is consistently good to exciting, the atmosphere is special, and there's a traditional craftsmanship practised there – I'm thinking in particular of Bob perpetually whirling round on his tractor. Eastbourne also has a genuine sense of community that can't be easily faked, although, so I'm told, like in every community, things could in the dim and distant past sometimes get a little wild or even tasty. It's best to speak about things as you find them, so I must say that this is something that I haven't personally encountered. The Eagles promoter and co-team manager, Jon Cook, has been supportive of my writing right from the outset. This made a book on the Eagles only logical and, in its own way, is also a general tribute to what it's like for any fan to follow their own particular sports club, whether it's a speedway team or from any other sport. As fans we're perpetually caught on the outside of what really happens in our club. We glean our information from what we read in the press, the programme and look at, if we dare, on the Internet. And there's what we hear on the terraces, in the bar and on the radio. We don't have the inside scoop and have to make presumptions, often incorrect ones, about motives and actions as well as relying on a rich seam of half-truths, rumours, and innuendo.

So, in a sense, this account of the 2005 season could actually be about the experience of supporting any speedway club or could cover any season. There's a mix of blind optimism, despair, only seeing what you want to see, complaints and mickey taking. Luckily I was frequently able to follow the Eagles on my own personal odyssey round the country as a fan, albeit not as much as I could have in the context of my other research and travel commitments for *Showered in Shale*. It was a season that had everything from fantastic racing, falls, injuries, fights, routine races, controversy, laughter, despair, weird decisions, tantrums, along with a rich tapestry of speedway people on and off the terraces and, of course, a dinner dance. Remembering the season here was quite a blast, and that's even without the luxurious and warm aural waters that the skilful Kevin 'KC' Coombes bathes you in from the tannoy.

The format of the book follows each month of the season in turn and provides an account of each meeting throughout the season. There were an impressive number of Eagles fixtures, arguably more than any other speedway club raced in any British league during 2005 (though I stand to be corrected). Many of these fixtures I attended. And like all fans, I inevitably missed some others, but these are still covered through my own research and by the comments I gleaned from those who attended.

It goes without saying that this book is intended as entertainment and, inevitably, must have observations you will disagree with. My intention has been to present my own impressionistic account of the season as I saw and remembered it, or heard about it afterwards. Like many fans, I not only appreciate the skill and bravery of the riders, but they also have my undying admiration for the matter-of-fact manner in which they put their lives on the line every week and every time they race. At the end of the day, this is just to earn a living and to provide our weekly speedway entertainment – they truly are, as KC invariably describes them at some point in the season, "handlebar heroes". I'm not fortunate enough to know any of the riders personally and, therefore, can only write what I see, what I heard, what was reported and what others surmise in person and in the press. Necessarily this is incomplete and partial; hopefully, you will still enjoy it.

I have retained the tendency to commit errors that everyone who has read or reviewed *Showered in Shale* has often kindly pointed out to me and, of course, I have chosen to continue with the poor resolution of the very small photos. That is my editorial decision. They are there "to be illustrative and break up the text" and not to win photographic prizes or hang in a gallery. Though I still think that remains a future possibility. Anyway, I like them and think they definitely capture certain moments about the ethos and atmosphere of a speedway meeting or a speedway season.

I hope that you enjoy this chance to dare like the Eagles team and dream like speedway fans everywhere!

2nd October 2006
Brighton

KEVIN COOMBES

"If it carries on like this all season we're going to have to issue everyone with tablets – for the heart, to stop it pumping!"

16th March

Steen Jensen and Adam Allott log some impressive laps at the Eagles press and practice day and so will share the No. 7 position at the opening Air Tek clashes of the season with Arena Essex. Since Steen will double up from the Premier League with the Isle of Wight, it's widely put around that his latent talent will quickly develop enough to take him to heat-leader status and that his Elite League average will slowly build along with his confidence. As ever, Ronnie Russell only has eyes on the "big one", the SkyBet Elite League curtain raiser against Poole on the telly.

Without Nicki riding for the Eagles, the Hammers lived up to their nickname. Floppy threw off the mental and physical shackles of last season's injury with four wins in a six ride 15-point return. Deano ruled out any Easter eggs from Thurrock with some skilful blocking manoeuvres, while Roman Povazhny battled and tangled with Deano in heat 6, only to then receive an injury that forced his withdrawal after he clashed with Mooro two heats later. Steen improved as the meeting progressed and gained a couple of thirds.

16th March Arena v. Eastbourne (AT Challenge) 53–37

19th March

Jon Cook remains upbeat about what could be gained from the challenge matches with Arena. He's keen that the team has an early opportunity to "look at ourselves" ahead of the "challenges that await in this very exciting season". Ronnie just hopes all of his riders exhibit better directional sense and actually find Arlington. This is after Roman Povazhny and Piotr Swist had to be rescued from Brixton via a *Tesco Express* near the Lakeside shopping centre, when they became lost as they vainly searched for their race suits in Purfleet.

With Nicki Pedersen back again, the result is never in doubt though the meeting is marred by an innocuous fall that causes a horrendous injury to Mark Loram[1].

Later on Sky they capture the true extent of the damage sustained by Mark when they say "you try dropping an engine on your hand from a few feet and see what damage you'll do". Ouch! The Deano–Shieldsy partnership looks strong, but Adam Allott fails to sparkle during a routine victory. He gains his only point in a three rider race forced onto Arena who manage to finish with only four fit riders.

19th March Eastbourne v Arena (Air Tek Challenge) 57–36

25th March

Though the score remained close at the end, this was a surprisingly comfortable home win for the Pirates. Deano was the centre of attention in the pits as he struggled with flu and also out on the track in heat 12, when Matej Ferjan collided with him on the first lap. The ferocity of the crash was so spectacular that Ferjan was adjudged to have had a miraculous escape and emerged largely unscathed though badly bruised. His bike was less fortunate. It was catapulted impressively over the safety fence in a manner that would have won

---

[1] Postscript to this incident – It was insinuated in some quarters that the Loram injury was caused by the red stop lights being applied whilst the riders were in the first bend, after an "unsatisfactory start" due to the referee detecting movement at the tapes. For a while it was mooted by the BSPA and SCB that to prevent a similar occurrence, the red lights would only be permitted to be displayed once the riders were on the back straight. There were two school of thoughts with this practice that prevented its incorporation, (i) the riders would actually be going faster when the lights were to be displayed and pulling up suddenly could lead to worst pile ups. And, more poignantly (ii) the supporters' backlash reaction at having racing restarted for starting infringements, after the riders were virtually in the third bend and almost established in their race positions. Imagine the ill feeling that would be generated when a team apparently gates for a 5–1 only to be brought back for a "roller", with the first notification being on the third or fourth bend! In jurisprudence, they say "laws made in haste in response to recent events make bad laws" – the same definitely applies to speedway and, arguably, many of the revolutionary ideas that have come out of the BSPA winter conference over the past few years!

high marks even from a hardhearted Soviet ice-skating judge. Floppy again looked impressive in support of Nicki and Davey Watt was a considerable threat at reserve. Less effective was Adam Allott who failed to trouble the scorer.

25th March Poole v. Eastbourne (ELA) 50–44

Plundered by Pirates

25th March

Hope springs eternal they say and what better way to get my speedway season underway than with a derby clash with south coast rivals the Poole Pirates. They are the reigning champions no less, again actually, and they have already established bragging rights by beating us at Poole earlier in the day across at Wimborne Road, but for keen Eagles fans there's nothing better than to join a huge queue outside your home track so that it almost seems like the good old days. In fact, the fine but cold evening with its beautiful full moon has drawn all the usual speedway suspects along with their families who appear about to enjoy an evening of racing.

It's a good mix of generations with steadfast senior citizens who mingle with their children, now grown up, and their children's children. It's almost idyllic. Well, the countryside that surrounds the Arlington Stadium is as bucolic as ever with its appealing mix of narrow country lanes, peculiar village names, rolling hills, country pubs and, the way I come, an unmanned railway crossing which is always a test of your nerve. It would be a completely unspoilt almost chocolate-box type scene, but for the great number of cars that now make their way to the large expanse of land that serves as a giant car park in front of the Arlington Stadium home-straight stand. The only sound that punctures the silence in this part of the country is the regular Saturday night roar of speedway bikes, and on quite a few other nights a week, stock cars smashing and grinding into each other.

Not that anyone who's lived in the area for any length of time would be surprised at this level of noise during the extended evenings of the summer months, since there's been speedway here since 1929. In fact, it's been a family-owned business as I understand it and throughout its history has been in the capable hands of the Dugard family. Responsibility has passed, rested or lain with Charlie, Bob and Martin in a variety of capacities over the years. Martin followed in his father's tyre tracks and was the star rider here for years and is still my all-time Number 1 Eastbourne rider, although as a fan you always reserve the right to be extremely fickle. Bob deserves his legendary status both for his speedway career itself as a rider and promoter and now for his track-preparation skills, among other things, the most visible of which is his love of driving round on his tractor on race nights. Something he does with great panache, aplomb and creativity.

According to friends not so close by, the noise from the track has recently become more of an issue and has been upsetting the local horses. I sense some exaggeration here but noise is a continuing problem in many parts of the country. You get plenty of chance to see the horses trotting along the lanes during many evenings throughout the season ridden by young women in jodhpurs and very shiny hair. It's fun to slow down to pass them but simultaneously rebelliously dream of getting some silly car stickers printed that advise 'I beep my horn at horses'. Just to even up, you understand, the stickers that continually nag you about road etiquette around horses that you see in the back windows of Land Rovers and other solely city-driven off-road vehicles in Waitrose car parks throughout the country. The horses housed in their stables haven't so much been upset by the sound of the bikes, but instead by the weekly end-of-meeting firework display and the club's loud bass public address speakers. These speakers appeared to be one of the few visible innovations brought to the club by the arrival of Terry Russell in his role as the owner of Eastbourne's speedway licence. Everyone appreciated the upgrade to the speaker system so that you could more easily hear the times and scores as well as be able to listen to thoughts, whimsical observations and the rider interviews conducted by our very own man with the mike, Kevin 'KC' Coombes.

Kevin is someone who has always fascinated me at Eastbourne, partly because of his relentless bonhomie, partly because of the wonderfully professional but slightly wedding disco attitude and feel he brings to his work, but mostly because of the things he says. Don't get me wrong he is one of the most mellifluous exponents of his 'craft' in the country. But, nonetheless, I can't make out whether these are insightful, naff or simply tow the party line, but I suspect that he has a gift for the work and is really just an enthusiast for all things speedway in general and Eagles in particular. Albeit one who's lucky enough to verbally shine at each meeting's proceedings throughout the season. He has considerable charm, though a notch less than he affects to project through his 'public persona', but one that nonetheless comes through in his choice of phrases and his facility to gamely chunter on irrespective of the circumstances. A less welcome innovation than that of Kevin becoming more audible, however, is the new fee of £1 to park your car outside the stadium. It's a change that you can't help but resent every week when you come through the gates, especially as it was always 'free' for so many years. Still, the also charge users on stock car nights, so it is equitable in that sense.

Still, while the council have been zealous in their pursuit of noise complaints they've had no jurisdiction over car-parking charges, which given the fiasco of the Brighton parking situation, is perhaps a small mercy. Inside the stadium the council safety officer has obviously also paid regular visits, along with the colleague who holds the noise meter, since the gap between where the crowd stand on the concrete stock car track and the safety fence has increased, to four metres, or approximately five yards in old money, which Jon Cook informs us in the programme is called a "safety zone". There's also "catch fencing protecting the track equipment" which I fail to spot or quite understand, although I appreciate it's all part of the council's ongoing Health and Safety campaign to wrap the crowd in cotton wool. Though that said, we can all recall the horrifying crash that Floppy had live on television, when he was flung over the fence and came to rest against the grader that was then parked outside the safety fence on the third bend. Other than to recall that 'the runaway train came down the track and she blew' and to doubt that either of the tractor maestros Bob Dugard and Roy Prodger would ever lose control of their machines, you can't help but be vaguely reassured. Though, come to think of it, it's maybe to protect the crowd against those rogue bikes loosed from the hands of even wilder speedway riders that's really at issue.

On the subject of speedway as a family sport, because I am a season-ticket holder, therefore I can join a shorter queue specifically reserved for people like me and thereby evade the sometimes massive queues. Often there are other fans too busy and important to queue, or wait a few extra minutes to enter, who cheekily ignore the small signs that demarcate the various entrances to the stadium and also join us in our privileged queue. Speedway folk, you like to think, aren't the sorts to wilfully disobey rules, except the riders of course, who are allowed to do whatever pride and cunning will allow. Well, that is if they're your team's riders, and if not, they're cheating bastards and you'll take the chance to point this out to them loudly. Manning the turnstile, or personing it as no doubt the council will soon advise, is Roy Prodger's brother who carefully scrutinises my season ticket. "That's either an old photo or you've aged dramatically over the winter," he says cheerily, as he points out the complete lack of grey hairs in my photo on the season ticket. Although going to the speedway should already signal that I was old before my time, I decide not to pretend that it's really innovative but fashionable use of grey hair dye in order to add gravitas to my appearance.

As a season-ticket holder, another privilege is that you receive a programme as you enter, and so do not have to briefly queue again just inside. It's one of those negligible time savings that you only notice when you're deprived of it, though today I appreciate this 'service', particularly given the size of this evening's line of expectant punters. Interestingly if, as a season-ticket holder you join the 'paying customers' queue, you don't get the free programme. Well, only reluctantly. This has trained me to strictly adhere to the demarcations. The crowds inside are such that it's impossible to see the new season's merchandise laid out on tables at the track shop. There does appear to be quite a bit of pent-up demand from a few children for Nicki Pedersen badges which, I gather when I overhear them chatter, they hope will be priced at 50p only to be told, "nah, they're a pound". Lots of these small transactions would build a huge track-shop business, but smaller numbers of mostly very reasonably priced items form the essential business model of the speedway memorabilia and paraphernalia market. Later, Kevin Coombes, whom I will try to refer to from this point on as KC (for ease of typing if not reading), breathlessly informs us over the tannoy that the item that possibly would fly off the shelves (well tables actually) the new season's Eagles replica shirts, are sadly unavailable and therefore not for sale at the track shop "for the next few weeks". Who but a business visionary could have foreseen that people would want to buy such must-have items as their club's new coloured replica shirts at the start of the season anyway?

We subsequently learn that it's an even bigger missed opportunity since this evening the Arlington stadium boasts the "biggest crowd we've seen here in a while", according to KC, when he convolutedly extends a "warm welcome to our country cousins-in-speed from Poole", many of whom are incredibly already attired in this season's new version replica Pirates shirts. I've noticed that we always accuse or suspect that the Poole fans enjoy inappropriate relationships with their close family members and may not be the sharpest knives in

the drawer. However, they seem to feel the same about the Eastbourne fans, which we affect to be ignorant of or laugh off as another telling sign of their mono-browed outlook. But, there's been no denying that over recent years they've consistently, but only metaphorically, had our trousers round our ankles and they have proceeded to give us a good smacking, while they win practically every available trophy in sight. They've also been pretty nifty around Arlington. Which is a level of success that you just have to admire or, alternatively, begrudge, as much as your current mood will let you.

As I mentioned earlier, tonight, under the brightening full moon, hope springs eternal and Jon Cook wildly predicts nothing more specific in the programme than Eastbourne will have a "top four finish this year that will be the envy of the rest of the League". We don't really go big here on covetousness, but it's claimed that the "new-look Eastbourne Eagles suits" will attract admiring glances as well, though sadly not yet when worn on the supporters' backs. Great prominence is to be given to the team sponsor's name, the ever-loyal South Coast Vehicle Hire, on the brightly coloured blue and yellow race suit. In fact, as the riders circle round on their bikes prior to the parade in the new "safety zone", you can see that their suits and bikes are festooned with sponsors' logos. These include the award-winning programme printers Fineprint, which Jon Cook always and sincerely name checks at every opportunity as the "best in speedway" and, "in their third year of sponsorship"[1], according to an apparently chuffed KC, are Kent Sweepers. As the fans chat to the riders in the pits, watch them on parade, or glimpse them as they ride slowly by in the "safety zone" prior to the introductory parade, is the best chance they really have to study these sponsors' logos in their full glory. The rest of the time, the riders and the sponsors' logos roar past at great speed in a blur of movement that makes close reading impossible. Still, they'll look good on the telly as intended when Sky Sports features the Eagles, as they contractually must, during the season ahead.

Sadly for Eastbourne they're not on the telly nor do they really raise their performance for the first home local derby meeting of the season. The end of March is very early for Eagles to leave their nests and to be racing competitively in the league but then, from a revenue perspective, the Bank Holiday provides a good opportunity to maximise early season attendance figures and thereby provide some immediate cash flow. Which, judged by the numbers here, there's no doubt tonight really helped to swell the coffers and the relative closeness of the meeting, albeit a defeat, should keep the crowd keen to come back again for more on a regular basis. Personally I think that English crowds most want to watch a winning team but with the continued added tension of the possibility of defeat to maintain interest and concentration. I definitely want to watch close meetings on a regular basis even more than thrashings, especially if our lot finally triumph. To be fair, Eastbourne would have won this meeting, but for the withdrawal of Dean Barker after one race, when he finishes in last place. He had decided to trojan on for the good of the team but is overcome with illness almost immediately. Deano has had the flu. Dr KC reports this to the crowd in the manner of someone who has to pass on news of an unexpected family bereavement and he makes the concept "under the weather" sound terminal. In fact, it does hamper the team's chances of victory when Deano fails to ride in heat 5. This episode raises questions about his self-diagnostic abilities, if not

[1] After the season ends, we all take pride in the fact that OUR programme wins the coveted 'Best Programme of the Year' award in the *Speedway Star*.

his commitment, and Jon Cook's faith in his determination, which on balance is probably a good early sign of confidence in the team and of its spirit.

The meeting rushes by quickly. Not only is it my first meeting of the season, but tonight's official is Frank 'Lightning' Ebdon. Notorious for running the meetings he works super fast, in marked contrast to last week's challenge meeting which, by all reports, was unfortunately held up by Mark Loram's innocuous-looking crash that actually resulted in a severe hand injury. As it turns out, the Eagles keep the score close throughout and the fixture generates quite a bit of interest through the appearance of many of Poole's so-called (and maybe actual) glamour riders. There's the vastly underestimated Bjarne Pedersen and the often over-rated Antonio Lindback. Well, that's unfair, he's still exceptionally young and gifted for his age group (19 until May) and extremely attractive to sponsors with his dashing looks. Understandably, he seems quite enamoured with his own good looks. Consequently, he's always lionised in the *Speedway Star* and even the national press as a future world champion. The story of his adoption from Brazil by his devoted Swedish parents runs this trope a close second as a frequently used journalistic article topic. He's still a bit wild and inconsistent, often brilliant, but can sometimes gate poorly, look nervy and not make up the ground. No doubt, he will overcome this with experience that he'll gain in the many years ahead. His even younger teammate, Edward Kennett, provides an interesting comparison between speedway's future fortunes in Sweden and England. Lindback rides in all the major leagues (Poland, Sweden and England) plus the GP series, whereas Kennett, from a rich riding pedigree and also gifted with talent, rides full time for Rye House in the Premier League and part time in the Elite League for Poole. This is an exceptional achievement by any standard but compares less well in contrast with the stage of development that Lindback has already reached.

They're both good enough to be roundly booed by the partisan home support every time they come out on the track. Mostly this is for the threat of their skills, so it's a compliment, but in Kennett's case it's his departure to local rivals Poole after he started to ride as a small child at Eastbourne, which is made all the more visible because of his long-standing family connections via his talismanic uncle Gordon Kennett with the club. At least the Eagles retain his contract, if not his services this season. Edward rides well in his opening ride and, later on, partners Lindback to another vital 5-1 heat victory in the penultimate race of the evening, to put Poole in an unassailable position in the match. The Pirates are helped considerably by the unfortunate Adam Shields who falls on the pits bend of the third lap, while he chases for the lead. With the chance of a home victory gone, KC remains in a philosophical mood as he notes, "that's speedway for you!" As well as a victory on the night, it's also an overall victory on aggregate that gains Poole five early but valuable Elite League points to the Eagles zero over the day. A great start to their campaign to try for a hat trick of League championship wins. Plus an away victory over your close local rivals easily gained without even having to win the last heat decider.

Nicki Pedersen and David Norris restore some hint of respectability to the score line when Poole have the luxury to rest Sullivan but, whichever way you look at it as a home fan, it's a disappointing result and bodes poorly for our season ahead. There has been some good riding on display, though, with some excellent passing by Adam Shields against Krzysztof Kasprzak as well as tactical savvy by David Norris when skillfully holds up the Poole pairing, in true Dugard fashion, to allow Nicki Pedersen escape in heat 13. The prophets of doom that surround me tonight at the trackside are quick to excitedly claim, "our season is already over". It's a perspective, which, like the first cuckoo of spring, you hear earlier and earlier each year. The riders are castigated roundly and evenly with Deano judged "too old, ill but still past it when well", while Adam Allott is already deemed "out of his depth". Andrew Moore rates as "out of touch", which ignores the fact that it's one of his first meetings since he has returned from a severe leg break sustained at the end of last season. A particular frustration for both Andrew (he's most definitely not an 'Andy') and the fans since he'd just really started to fly round Arlington though, if his confidence returns, it should resume once more. The home riders of the night are Nicki Pedersen and, also on his return from injury after a brilliant campaign last season, David Norris. Two swallows don't make a summer though, and the large home crowd serenades itself with some spontaneous early season moans as it troops out of the stadium towards the car park.

25th March Eastbourne v. Poole (ELA) 44-46

30th March
Not exactly a happy hunting ground for the Eagles in the past, rain caused this fixture to be abandoned, but not before the team had assembled in the pits at the East of England Showground. So with this cancellation honours remained even for once after a trip to the Showground, albeit with much gnashing of teeth for all concerned before the Eagles riders' headed back down the A1.

30th March Peterborough v. Eastbourne – postponed: rain

April

JON COOK

"There's garbage on the Internet, I can't be bothered to reply"

The Toys Leave PK's Pram or How not to Park a Bike

2nd April

I arrive slightly late at Arlington for the Elite League 'A' fixture clash with Peterborough. A beautiful red sun hangs low in the clear sky, as I negotiate the quiet and, for once, horse-free country lanes that lead to the stadium. The only notable feature of the journey along the A27 from Brighton were the fleets of stretch limousines that I imagined were headed to the bright lights of the seaside, even as I left them. I can't recall seeing any limos in Brighton before, never mind four of them, but then I'm not often down by the weekend seafront bars and nightclubs so I usually miss the hen parties and riotous girls' nights out that journey from all parts of rural East Sussex to disport themselves in the fleshpots of my city. In fact, I myself am off to the country for a Saturday night of speedway spent with fellow Eagles fans, which is the sign of either great sadness or great sense, one that depends upon the likelihood of my being invited along with the girls anyway, or, for that matter, how well I could easily fit into a strenuous evening of alcopop consumption, smoking, and dirty laughs. Though I'm sure that this would present no difficulties of adjustment for the Eastbourne rider closest to my age, Dean 'Deano' Barker who would be just as comfortable on the town as he will be in the pits or on the track tonight.

Inside an undebauched Arlington, my usual spot has already sadly gone, but nonetheless I'm just in time as announcer Kevin 'KC' Coombes is, unsurprisingly, confirmed as "our host for the night". I love the rather old-fashioned description of his role which conjures up images of KC as some sort of glorified Butlins Red Coat or an avuncular cruise ship entertainments officer who remains robustly energetic throughout a long voyage. He straightaway thrills us, from his first words into the microphone, with the news that it's Nicki Pedersen's 28th birthday today. Where the cake and candles are located remains a mystery, though KC wittily notes, "some people go for a meal or have a party but not Nicki – he rides a 500 cc bike with no brakes!" Instead of this adrenalin rush we're all advised to "give ourselves a pat on the back", in a kind of group hug, for last week when we were part of the largest crowd seen at Arlington since the 1992 Bank Holiday meeting also with Poole. There's evidently fewer of us around tonight to congratulate ourselves, but KC is probably correct in his assumption that we were all devoted enough to have been along at that meeting too.

Jon Cook in his programme notes cannot explain the reasons for Deano's rapidly debilitating flu. He also provides an insight into the details of Edward Kennett's loan to Poole, which bit Eastbourne in the bottom last week, and which is so convoluted that it could be made into a long-running series or a book in itself.

Heat 1 begins with Andrew Moore, who lucklessly ended last season with bad injuries, and now gets the opportunity to improve his race fitness and try to recover the sort of form and triumphs that previously excited the Arlington faithful. He gets a vote of confidence from Jon Cook in his programme notes that would be dreaded if this were football. But as it's speedway we gather Jon can indeed simultaneously have an "obvious concern" about Andrew's riding while he sincerely offers "our full support". Sadly, as gating isn't Andrew's strong suit on the best of days, he doesn't manage to get anywhere close to the experienced Peter Karlsson who skilfully uses his elbow to exaggerated and exemplary effect, as he cuts across David 'Floppy' Norris in the first turn. This upsets Floppy's always finely calibrated equilibrium so much that as the race ends he pointedly gestures to the referee, Phil Griffin, in his box that overlooks the track that he should make an emergency appointment at the opticians without delay.

Heat 2 sees Davey Watt win easily and indulge in a wild lap of celebration. Bob Dugard celebrates in his own way with over ten laps of grading the track on his tractor. The results of this work are immediately difficult to gauge as an unsatisfactory start has Adam Shields clip the fast-gating Ales Dryml's back wheel to send himself careering into the air fence with some velocity. The woman to my left, Jane, screams in anxiety but, apart from a while on the floor to check his vision and "getting his breath back" according to KC, Shields appears well enough to participate in the re-run of the race. KC uses the time to make a few announcements that typify the sort of crowd that speedway attracts. First there are some congratulations for Frank Quinnell who's has his 80th birthday and celebrates with a visit to the track as his birthday treat. It's going to be a big year for him too, since he will reach his 50th wedding anniversary later in the summer with his wife Morag. We also hear about Liam, who has made his first trip to the speedway this season to celebrate his 12th birthday with his dad and granddad.

Eventually the race is re-run and Shields is loudly applauded as he glides back to the start gate, with considerable quantities of dirt on the back of his kevlars and his right leg, a compliment for the dirt that remains on the track air fence or hangs as a light cloud of dust in the evening air. He wins a consolation point after Dryml suffers an engine failure while the Peterborough guest, the ebullient Billy Janniro, celebrates his win with the longest wheelie of the night so far, down the length of the straight. Heat 4 sees a surprise victory for Watt, who is urged on by Jane who repeats her screech of "go on Davey, go on Davey". With only three other races to choose from so far, KC declares it "the race of the night" before he sagely identifies that "he's got a bit more speed on him this year". The next race sees a superb example of team riding for two laps from Deano and Shieldsy, which is only spoilt by the fact that they're actually a long way behind the Peterborough riders, so they should, just maybe, really think about chasing them down. As they belatedly wake up to the need to urgently make up lost ground, they indulge in a superbly choreographed example of repeatedly getting in each other's way that contrasts with their earlier smooth exhibition of controlled riding, albeit at the back of the race. Joonas Kylmakorpi can't quite reach the celebration wheelie standards set by Janniro, but he wants to emphasise the emphatic nature of his victory to the Eastbourne crowd, especially since the Eagles had to let him go during the close season due, most likely but you can never be sure, to the iniquitous logic of the Elite League points limit dictated by team averages.

KC interviews Davey, an encounter where enthusiastic Queen's English meets lilting but reticent Aussie, and in the process manages to tease out from him the world exclusive information that "I'm riding well so far this season"[1]. Shocked by these revelations the starting gate mechanism decides to go on the fritz before heat 6. This gives us the chance to watch Eastbourne's legendary Start Marshal, Alan Rolfe, in his calm problem-solving mode, which contrasts sharply with his usual calm, pantomime crossed with Marcel Marceau style of gestural management of the riders when they line up at the start line. I'm always fascinated by Alan's elegant but distinctively pleading but instructional arm gestures or those frequent tape touching and tapping motions that silently communicate with the crowded, noisy start line. In coordination with the referee, the tapes are repeatedly tested to see if they will operate smoothly again, a total of 15 times before they finally stop only going up at one side. The speedway obsession with numbers trains you to note every activity numerically. The tapes test takes place each time after Alan has tinkered further. This involves Alan either spraying lubricant down the start poles (usually enough for it to waft back towards the crowd like dust), check the electrical box, talk at length on the trackside phone, or painstakingly study the metal start mechanism as if about to paint it as a still life. Oiling the start poles appears the favoured solution.

Meanwhile nothing bypasses KC who notes, "there's nothing worse than sticky gates" before he dons his metaphorical doctor's white coat for a lengthy run down on Deano's continuing flu ailment. In the light of his reputation on the terraces, Deano would definitely not be the first man you'd automatically associate with the ingestion of the "herbal remedies" cure that KC painstakingly outlines. But, given the stringent regulations in the SCB rulebook about the use of stimulants within the sport, other than a reviving can of Red Bull, homeopathy is the only solution other than to let nature take its course. As he desperately thumbs through his pre-meeting notes and mentally riffles through his bank of tried and tested phrases to try to meaningfully fill the delay, KC then revisits the current availability crisis that still has no replica shirts in the track shop. Sadly these won't arrive at least until the end of April, due to unspecified "gremlins", but for those who desperately pine for this season's Eastbourne merchandise the "new style hats" will manage to arrive on April 7th. Just before KC resorts to a search of his briefcase for other interesting titbits, the start mechanism is fixed and the meeting recommences. The delay hasn't benefited Floppy who trails as a very distant second to the speedway's second oldest rider, the evergreen Sam Ermolenko.

Between races Alan makes great efforts to lubricate the starting gate release mechanism and study it even more closely. Along with KC, I'd personally say that to watch Alan Rolfe work is one of the delights of speedway at Arlington. However I imagine that he's the reason, apart from decorum obviously, that the Eagles sadly don't indulge in the fripperies of having scantily dressed start line girls. Given that there's a pit full of speedway riders every week and that we also have Deano in our midst, their absence is certainly not due to political

---

[1] At many Elite League tracks the fans are often puzzled by the fact that while their riders are always only too happy to drop everything, including the bike, to rush to be interviewed live after a race at any EL fixture televised by Sky Sports, they're often very reluctant to be interviewed by the stadium announcer. Basic economics dictates here, since an appearance on television with your kevlars and cap festooned in the logos of your sponsors pleases them and, by extension, financially benefits you. Whereas an interview in the stadium generates no national exposure and no monetary benefit. It's also human nature to become shy about interviews if things aren't going so well for you on the track. KC appears to have very little problem persuading the members of the Eastbourne squad to be interviewed. It's not always that illuminating but it provides a connection to the riders for the loyal fans and reflects well on the approachable ethos that characterises Arlington before the meeting with the 'open' pits policy and afterwards around the pits, car park and in the bar. It's not like this everywhere and KC takes full advantage of this access throughout the season.

correctness, although cost might be a contributory factor, given the notoriously exorbitant price of skimpy costumes. I suspect that the real reason is that Alan is so brilliant at what he does with his exaggerated gestures, smiles, and studied quiet competence that the club doesn't need the additional entertainment of the girls. Alan's an institution at the club and always has time for a chat and a laugh with fans in the crowd as he prepares for another evening's performance, and the way he does it so elegantly, it's near as damn it to being a piece of performance art.

Apart from Alan who again gets high scores for artistic merit and competence as he lines them all up at the gate, in the next heat Janniro shows artistic merit when he deliberately stays lying on the track to force a stoppage after a fall. It's a tactic that enables the other Dryml brother, Ales, to try to gain a better position in the inevitable re-run of the race, since he'll now no longer have to ride Kylmakorpi's second replacement bike which was kindly provided at the last minute after his packed up during the two-minute warning before the initial running of the heat. Even though Eastbourne's riders would do exactly the same, in true partisan style, the crowd loudly boos Billy Janniro – while he's laid out prone on the track, possibly injured but most likely not – for his successful attempt to stop the race. But with his relaxed, devil-may-care approach to life and racing, Janniro despite the predictable exclusion, relishes the abuse as a badge of honour and gleefully waves to the crowd as he slowly ambles back to the pits. With only three riders in the race, Steen Jensen is guaranteed at least one point but decides instead to try hard to link up with Nicki Pedersen for a rare sight at Arlington among the home riders of a Danish 1-2. Right beside me, Jane screams encouragement with varying degrees of ear-splitting volume throughout the four laps, as she successfully and slightly hysterically implores him into second place. Steen reacts as if he's won the lottery with lots of arm waving and animated gesticulations during his celebration lap, conducted without Nicki, who has returned to the pits after another expected bread-and-butter victory. After Steen celebrates in a wild, joyous manner that wouldn't disgrace the citizens of a newly independent country, KC can't help himself so observes, in deadpan fashion, "Steen is very pleased". Given that Mr. Jensen has been presented to the Eastbourne public as a great speedway prospect for the future, someone who we can confidently anticipate will develop before our eyes as the season progresses to become a true force in the future of the sport, I expect that this will be the first of many joyous celebrations.

The excitement in the next race occurs on the back straight when Henning Bager's chain snaps and he executes a strange mid-track wheelie cum broadside that allows the trailing Mooro to demonstrate his lightning reflexes when he manages to miss Bager by a fraction of an inch. Jane gasps audibly but it happens too quickly for her to get off a decent scream.

The early interval gives me the chance to chat to the 'new' people who have stood next to me tonight close to the start line. They're three generations of the Simmonds family, the eldest member Tom who's 78, started to watch speedway when he was 19 and stationed with the RAF in Norwich. Just for fun he went along to pass the time at The Firs on a Saturday night and has been hooked ever since. He's nostalgic for the old days as "there were so many good sides" but continues to love the smell and excitement of the racing. He went for years to the Canterbury Crusaders, until they packed up because of noise objections by the council. He took his son Nick, now aged 46, along for the first time 30 years ago and in his turn he's passed on the speedway bug to Sam, Nick's 11-year-old son. Doing things together as a family runs in the blood though, as Tom and Nick have worked together in the same building at the family ceramics business for 26 years. It's a business that's travelled in the diametrically opposite direction to speedways fortunes, because years ago there was hardly any call for floor tiles whereas nowadays the demand is huge. To strain my comparison further, almost similar to contemporary speedway, many of the loveliest floor tiles come from overseas, although there is still a need for English quarry tiles. Stoked by everyone's desire for improvements to the home, tiles have now started to even decorate the walls (where the best come from Italy) as well as the floors (where the best come from Spain). When the Simmonds family don't enjoy the speedway together as a break from work, they golf.

Right by us at the start line there's quite a gaggle of Eastbourne riders, who have ventured unusually far out from the pits; here are Nicki, Watty and Shieldsy. They have all gathered to study the starting mechanism with great concentration, they stand around as if contemplating a fine painting and, more prosaically, peer into the innards of the start gate. No test of the equipment is actually conducted, but their concern appears deeply held. The Start Marshal Alan offers occasional comments and smiles a lot, as is his wont.

Shieldsy is out in the next race after the interval only to finish third by the merest fraction of a tyre width in a tight race for the line with ex-World champion 'Sudden' Sam Ermolenko. In the next heat Floppy displays something approaching his sizzling form of last season before it was blighted by injury, when he passes Ales Dryml on the last bend of the first lap. KC coos appreciatively, in that voice of his that mixes sycophancy, delight and satisfaction that he reserves for his descriptions of Eastbourne heat wins. He labels it "as a superb drive round the outside". This is not quite up to KC's usual linguistic standard where the flamboyancy of description matches the vibrancy of the ride, but then, like the riders, he's still blowing off the winter cobwebs. Homeopathy and Red Bull apparently continue to work well for Deano as he surges to his second successive heat win, albeit one that's awarded in heat 12, when Watty gets caught out by his own winter cobwebs, and falls heavily when he tries too hard to overtake on an imaginary dirt line by the fence.

With an Eastbourne victory in the meeting starting to look more likely, Peterborough's usually taciturn Peter Karlsson suffers an extreme and severe temper tantrum – not only are his toys thrown from his metaphorical pram but the pram is trashed beyond repair – after a crowded first bend start to heat 13. Clearly unhappy with the way the tapes rise and with the visually challenged referee who did not stop the race, PK decides to park up his bike and indulge in a sit-down protest on the first bend, right in the middle of the track. To this admittedly partial observer, since I've already seen many other similar incidents with apparently weirdly rising tapes this evening, for once the tapes did appear to rise evenly so Karlsson's extreme behaviour has a strong hint of gamesmanship cum student protest about it. Though, that said, there's no doubt that theatrically parking up is a dangerous and petulant reaction, out of character with his usual studiously calm demeanour, and an infraction that should be punished with an exclusion. There's a loud outbreak of outrage among the home crowd and many vociferous reactions surround me. It might be a family sport but the language at the moment isn't at all family friendly. Group equanimity doesn't improve when the referee, Phil Griffin, "bottles it" as a politer crowd member near me puts it, when he allows PK a place in the re-run. This decision KC relays in that querulous doubting voice from his repertoire that he reserves to signal his complete disagreement without actually uttering any words of objection. In this instance, the referee's decision is relayed to the crowd as, "due to the starting gate not going up satisfactorily".

A subsequent call from the referee's eyrie to Alan at the start line has Karlsson tokenly "reprimanded" but otherwise unpunished. The benefit of having an older clientele who watch the sport is that outrage can always be historically comparative, in this instance the keen Elvis fan, David Rice from Dorking, who regularly stands near by to me recalls, "seeing Eric Boocock thrown out of a meeting for parking his bike like that!" David is always a mine of information, since he's watched since 1953, when he was 11 and still counts himself fortunate that on his introduction he saw two-times Welsh World Champion Freddie Williams ride at Wimbledon. To his mind, it was "the golden age of speedway", an era he technically defines as being the "late 50s to early 60s" when "you have to remember that the great riders like Moore, Fundin, Briggs and Craven used to have to start each race from behind the others with a 30-yard handicap". Years later he was "forced to move to Eastbourne" as a fan, along with the Wimbledon team who became the Eastbourne Dons for a while. But you can't doubt his commitment to the Eagles or his Eastbourne credentials nowadays, as he fairly but measuredly criticises the weakness of the referee.

Justice isn't really served in the re-run when Karlsson gains the two points that temporarily delays the inevitable Eastbourne victory. We then again get treated to see PK race in the next and penultimate race; this time he wears the black-and-white helmet colour as a tactical substitute (or tactical ride). Though, it's all to no avail and the crowd roundly barrack him mercilessly throughout. He subsequently lines up for the third time in three races for the nominated heat, booed as the pantomime villain would be at a matinee, but immediately finds

himself thrown from his bike by a hard-charging Nicki on the first bend, who is excluded for the incident. But, on a night of repeatedly scattering his toys about, Karlsson stays down for a while before he rises, Lazarus-like, from the track in his case, to angrily gesture at Pedersen. Apparently maddeningly for PK, Nicki has immediately returned to the scene of the crime to offer sympathy for inadvertently parting man and machine having apparently forgotten his own significant role in the incident. Karlsson limps back to the pits with due theatricality, as if his steel shoe had become a platform soled boot on just one of his feet, serenaded by loud catcalls and uncomplimentary gestures. Floppy wins the re-run, and Eastbourne triumph easily, 51-40, after a few unconvincing moments earlier during the evening. The crowd meanders back out through the turnstiles, and probably makes a mental note to add Peter Karlsson's name to the list of people we love to boo. Except, for times of temporary amnesia, when he guest rides for us, of course.

On the subject of unexpectedly parking, as I head back to Brighton the limousine mystery deepens, when all four of them that I'd spotted earlier in the evening are parked by the side of the A27 in the direction of Eastbourne. Even more strangely they're all parked a mile or so apart from each other. It really must be a lonely job being a limo driver. Apart from the Parker style hat modelled in Thunderbirds or maybe the Bond film *Goldfinger*, either everyone's too busy enjoying themselves in the back seats, with a spell of drinking and bonking, too occupied to pay you any attention. Or, on the other hand, you can find yourself parked late on a dark Saturday night, in the middle of nowhere, alone. Just waiting to be summoned to pick up your charges, once more, after a debauched night of fun and frolics.

2nd April Eastbourne v. Peterborough (ELA) 51-40

7th April
A waterlogged track led to the early postponement of this fixture and allowed Nigel 'Waggy' Wagstaff to continue his early season quest to scour the globe for suitable replacements for back injury victim Billy Hamill and any other new talent to refresh the ranks of the Oxford Silver Machine, should the need ever arise or the whimsy temporarily take him.

7th April Oxford v Eastbourne (ELA) – postponed: waterlogged track

Cold Night for the Season's Slowest Lap

9th April

It's a cool evening with fresh winds that blow through an array of clouds that, given the forecast of rain, you would expect to see. The Eagles line up tonight against the Oxford Silver Machine team who are fresh from a recent impressive away win at Arena Essex. Oxford is a team that would have high hopes for the season ahead, but have been struck by some early season bad luck that has already seen one of their key riders, Billy Hamill, struck down by injury. Quite a serious injury it is too: involving four chipped vertebrae, one compressed vertebrae, four broken ribs and a collapsed lung to briefly list the damage inflicted by his crash at Swindon.

I've brought along a first-time visitor to speedway and I hope to induct her gradually to the delights of the sport. I hope to achieve this by only concentrating on the bare minimum of explanations of who rides for whom and against whom. I already know from bitter experience that any attempt to explain tactics, even seemingly simple rules, or how to fill out the scorecard immediately bogs the novice down in a distracting level of detail that doesn't really make for an enjoyable evening. When, or if, these visitors ever become hooked enough to want to return to another meeting, then that's the time to gradually immerse them into the ways of the speedway world. The safest bet would appear to be a trip round to the snack bar, or more exactly the snack hut as it forms part of the building that houses the bar area at Arlington, and to queue up to buy the country's most delicious baked potatoes. Well, that's always been my opinion of them though I can't quite decide whether it's the innate tastiness of the potatoes they provide here or the basic fact that food always seems to taste much better when you eat it outdoors.

Before we sample these culinary delights, there's just enough time to take advantage of the Arlington open pits policy that allows the interested fan, obsessive stalker or first-time visitor to mingle with the riders, their machines and mechanics. There's the usual mix of ages from young children to pensioners and every age in between. This part of the evening always attracts autograph hunters and people who want their photos taken with the riders, who, on the whole, are mostly only too happy to oblige. Sadly, we only get a few minutes to jostle our way along to an always entertaining area, namely Floppy's part of the home pits and observe him as he warily greets spectators or indulges in his own rather unique but trademark warm up routine. At most home meetings this consists of him dressed in trainers and jeans, plus his riding gloves set off with a zipped up dark anorak cum jacket, for as long as possible. In order to limber up and loosen his muscles for the exertions ahead, Floppy likes to exaggeratedly whirl his arms windmill fashion or hold them out, as if about to be crucified, while he traces small clockwise and counter clockwise arcs. Undoubtedly a vital part of his psychological preparation and routine, this is all fine and dandy but does look extremely incongruous when you are in your civilian clothes except for your gloved hands. Then again, the pits like the terraces are a broad church that welcomes eccentric behaviours and foibles. Floppy's impression of a speedway version of Alvin Stardust, although minus the leather jacket and with differently coloured bleached hair, adds to his air of mystery. His natural wariness lends authenticity to the rumours of his occasional pre-meeting conniptions that can result from inopportune interruptions, well-intentioned comments, or misplaced criticism, that the more pushy fans feel free to share with him during these final few vital psychological minutes before the bikes get warmed up for the impending fixture. Reputedly Floppy is much calmer than when he was as a junior rider learning his trade at the club, but glimpses of his old volatility intermittently pierce the great calm he usually studiously projects nowadays in most of his 'public' appearances. Part of this success at keeping his emotions and feelings in check appears to involve the affectation of distance and absorption in these elaborate pre-meeting rituals and preparations, especially the gloved calisthenics.

Tonight Floppy is all sunshine and smiles – he poses for photos, jokes with the children, which, even on a slightly darker mood day, always comes easily and naturally to him, flirts with the ladies and offers a few words of wisdom or witty comments to the besotted hordes of men in anoraks only to keen to start up a detailed conversation. If I was a speedway rider, I think I'd find that the access these more obsessive males continually have and expect to have with the riders extremely irksome.

After he dispenses his time and attention with good grace and some largesse, Floppy embarks on another favoured aspect of his warm up – he sits astride the machine, pretends to either release the clutch as if he's involved in another vital start from the gate or instead adopts the aerodynamic, elegant body profile of a rider who races full out at considerable speed. With the advent of sports psychology to try to gain that vital mental edge, competitors in many different sports have now started to use visualisation techniques, usually in the privacy of their own space or imagination, where they win or execute some repetitive behaviour with a view to excellence. I like to think that Floppy has taken these widely adopted visualisation techniques a logical stage further. Particularly since he performs these cameo tableaus in full public view and deliberately uses his actual gloves and race bike, albeit that it remains stationary throughout. I like to think that he imagines his imminent triumphs in the racing ahead.

Another rider also prone to a strange ritual warm up before every meeting he takes part in is Steen Jensen. We all have our peculiarities and foibles and Steen has his too – sadly they don't appear to have the impact that he'd like them to have. Though each time, as the sports psychologists instruct us, the approach and activities remain repeatable and unvaried. His routine involves either the melodramatic adjustments to his racing gloves, as though he were a fighter pilot. Or, alternatively, he strikes the sort of elegant, aerodynamic but completely stationary poses on his bike that you imagine he later hopes to reproduce on the track when his bike is travelling at high speed. Perhaps, it's some advanced form of sports visualisation exercise? Whatever his intentions, though not the tallest man, before every meeting Steen is content to twist his body into the various shapes required for this simulation, all of which can be accomplished without the need to start his bike, or to take off his dark coloured anorak. In fact, for some reason Steen prefers to undertake these psychological exercises in his civilian clothes rather than his kevlars. He will repeat this process endlessly throughout the season.

It certainly stands out as distinctive behaviour to my visiting friend as we discuss her impressions in the baked potato queue. I've tended to find that if you bring male visitors to the speedway at Arlington they concentrate on the power of the machines or studying the racing itself and whatever is in hand on the track. The reaction of female visitors is pretty uniformly "Is that it?" once they've seen a couple of races. The fascination doesn't tend to grab them at all although they do allow themselves to get distracted in the summer when the heat of the night's work often leads the riders to parade about the pits topless or in tight fitting tops, rather than the speedway itself, which is a much more gradually acquired taste if it's not instilled from childhood. My ex-girlfriend, the lovely Fiona, developed quite a disconcerting and unhealthy obsession with the dapper Mr Smooth himself, Olli Tyrvainen, Eastbourne's previous team manager, who was eventually lured away from Eastbourne by the temptations of the chance to manage the endless grind of Tony Rickardsson's relentless Grand Prix campaigns. Fiona used to become quite giddy if we got close to him when we visited the pits or if his management duties called him over to the start line or referee's box.

Back at the start line in my usual position, my neighbour Dave Rice attempts to briefly sketch out the enduring appeal of speedway from his perspective. It's mostly a trip down memory lane that involves the Golden Years when you could watch various London teams compete in front of huge crowds on the terraces. He believes that "those days were better" with so many tracks to chose from if you happened to live in London. Most of these teams it seems, with the exception of New Cross, to be truly acclaimed in later years had to begin their name with the letter 'W' or 'H' – whether it was Harringay, Hackney, Wimbledon, White City or West Ham ("a brilliant fast track"). While I half read the programme, Dave relives his memories that feature a happy past of close racing, camaraderie and modest but brilliant riders who did and didn't become deserved World Champions. I gather that Jon Cook's opinion on last week's referee has led him to think of using another word that begins with W. Instead, because the programme is produced for a family sport, JC notes that Phil Griffin was a "referee who was experiencing a bad day at the office". After he identifies that Peter Karlsson's actions caused "controversy aplenty" Jon asks the difficult question, namely about "who was in charge last Saturday". At this early stage of the season, the club remains cautiously optimistic on the rider form front, particularly with the green shoots of recovery and improved performance that have started to sprout up in the form of the team's reserves, Andrew Moore and especially Davey Watt who provides "a real sting in the tail". Cooky is more cautious when it comes to Steen Jensen and, in man-management terms, this year intends to "tread carefully" – hence the Dane "retains his place" – to avoid the situation where last year's early promise rapidly turned into dire performances after the application of "too much pressure on him". JC is also keen to celebrate this season's technological innovation in this part of East Sussex, namely a text messaging service about the forecast weather for all Eagles meetings. Apparently, this has already had a very encouraging start if judged by one metrologically inclined fan, a lady who's been fooled by the texted promise of a fine evening tonight, who totters past with bare feet in her impressively high heeled sandals. It's an unusual sight at any speedway meeting and remains the dress of an optimist (or exhibitionist) at this time of year when the Arlington evenings rapidly become notoriously chilly after the sun sets.

The meeting is just about to start when "our host", the ever genial often super jovial Kevin 'KC' Coombes arrives late, and bounds onto the centre green only to announce in his dulcet, though tonight slightly jaded, tones that he's "knackered". We have to use our imaginations about the source of this fatigue since it's highly unusual for KC to voluntarily forego any airtime with the Arlington faithful. The smart money in the nearby crowd has the most likely explanation as another late night of wild partying in his capacity as a local DJ in control of his mobile disco decks and the attendant partygoers, skilfully controlling the dance floor to ensure he works everyone into a frenzy (probably "doing it to the boogie") with his choice of many exquisite sounds at some 'chicken in a basket' type event at a neighbouring village hall or marquee. Whatever the reason, interest in this mystery subsides after an easy win for Floppy in heat 1 where he, now out of his civvies and dressed in his team suit kevlars, uses his race gloves to great effect, albeit without need of too much aerodynamic slip-streaming on the bike because of the ease and distance of his lead.

From this point onwards, it's too cold for KC to brave the elements, specifically the freezing cold on the centre green, so he retreats to the comparative warmth of the pits. From then onwards, he's not his usual ebullient self so we have to content ourselves with a subdued presentational evening that matter of factly deals with information and results rather than his trademark gnomic comments or imprecations to rouse the frequently silent crowd. Heat 2 sees Jon Cook's worries made flesh as Steen falls then remounts to finish comprehensively last, while Watty still stings the opposition, who then celebrates with a series of wheelies on his celebration lap, which has hardly ended before a skilful display of team riding from the Deano–Shieldsy combination gives the Eagles an early lead. The scoring is already confusing my visitor but she tries to get into the spirit of things by excitedly noting, "when they start I like the way it makes your ribcage vibrate". As experienced regulars we're all too cool to say this, though we also appreciate and notice it. Eastbourne take effective control of the meeting from this point onwards, a dominance emphasised by Shieldsy who beats the current world number 3, Greg Hancock, almost straightaway with a daring outside pass when he exits the very first bend in heat 5. Hancock then makes no impression on Shieldsy after his initial overtake. As he crosses the line Shieldsy is clearly delighted with the win and Hancock sportingly makes a point to mark this achievement with handshakes and vigorous pats on the back for the length of the back straight.

The starting gate gremlins from last week threaten to reappear in the next heat, but the referee fails to spot the fractional delay that afflicts the inner side of the tapes. On gate 3, Floppy makes an absolute flyer of a start, but then seems to ride in cement (or with a heavy bag of it as additional ballast) as Jesper B. Jensen almost instantly passes him with exceptional ease and evident high speed. KC upholds a great tradition of investigative journalism with an interview with Shieldsy. His close questioning manages to get Shieldsy to admit, "Greg is on my list of people to beat so I'm pleased to have done that" before the shy Australian reverts to his default setting and so becomes very guarded when quizzed about practically any topic. Even though he hails from Down Under, which we all just know is the vastest country in the world where you find yourself hundreds of miles from the paper shop and think nothing of it, nonetheless, he is still probably the only speedway rider in the world who has the opportunity to practise on his own speedway track built in his garden. Most people, never mind speedway riders, don't have gardens large enough to accommodate a model railway track, let alone a full sized speedway one!

By the half-time interval, the Eagles are comfortably ahead and only the distinctive leg-trailing style of Niels-Kristian Iversen has stood out. Temperatures feel close to freezing, so we're treated to the sounds of the song *Summertime* sung by Jazzy Jeff and the Fresh Prince. My guest enjoys the racing, if not the temperatures, and is most taken with the choreography of the starts. The intense revving of the bikes, the synchronicity of the riders as they glance down in unison at the start gate mechanism and the dramatically flying start they all try to make into the first bend to jostle for position. She's impressed by the atmosphere of racing at night under floodlights as well as the noise and the "peculiar but quite nice smell". However, she's not so keen on the shower of shale that regularly flies through the small gap in the fence as the riders repeatedly pass the starting gate. She's also not a big fan of the two-minute warning equipment, "I don't like the klaxon thing".

Straight after the interval there's the first of the many eagerly anticipated clashes between Nicki and Greg Hancock. They've ostentatiously gone out of their way to build bridges back to one another since the infamous falling out they had last year in the Grand Prix series. No matter what their protestations, you know that the history between them still lingers every time they race each other again. Whatever the circumstances or the respective psychology of their individual approach to their clashes in Poland, Sweden, England and the GPs – you can be, as a spectator, certain that you will definitely witness a dramatic and compulsive first corner. More drama comes with Hancock's nomination for Oxford's second tactical ride of the evening. It's the last throw of the dice points-wise when it comes to trying to get back to level terms. It's a possibility that lasts as long as it takes Hancock to be outfoxed by Pedersen and fall, when he misjudges a sharp cut-back manoeuvre, on the second bend of the initial lap. When Hancock remounts he's so far behind that he's even unable to make up the distance required to catch Steen Jensen who takes his second consecutive third place against exalted opposition.

That effectively ends the meeting as a contest, while Deano and Watty ensure that it's all over bar the shouting with a dominant ride together in the next race. Watt wheelies once more in celebration while Deano heads back for some more rejuvenating herbal remedies to combat his lingering flu. With the result no longer in doubt, by the next race had KC cast off his comparative presentational torpor after he witnessed Nicki get elbowed aside by Jesper B. Jensen, just as he approached the bend, before he then regrouped to ride round the outside of everyone else ahead of him and then cut back through a non-existent gap to take the lead. It's a stunning and gifted ride at high speed that KC styles, fully justified and practically without hyperbole, as a "superlative manoeuvre". The penultimate heat then descends into farce during its re-run, when a three-rider sandwich on the last lap has Steen Jensen and Tom P Madsen both fall in Keystone Cops fashion. Iversen continues on in stately fashion for a heat win and, after he promptly remounts, Madsen rides home extremely slowly but still fast enough to beat Jensen who'd set off before him but now pushes his stalled bike to the finish line. Madsen finds time to gesture at referee Dale Entwhistle when he passes the finish line. The riders are so slow to finish that there seems a real danger that Bob Dugard on the grading tractor might be able to set a comparable race time. The race time was finally announced in minutes (1 minute and 1.2 seconds) rather than the usual seconds. This is an eon in race terms at Arlington.

As he goes through the motions, Pedersen beats Hancock for the third time in the last five heats before the crowd starts to leave for the comparative warmth of their cars. As she leaves, my guest praises the family atmosphere of the evening, and then adds that she likes the "bonfire night eerie feel of the darkness". The chance to get a simple cup of coffee when "at an outdoor event in the country" also impresses her but it's the glamour of the noise and the speed that most surprises my novice visitor. She ponders another trip in the summer when it's warmer.

9th April Eastbourne v. Oxford (ELA) 55-39

A Work Out with Floppy, Followed by a Curate's Egg

16th April

I'm early enough into the Arlington pits this evening to find that there's only a comparatively small crowd around the ever-popular David Norris. He's attired in his usual outfit of trainers, jeans, and black jacket set off with a pair of his trademark black racing gloves. Once again, the process and mystery of his own unique but almost unvarying pre-meeting performance to gradually psyche himself up has just commenced. First there's the rocket booster phase with a bit of restrained flailing of the arms. Then there's a little of the sitting akimbo on his race bike while he holds the handlebars in a slightly mesmerised, but an almost OCD manner. He looks so comfortable and yet, for once, simultaneously so susceptible to interruption that I almost finally break my self-imposed duck of never having spoken to him. I'm not quite sure what to say so that I don't come across as too earnest or too obviously anoraky. While I rack my brains for something suitably light and appropriate, another bloke nips in to ask Floppy to pose for a photograph with his girlfriend. He is more than happy to do, which itself then provokes a rash of requests from people who all want their photograph with the man from Hailsham.

If the digital revolution has swept the board when it comes to photography, at least everyone appears to use the camera technology appropriate to their age group in the Arlington pits. The teenagers use a mobile phone with a camera, the couples have compacts and the pensioners use Box Brownies. Well practically their present-day equivalent, namely a beaten up camera that still uses film! I've yet to invest in my digital camera but again in the pits I spot the black-haired slightly goth and almost punk-looking teenage girl who always appears to be in the pits or on the terraces taking yet more photographs with an impressively large camera. I'm convinced that she must work on behalf of the track shop or is perhaps training to be the club's track photographer since she's absolutely everywhere with her impressive bag of equipment. She gives each rider her camera's thorough almost loving attention as they warm their bikes up, chat among themselves or with their mechanics.

She spends quite some time snapping an unshaven Nicki Pedersen from every conceivable angle, except prostrate, as he stands around chatting, dressed in some strange Euro-fashion stone-washed effect sort of jeans that single him out simultaneously as unfashionable and foreign. It must be great to be a speedway rider and get special work clothing to wear, like working in a shop but much more fetchingly deluxe; particularly when you bear in mind that sponsors will actually pay you to put their names onto your work clothes. And everyone who watches you work will unconsciously agree to only ever judge your individual style as it relates to your exploits, ability and appearance on the track, which, where those sorts of judgements are concerned among Eagles fans, is mostly reverential. Apart from that you can just turn up to the track in whatever you fancy or whatever is comfortable or practical, although – as a speedway rider worth your salt – you should need no reminder that the pits area is pretty dirty and messy so there's a good chance of spoiling your clothes for special occasions, if you choose to wear them. Only the younger more preening riders (and Deano, of course) make a point to wear their most fashionable and expensive clothes in the pits for reasons of performance cum parade for adoring female eyes and rival contemporaries, apparently without a care about potential damage. Nicki appears not to have a care in the world. He's perfected an unsmart casual look that wouldn't lead you to glance at him twice in the street, garage or shopping centre. Whereas, on the other hand, if I stop to consider, there's no doubt that both Floppy and Deano have a much sharper sense of self-image than their teammates and somewhat greater pride in their presentation, clothes and general appearance when dressed in civilian clothes away from the track. They're not quite metrosexuals, but there's definitely much more mirror time than you'd expect that Nicki, Shieldsy or Mooro would put in on a regular basis. With Deano in particular, you just know that he definitely shares at least one thing in common with his partner, which is a love of Deano.

Even when he was out injured last year, Floppy had just become the flavour of the moment everywhere and had finally gained his due recognition throughout most speedway circles, after years as an acquired taste. Among other things, this resulted in his well-merited selection to represent his country as well as an increasing number of appearances in the Sky Sports commentary booth as an expert analyst. It was something that he took to naturally, with humour, genuine wit, great insight and plain speaking in equal measures. It's a

refreshing change from the blander approach taken by some other commentators regularly used by this satellite channel. In my opinion, he's always good value and should probably seek to get a bit more involved on the television side of things, since this is something he could pursue more intensely when he retires, but that's an idea many older riders have already had as their career winds down and they desperately try to guarantee an alternative future for themselves. Many of Floppy's contemporaries are much more obvious about and transparent in this desire for future work and preferment on Sky Sports than he is, if judged by their relentless bonhomie, platitudes and hyperbole when watching even the dullest televised races and fixtures. All his erstwhile rivals are equally informed about the reality, techniques and travails of the sport but few have Floppy's brio, insouciance or élan, never mind his hint of on-screen arrogance[1].

As a case in point, to give an exciting insight to armchair fans at the start of this season, Sky had bravely kitted Floppy out with a camera and microphone so that he could talk the viewers through an actual typical four laps of speedway action on the track itself from a contemporary rider's perspective. Sadly for Sky, who are forever vigilantly on guard to ensure that they expunge all expletives from their live commentary and post-race reactions, Floppy had almost forgotten himself or where exactly he was when he accidentally swore, live on national television, while he gave the viewers this additional visual and aural insight into the on-bike experience. This thereby further boosted his credentials as an ordinary man of the people, just 'one of us', who also happens to ride a speedway bike. During that evening he'd also used the attractive but somewhat elliptical phrase "Elvis has left the building!" when he described the fruitless chase of one rider in pursuit of another rider that he could never realistically catch. He confirmed his idiosyncrasy and independence in a single phrase.

So, when a gap appeared in the space–time continuum that was the avalanche of admirers queuing by his bike, I plucked up sufficient courage to engage the great man in conversation, all under the pretext of politely asking him to kindly autograph his photo in the programme where he appears in an advert for the club's long-time sponsors, who use the cheesy tag line "Class Acts…". Fineprint are a local printing company, owned I imagine by an Eastbourne speedway fanatic, who produces the colourful match programme that JC never misses a chance to praise[2]. Close up Floppy appears slighter in the flesh than I'd imagined which I ascribe to all that zealous attention to his diet and fitness that he's discovered later in his career, as well as the renowned abstinence from alcohol that we heard about so often last season. I make a point to praise his commentary work and note that he makes a good combination with Tony Millard. Quick witted but also reluctant to accept undue praise he laughs, "I'm pleased that you didn't say couple!" He diplomatically notes that he combines well with the other regular Sky commentator, the ubiquitous Nigel Pearson, who I say can be pretty histrionic in his commentating style. Floppy avers "he's a really great bloke who's just very, very excitable when he's working on air". Floppy enjoys the change of television work but is, "taking it one gig at a time". As I leave him to his impressive line of admirers, I pass the unshaven Nicki Pedersen still deep in animated conversation, and then I stop to watch the preparations of the Ipswich Witches riders and their mechanics. The away side of the pits is a bit

[1] Though equally Gary Havelock and Chris Louis are also gifted and insightful commentators.

[2] As noted earlier, this is deservedly so, since the programme was awarded the *Speedway Star* 2005 prize for the best speedway programme.

When Eagles Dared

more tucked away and inaccessible to the fans who choose to wander around prior to the meeting, though you can almost overlook it from the snack bar queue or you can press against the wire fence and gawp at them all, but it's also noticeably much more frenetic than the studiously relaxed Eastbourne part. Tonight the Ipswich team are obligatorily without both their Polish riders because of rearranged Polish League fixtures, originally postponed because of the death of the Pope. It's not often that you can mention religion and speedway in the same breath or have such a magnificent reason for the non-appearance of riders. So Ipswich will use their long-time local boy made good, Scott Nicholls, as a guest for the first time this season since his acrimonious departure from Foxhall Heath to the new pastures of the Coventry Bees.

Scott has arrived early, for a change, at the stadium and chats happily through the mesh of the fence to a man with close-cropped hair and his girlfriend. Scotty is still dressed in his jeans and unsurprisingly, like the majority of the star riders in the pits, hasn't seen a razor for some time.

Back at my place close to the start line, I take the chance to study the nuances of Cooky's column in the programme that he has again written in a manner that combines frankness and a careful, almost lawyerly turn of phrase. The review of the individual team members has Mooro on the cusp of "turning his undoubted efforts into points" while Steen is "still way above last year's form and continues to keep his place". If I were Steen I'd find the use of the word "continues" a bit of a worry and a pressure on my future performances. Still, the last thing the riders want to pick up, never mind read, is a match programme; so whether this message would ever get through using this medium is extremely doubtful.

What isn't in doubt is the terrace chatter from Margaret Rice who hopes that Andrew Moore soon gets the chance to ride at reserve, so he can escape speedway's notoriously "difficult" number 2 position. It should happen when the new averages come into play shortly. She "feels sorry for Moore" since she noticed an increased nervousness about his demeanour that isn't solely attributable to his anxiety as he returns from his injury. This perception isn't dispelled when he trails behind by a long way in last place during the first heat, after he failed to make an impression on the comparatively inexperienced visiting number 8 Kevin Doolan. KC on the microphone for his announcing duties is also again strangely subdued tonight, although nonetheless he can't resist an early run out in the season for one of his favourite stock phrases about the inflatable air fence, which loves to refer to as a "bouncy castle". KC wilfully uses this phrase throughout the season with a studied irreverence cum casualness that deliberately belies the ever-present danger of rider injury. This simultaneously communicates his familiarity with riders who laugh in the face of terror and everyday concepts of fear; while it also exhibits that KC is 'on the inside' and in the know – a state of affairs characterised by Bryan Ferry of Roxy Music as, "I'm in with the in crowd, I go where the in crowd goes".

Since he had crashed the previous week, KC can introduce Shieldsy as he trundles out to the start line in heat 3 as "having recently had a touch of the bouncy castles". In the race itself, Shieldsy successfully avoids a collision with the plastic of the air fence, but like all the other riders he's left to trail behind by some distance by the quick start made by Chris Louis. Chris's flying departure from the gates is greatly aided by his illegally rolling at the tapes, something that the crowd vociferously reminds him and the referee of with a sustained bit of booing. In the next heat, Scotty Nicholls manages to temporarily thrill the visiting Ipswich fans on the third bend almost back into loving him again with an exhilarating pass of Watty at high speed, through the narrowest and most illusionary of apparent gaps. This allows the Ipswich faithful to indulge in their traditional victory celebration that requires that they throw armfuls of torn paper into the air. I'm not clear whether they bring the paper ready torn in the manner of the bedding that you can buy for guinea pigs in pet shops, actually tear it up while they're at the stadium or just hope that there's something convenient to hand to rip up in the event of an exciting heat win by an Ipswich rider. Whatever the answer to this mystery, they create a mini paper storm of the sort that you see at overseas football stadiums when the excitable Latin temperament of the crowd get carried away in a blur of confetti. KC very much takes a 'Keep Britain Tidy' approach to the whole situation and prefers to discourage them with humour and leaden irony, "the large Suffolk contingent are causing havoc over there with the paper".

The paper stays firmly in the Ipswich fans' pockets after heat 5 when their strong-minded GP star Hans Andersen loses to another consistent performance from the Deano and Shieldsy combination. Mooro's nervous night continues in the next heat when he appears to be unfairly excluded for touching the tapes at the start line. The crowd is not amused. It appears that Floppy must have been shouting at himself in the pits tonight, as he's reputed to do sometimes in order to motivate himself for the racing. In the re-run of this race, he passes Nicholls on the back straight of Lap 1 through a gap that not only doesn't appear to really exist and is one that he has to literally stand up on the bike to take advantage of, so narrow and perilous is the space between Nicholls, him and the fence. Scott is obviously surprised by Floppy's determination, since they speak at length after the race as they almost meanderingly return to the pits.

Shortly after this race ends, we're unfortunate enough to be joined on the home-straight terraces by a family that I hadn't previously seen at Arlington. The overweight parents wear replica England shirts and struggle to control their small child and teenage sons. As if to confirm this, the adults chatter throughout the rest of the meeting, swearing loudly, while the lad's prat about and chain-smoke although they're much too young to smoke. Speedway is a broad church, but continual interruptions of everyone else's enjoyment isn't the best way to worship and I find myself very distracted from watching Pedersen's easy win by a country mile. The arrival of Mooro once again onto the track has Jane shout and scream "go on, Moore" at least ten times as she urges, implores, cajoles and encourages him to try to succeed. He finishes second behind Watt and apparently is very pleased with this result, since his mood rises above morose and for once he performs his part of their victory celebration during which they indulge in some wildly extravagant wheelies. I think this is the race that signals both to the rider himself and the crowd that he's finally back mentally as well as physically from his badly broken leg. His teammates make a point to applaud Mooro's success as he comes back to the pits area.

The next heat, as the saying goes, "has it all" and is the most eventful of the night. Chris Louis approaches the start in his traditional fashion with an extensive display of relentless pre-race fiddling with practically every part or item on his machine. After doing everything but change the tyres or clean his bike cover, he's finally ready to deign to come up to the tapes to start the race. Kim Jansson then takes his turn to excessively delay the start, which provokes the usually placid Start Marshal, Alan Rolfe, to have a quick but instructive word on race etiquette and, doubtless, threaten him with the 'naughty step' back in the pits. All the riders then race from the tapes to the first bend only for Floppy to fall heavily on the corner. This is the signal for Watt and Jansson to duel aggressively for second place behind Louis. Jansson crosses himself off the home crowd's Christmas card list when he cuts up Davey Watt on lap 2, having clipped the back wheel that suddenly presents itself in front of him. Watty just about manages to stay on and stop his bike from flying over the safety fence. The crowd boos Jansson vociferously. When they both recover sufficiently to resume the chase, over confidence gets the better of Jansson on the final lap where a shockingly misjudged corner serendipitously allows Watty back through for second place.

The rash of Eastbourne fallers continues into the next heat, which again brings KC's considerable powers of understatement into action when he describes Steen Jensen's spectacular fall as "he took a bit of a purler". Before he adds, with accuracy and well-observed dramatic timing for effect, "he's dislocated his thumb, it was hanging off at a strange angle making us all feel sick". Whatever the status of everyone else's stomachs, Steen certainly didn't feel too great since this injury took him off to the A&E department at the hospital for some vital medical attention. KC then distracts, entertains and enlightens the crowd with some waffle during which he introduces his very own definition of what defines financial independence and being comfortably well off, when he recaps what he's seen on that week's televised match on Sky Sports, and admits his own privileged status when he notes, "you'll also have seen this if you're posh and you've got the satellite system running". I hadn't realised that this was the criterion by which you could judge comparative levels of contemporary material success. I immediately resolve to finally arrive in the world and subscribe post haste on my return home.

Heat 12 has Jansson serenaded out to the tapes with a chorus of jeers and boos for yet another race with Watt. However, while repetition doesn't dull the crowd's enthusiasm, we do then all watch Jansson wildly slew all over the track throughout the race and he genuinely appears barely able to control his bike. Clearly the previous incident in the last heat took place more due to lack of control combined with inexperience rather than malice. While he's still getting a feel for this track or, indeed, a speedway bike in general, most riders would be sensible to avoid getting too near him at all costs. An inconsistent evening of brilliance followed by surprisingly basic errors continues for Floppy with a start so poor you wonder if he's riding a lead bike. However, he recovers to superbly relegate the ever-threatening Nicholls to last place. The result of that race, despite a tactical ride win for Hans Andersen, effectively ends the match as a contest. As the meeting fizzles to a conclusion, Shieldsy finds time to fall and remount in the next while Watt wins to the mad enthusiastic cheers from both Jane and Margaret next to me.

The last heat has quite a bit of tension and gamesmanship that initially results in the all the riders being called back for a re-run due an "unsatisfactory start" with Floppy as the main culprit, after he moved on gate 4. From gate 3, Andersen demonstrates that tonight he is definitely the master of Pedersen's psychological outlook when he lines up very close to the gifted Dane, who occupies the adjacent gate (gate 2). This prompts Nicki to rather petulantly complain to Alan Rolfe, the Start Marshal, about Andersen being unfairly and illegally too close by encroaching on his start lane. After he's looked closely, Alan Rolfe confirms all is, in fact, completely legal with Andersen's position. In order to extract instant revenge, as Andersen clearly surmised he would, in the first corner Pedersen immediately tries to aggressively sweep Andersen towards the first bend air fence ("bouncy castle"). This plan is thwarted when Brer Andersen slows at the very last second to cut inside, leaving Pedersen literally high and dry but barely able to stay on his bike as he super-aggressively broadsides his bike at the fence. Suitably embarrassed and comprehensively out-thought, Nicki gets one of his season's rare last places out of the way in the last race 1-5 that allows Ipswich to dramatically narrow the result to 48-45. It's a score line that doesn't reflect the ease of the Eastbourne victory but illustrates the determination of the Ipswich Witches team on an extremely cold April night. It's a late meeting turn of events that bodes poorly for any chance of a bonus point for the Eagles in the return fixture at Foxhall Heath.

The star of the night for Eastbourne is Davey Watt with some support from Nicki. Floppy's evening is a curate's egg of a performance below his usual standards that, in this case, probably also ultimately disappoints the curate with only seven points and a bonus to show from his five rides. Andersen and Louis star for the visitors while Scott Nicholls temporary return to the Ipswich side ends in comparative ignominy when he only posts a very disappointing seven points. It's difficult to know what to make of it all tonight or what this might forecast for the rest of the season's prospects. I think about these matters while I drive home. Like the last meeting, I'm continually passed in the other direction by an armada of limousines.

16th April Eastbourne v. Ipswich (ELA) 48-45

21st April
Raced on the 20th anniversary of the death of Ipswich Australian legend Billy Sanders and after a moving and heartfelt tribute from John Louis, the Witches were overcome by an all-round Eastbourne performance that had every rider score points. The quartet of Norris, Shields, Pedersen and Watt contributed most of the points. Expectations of a win on the road at Foxhall Heath weren't high and Jon Cook talked beforehand of going there "for our annual drubbing", though afterwards he was still eager to remember "it has never been a happy hunting ground for us".

Amazingly, the Eagles did achieve the improbable and showed that it wasn't impossible to outfox the Witches at Foxhall Heath. This is the sort of early season triumph that augurs well for the campaign ahead and builds the confidence of the team for next week's 'Battle of the Birds' at Blunsdon.

21st April Ipswich v. Eastbourne (ELA) 41–50

25th April
Another venue that doesn't make the hearts of any Eagles fans sing with joy is a trip to Gorton to the home of the Belle Vue Aces, Kirkmanshulme Lane. Again, contrary to expectations the Eagles ran them close until the latter stages, after which the wheels came off the wagon. The always gentle but tactile Andy Smith got into a tangle of men and machines with Deano in heat 12. The subsequent exclusion for Deano was taken badly by JC, but in a Zen manner by Smudger, "he was out of the race and I wasn't".

Earlier the sombrero wearers and their often witty but surreptitious microphone were silenced by Nicki and Davey in particular, who relegated Jason Crump to a surprise third place in their initial encounter. Crumpie gradually recovered his equanimity before what the Aces deemed "hard riding" from Nicki in heat 15, restored some pride in the score line. In the race itself, the apparently exceptionally keen-eyed Richard Frost saw Crumpie "shoot a glance" at referee Dave Watters, maybe quizzically, but certainly hard to discern during a speedway race with a helmet on, after "the pair appeared to rub shoulders". Talkative as ever, a "clearly angry" Crump said: "I don't want to comment".

25th April Belle Vue v Eastbourne (ELA) 49–41

An Ornithological Encounter

28th April

The only teams in the Elite League with ornithological nicknames come head to head, or rather beak to beak, for the first time this season at Blunsdon when the Eagles visit the Robins in a 'Battle of the Birds'. From the point of view of ownership though, it could also be billed as Terry Russell vs. Terry Russell. He cuts a distinctive figure as he strides about the pit area or chats earnestly on the track with Jon Cook. Mostly because we all know he's a 'big cheese' and because he's the smartest dressed person in the stadium, albeit with a hint of smart casual since he doesn't favour a tie. Unlike many of the local fans, he doesn't sport the apparently *de rigueur* beard and ponytail favoured by men of a certain age (roughly his age) or one of the many bright red Robins anoraks that pepper the terraces.

The Robins, of course, have their big top two in the form of Leigh and Lee. Although they spell their slightly recherché Christian names differently, on their respective days they are both a force to be reckoned with and on the paper that you imagine promoters use to draw up their teams in pre-season, doubtless look jolly impressive. In fact Leigh Adams, born under the sign of Taurus and 34 today, is consistently impressive in Elite League racing. But the personal flamboyant and confident skill he displays on the track often deserts him when he is off it. He is a bit dour and often a slightly put upon grouch in interviews as he tries to see the 'bright side' through his words but doesn't quite manage through his demeanour. On the track he is superlative. If the Eagles are to triumph, both Floppy and Nicki will have to head him on a regular basis. Lee Richardson is a different kettle of fish. Obviously, I admire his granddad as he played football for Sunderland AFC. In the world of speedway, Lee seems to have made the inconsistency mantle his own when he rides for the Robins. No wonder the locals grow so many pony tails, as they need all the hair they can grow to have enough to pull out on a regular basis as they watch Lee compete with "inconsistency" often his watchword.

Although there's a strong threat of rain, the crowd are treated to the first of many bursts of aural clichés with a rousing march out to the tune of *When the Red Red Robin Comes Bob Bob Bobbin' Along*. The use of this tried and tested musical favourite is echoed in the programme by Alun 'Rosco' Rossiter whose name always conjurors up thoughts of the Emperor Rosko radio programme of a certain era. Drawing deeply from the Manual of Inauthentic Programme Notes, he advises: "Once again, I think the supporters will be the winners, with our super raceway serving up another generous slice of excitement". Read this sentence out loud in a monotone, dear reader, and you are just about there yourself.

Although the calibre of riders assembled by both teams bodes well, sadly the meeting remains notable for mostly the wrong reasons. The meeting has barely started before the events of heat 1 fatally compromise and undermine the 2005 season for the Eagles, scarcely before it has had the chance to begin. On the first lap, David Norris careens into the bend 2 air fence as he enthusiastically chases the home-track hero Leigh Adams. It's another one of those innocuous looking crashes at speedway that has long-term repercussions far beyond the apparent seriousness of the injuries sustained by the rider. Despite the cushioning effect of the air fence (manufactured by Terry Russell's company), Floppy suffers a concussion and withdraws from the meeting with what the announcer calls with masterly understatement "a knock on the head". It is an immutable law of speedway that the most innocuous-looking crashes are often the worst. The result of this crash is that Floppy suffers with continuing symptoms as well as the psychological effects from that moment on throughout the Eagles campaign and is never quite the same again for the rest of the 2005 season. Subsequent tests reveal that he has damaged three small but vital bones in his neck.

This is more than a metaphorical pain in the neck for the remainder of the Eagles team. Given that the notoriously larger and faster spaces of the track at Blunsdon aren't conducive to equipment set up for the tight confines of the Arlington track, most Eagles fans in attendance that aren't blind optimists would have sighed in resignation at the expectation of the defeat that must now inevitably follow. But rather than this being the signal for a general collapse and rout, we're treated to a pugnacious performance from many members of the team as well as some shrewd shuffling of the remaining riders available to them by Cooky and Trevor Geer.

This mainly involves a succession of three drawn heats that the Eagles fans on the terraces enthusiastically greet as a moral victory. Most noticeable is Davey Watt, at reserve, who is rarely off his bike for the rest of the evening. This suits him well since he scores in all seven rides. It's clear that the side will have a potent threat with him riding at reserve. It's a shame that the same can't be said of the rider in the other reserve position on a night when scoring power in this position is even more at a premium than usual. Steen races to a final score of one paid two, which counts as high by his own standards but poor by any reasonable measure, as does a surprisingly out of sorts Deano. Reportedly on a bike with a revolutionary aluminium frame, Mooro is involved in the only 1–5 win for the Eagles in heat 8 when he shows considerable determination to follow Davey Watt home. Adam Shields also rides with gusto until his only blip of the evening in heat 15, where a last ditch 1–5 would have secured a surprise draw for the Eagles.

The Eagle with the bit really between his beak, who rides to a flawless maximum in flowing style, is Nicki Pedersen. On a fast track that favours competitive riders, he overcomes the natural home track advantage and knowledge of Swindon's top two riders, when he beats Leigh Adams three times and Lee Richardson twice during the evening. He establishes complete mastery over them from the outset and ruthlessly exploits his psychological advantage with some brio and considerable élan. When he's in this sort of form, he is worth the admission money on his own and it's unlikely that both Adams and Richardson will be defeated so often on their home patch throughout the rest of the season. If the Eagles can sustain this level of performance without Floppy's services and if the riders who had an 'off' night can regain some form then a successful season in the challenge for honours and silverware in 2005 looks definitely within our grasp.

28th April Swindon v. Eastbourne (ELA) 48–44

Another different chapter about this fixture appears in my book *Showered in Shale*.

Riders on Parade. © Jeff Scott

Start Line at Blunsdon. © Jeff Scott

Another Distinctive Robins Anorak. © Jeff Scott

May

KEITH HUEWIN

"At the end of the day, it's not flower arranging is it?"

Battle Royale in the Black Country

2nd May

They say that if you can remember the 1960s then you weren't there. In years to come, many people will claim to have been at this meeting between Wolverhampton and Eastbourne. I was there and witnessed the events as they unfolded from beside the pits as the invited guest of Jon Cook and the Wolves management of Chris van Straaten and Peter Adams. It was a meeting of contrasts that had the best of speedway on the track and the worst of speedway off the track. Long after every rider involved has finally retired, this fixture will be recalled as one of those very special matches and the telling of the tale will become inflated and exaggerated over time. It will live in the collective memory for many things, but most memorable and prominent will be the fight that erupted trackside after the initial attempt to run heat 9.

The sky was cloudy when I arrived for an interview with the Wolves manager Peter Adams. He's the sort of man's man that you instinctively admire, both as a result of his demeanour on live Sky television — where he's taciturn and reserved, but clearly very acute — as well as his articulacy and his sophisticated reading of the sport in general. You just know that he has thought about things deeply and that he affects a slight air of ponderousness to give him additional time to think in every situation, time that in reality he doesn't really need. I report straightaway to Chris van Straaten's office to have a brief interview with him and to thank him for his hospitality and to search for the whereabouts of Peter. Chris is a speedway 'big cheese'. Long in the tooth and someone who's been there and done that and worn the proverbial upper clothing garment. Consequently he is respected and vilified in equal measure. He long ago perfected a patrician attitude that could be seen as unwelcoming by those with an anxious or nervous disposition like myself. His is a man of few words in public. Although there are a couple of hours before the gates even open, Chris is very distant, pretends that he has no idea of our appointment to speak briefly, and affects that this is Peter's appointment and reacts as though I've come to steal something or have just broken wind. Probably a helpful standard response and sensibly protective initial attitude to have, particularly when you are naturally suspicious of any writers and journalists that you don't know from Adam. I am dismissed in short measure.

No sooner am I outside the office door, than Peter shoots by purposefully and at an impressive speed for a man of his size and demeanour. I gather he has important business to discuss immediately with CVS. He's politely brusque and says, "I'll see you for a coffee in a quarter of an hour or so after I've finished in the office" or words to that effect, as he nods to the benches beside us.

I retire back to the trackshop where just earlier the avuncular owner Dave Rattenberry and his charming sidekick-cum-star-employee John Rich have immediately made me feel welcome and part of their corner of the speedway community. It is a special skill to be able to do this so spontaneously and naturally, while all the while asking innocent, open questions whose answers will immediately metaphorically reveal you — who you are as a person, how you approach life and the purpose of your visit. The arrival at that moment of the knowledgeable SCB official Chris Durno, who will be tonight's referee, and Shaun Leigh the stadium's flamboyant announcer, causes them all to have a conspiratorial confab that, if they were women, would gain them reputations as gossips. It quickly becomes clear that the Wolverhampton promotion are about to reap the potential pitfalls of their "British is rarely Best" employment policy.

Basically a rare lull in the manically busy schedule that is the spring, summer and autumn for every half-decent speedway rider, has understandably led the Karlsson brothers — Michael, who has adopted his mother's maiden name Max, for reasons that have never been satisfactorily or believably explained but that excite my curiosity, and Magnus — to spend a long weekend relaxing. The place that they choose to do this in is Sweden, at home, far away from England never mind the Black Country. It is human nature to try to maximise your enjoyment and minimise time wasted at work which, in the case of every speedway rider's normal work life means endless waiting around at airports, workshops and speedway tracks, for a few intense minutes of dangerous and possibly life-threatening activity. Rather than come back on the Sunday night for a Monday night meeting, they elected to opt for the morning flight back over the sea. Fair enough if all goes to plan but horrendous if your aircraft develops a technical fault, which sods law had dictated that theirs had done. Collectively we contemplate the vision of a roused and angry Peter Adams, who would definitely have no problem verbally striping the paint from the wall, never mind when he's thoroughly admonishing a couple of sheepish Swedish speedway riders for whom English was not a first language. A severe scolding from CVS who allegedly can be aloof and coldly cutting would also not be an appetising prospect, even if you ignore that he wields considerable power over you, the club, and the sport, would also not be something anyone would relish, let alone a penitent speedway rider.

However, unable to send their absent star foreigners to the naughty step, the Wolves management found themselves left hamstrung by the league rules and their own strategic employment practice, with the additional nightmare that they could only replace the absent Swedes with riders of much 'lesser' stature. That is in terms of skill and expertise, not height. With the help of malfunctioning parts of a plane far away, they had metaphorically but effectively kicked themselves in their own groins when it came to the likelihood of beating Eastbourne. Given the similarity of the tracks at Monmore Green and Arlington, the widely held theory is that "they both ride each other's tracks well". In fact, Wolves hadn't been beaten at Arlington for two years now, so it would be more accurate to say that it was highly likely that with a full strength team they could confidentially expect to easily run out winners on the night against the Eagles.

Very few options presented themselves, but Peter and Chris took both with alacrity. They called up at short notice a couple of replacement riders who were available to race and based reasonably near by. One was Conference League rider, Jon Armstrong, who would at most of the clubs he ever races at be the smallest and attract the sobriquet "diminutive", but for the fact that Wolves already had the impressively much smaller Ronnie Correy in their team. They had also called upon the services of Tony Atkin, who kindly and impressively dropped everything to help the Wolves in their hour of desperation. I always have a pathological desire to refer to him as Troy, for reasons that escape me but come from a deep-seated confusion with the American Football quarterback I never quite saw the genius of as much as everyone else did (I think I just held his initial season against him). Anyway, these replacements wouldn't gladden the heart of any manager or promoter if directly compared with the firepower of the Karlssons or, to be technically accurate because of the relatively recent but inexplicable deed poll name change, the Karlsson-Max combination. The other things that could be done were being done; notably to excessively water the track in the hope that the forecast of possible rain came true and, with a brief deluge, provide the excuse to postpone the meeting due to a waterlogged track and the handy canard of "rider safety always being paramount". I expected Jon Cook to be outraged at this gamesmanship, but he just shrugged as he looked across at the bowser as it deposited yet more water on a well-watered track and phlegmatically said, "we'd do exactly the same in their position!"

Oh, to have been a fly on the wall as CVS and Peter Adams discussed the situation in the inner sanctum of the Monmore speedway office adjacent to the pits! Not that Peter breathed a word about what was troubling him – even when enough steam is being generated at that very moment from his ears to generate sufficient power for the whole town – since he still has the studied but professional equanimity to drink his coffee, draw very deeply on a rapid series of cigarettes and suggest that I send him a list of questions for an interview at another date.

The Eastbourne riders prepare at Monmore. © Jeff Scott

Chris Geer, Floppy's mechanic at work. © Jeff Scott

Trevor Geer greeted with Black Country headlock. © Unknown

You don't have to hang around any speedway pits in the build up to a meeting, let alone during it, for any length of time to quickly get the feeling that you're as useful as a spare prick at a wedding. Without an interview to distract me, I could observe at close quarters all the different styles of (elaborate or otherwise) preparations that the mechanics, management and riders go through individually in the minutes that lead up to the meeting itself. I have observed elsewhere the uniquely personal physical and psychological routines that Floppy and Steen Jensen regularly, ostentatiously pursue. Mooro uses all his Zen training to cast himself into a catatonic and completely disengaged state, while Deano remains laid back though you sense always slightly watchful. Davey Watt behaves like he's the new boy at school pretending that he's already part of the gang, Adam Shields shows earnest and careful maintenance skills and Nicki does his cool as a cucumber routine. This mostly involves him in extremely fastidious preparation of his tear offs, a comprehensive helmet inspection and lots of sucking on a giant black hair-dryer that he appears to bring along solely for this purpose. In fact, I'd expect that he's the only one with such a machine on either team, though Floppy or Deano might have some tonsorial equipment with them for after they've had a shower. I genuinely feel that I'm supremely privileged to have this unique access behind the scenes, though obviously to all intents and purposes I'm completely redundant. I'm so much a part of things tonight that I can't help but notice Nicki have a quick slash into the surprising verdant hedge-cum-shrubbery type growth that they have dooted about the place at Wolverhampton. It is an activity he leavens with lots of loud clearing of his throat and some slightly machismo spitting.

It is safe to say that out of all the riders on display, the greatest weight of expectation rests on Nicki's shoulders. Those favouring the Eagles hope that he will succeed and, for those of the Wolves persuasion, they definitely hope he doesn't do so well. In fact, they affect to hate or, indeed, do hate him. Maybe they have only taken severe dislike to a whole new level. Because of his previous time with the Wolves, Nicki has gone from hero to zero and then beyond to pariah status multiplied many times over. It is, ultimately, a huge sign of the greatest respect but, unfortunately, caught up in the moment it can turn the atmosphere and things rather poisonous. So it would transpire this night, though it has to be said that Nicki as a true competitor always appears to thrive on this, raise his game, and channel this opprobrium into even better performances.

Since I have covered and analysed the events of this evening in copious but slightly self-righteous detail in my book *Showered in Shale*, the following is only a brief impressionistic account. It's not meant to belittle the seriousness of what occurred nor to deliberately alter or exaggerate it unnecessarily, particularly as elsewhere I've already taken the mickey out of people that deliberately do that. Though that said, like most people, I'm sure I am to some extent a hypocrite really.

Tonight is the best night I will ever have to exchange a few words with the riders that comprise the Eagles team, albeit this will have to be on a work night when their minds and concentration will be off elsewhere. I stood next to a number of riders as they overlooked the track. Notoriously a man of very few words, Adam Shields was true to his reputation when he replied "yup" to my introductory gambit. It was a reply that immediately left me in no doubt that our conversation was over. Really touchingly, the solicitous and unfailingly polite Steen Jensen mistook me for someone who knew a lot more about speedway than I do when he engaged me in conversation himself. It only lasted a few brief sentences but, in comparison to any other exchange, it was equivalent to reading all of Finnegans Wake aloud. Steen took a rather nationalistic view of the later events, typical of many smaller countries' attitudes to their larger and prosperous neighbours, which he parochially put down solely to the presence of "dirty Swedes". This was an attitudinal criticism rather than some reference to hygiene problems. The chance to stand close by Davey Watt made me worry that he has some kind of expectoration problem that causes him to have the spitting equivalent of Tourette's Syndrome.

Anyway enough of standing around nearly talking, the unpredictability of Floppy's injury sustained at Swindon is such that not only can he appear for the Eagles in this important fixture, but he also immediately sets a new track record for the Monmore Green circuit. Not that I'm aware of this as the intensely feverish activity in the Eagles pits is completely absorbing – particularly as I stand right next to them and can then run a few yards to watch with the riders of both teams the action on the track over the perimeter wall – but, more importantly, the speakers waft Shaun Leigh's well-crafted verbal gems away into the night without leaving any sound of them in this part of the stadium.

There is a bad accident that has Jon Armstrong tangle with the fence in dramatic fashion. His tiny body lies prone on the track for an inordinately long time while it receives the ministrations of the St. John Ambulance staff. Floppy demonstrates a compassion for other riders that I hadn't picked out in him before when he sprints over to the stricken Armstrong. I mistakenly assume that this is out of acute concern as well as to offer words of encouragement and solace. I quickly learn that it's out of suspicion that he's playing for time and tactical advantage by spinning out his recuperation period before he stands back up onto his almost child-length legs. Still, they say that like jockeys, the ideal size for speedway riders is small and the optimum weight is light to anorexic. You never really see them astride a speedway bike if they're the size and weight of the Wolverhampton security man. We see quite a bit of him just in front of me within a minute of the initial running of heat 9. It's a race that results in an introduction to the track surface and the air fence for Freddie Lindgren, after he's tangled with the always combative Nicki P on the first corner. As public enemy No.1 the crowd immediately bay for swift retribution from the referee, unlike the tannoy system, the sound if not the detail of their requests is very audible in the pits area.

Lindgren reacts with anger and aggression at his enforced chew on the well-watered surface but, almost before their handbags can be drawn for action, the fight takes a turn for the worse with the frantic, flailing arrival of Lindgren's mechanic who decides to meet out some summary street justice upon Nicki P. This just isn't the done thing and lights the blue touchpaper for a five-minute or so episode that disgraces the name of speedway, drags it through the mud and leaves it quivering in a pile of ordure forever more. Well, it does if you ascribe to the high-minded slightly moralistic outlook that I mostly affect to in *Showered in Shale*. Or, it is a truly shocking but nonetheless memorable event to witness. In fact, it remains the most extremely violent event that I have had the misfortune to see. I've never seen this level of violence before, and hopefully, I never will again. Lindgren's mechanic used to share a house with Nicki and might have even been his mechanic at one point, the urban myths about this night get so mixed I can't really decipher them anymore. Whatever the exact nature of their previous relationship, Nicki shouldn't wait expectantly by his letterbox for birthday cards in future. Particularly if this is the way that this mechanic lets petty house-sharing resentments fester over time – so that not doing your share of the washing up, shopping and tidying or, maybe, always using the last of the milk and taking too long in the bathroom – explodes in this violent and extremely unhelpful manner. This barmy reaction only provokes the riders and staff from both sides to immediately involve themselves in the contretemps. Showing surprising speed and agility for his age, Trevor Geer is one of the first to arrive at the scene trackside. This is unfortunate for him. Particularly as the man mountain that is the security man employed by Wolverhampton (again the urban myth has it that he already had a record of misbehaviour at Monmore and is still often seen there) appears not to have been issued with a job description or not to have read it, since his version of mediation in a conflict is to go in there all guns blazing to lash out psychotically at everyone he deems to be a legitimate target. Like the beast in the film Predator, his definition of prey is rather hazily wide and so catholic that it appears to include anyone in the vicinity that has any association with the Eagles or might have in the future.

My old boss used to say: "It looks like a dog, it hunts like a dog, it smells like a dog – it is a dog!" You should sunstitute the canine variety in this saying with the violent thug variety. The avenger immediately started to savage Trevor rather than try to break the fight up in any meaningful fashion. In fact, rather than placate the situation, he magnified the latent anger and violence of the incident to a whole new level. If he had calmly interceded between the two riders and the mechanic, as you would imagine he should was in his job description as the security man, then the trouble would have died down almost as soon as it flared. Instead he picked his Eagles targets indiscriminately.

Throwing himself into the breach with great bravery and chivalry to protect his father was Floppy's mechanic, Chris 'Geernob' Geer. His quickness of reaction and desire to protect his father limited his own strategic options and the incredible hulk, who wasn't fighting according to Queensberry rules, immediately felled him. In fact, in true street-fighting fashion, once a man is down the ferocity increases to decisive levels. Geernob soon found himself at a greater disadvantage, even more than their respective differences in size would automatically create in the natural course of things. In a sickening display, the Wolverhampton employee repeatedly kicked him in the head with a zeal that would make you look completely bonkers on a football field. Geernob sustained so many extreme blows that there was instant worry that he might be dead, brain-damaged and, at best, unconscious. It was the most savage brutality towards a helpless person I have seen and, unlike a boxing match, there was no referee to stop it.[1]

Deano and Floppy did try to intervene, as did Jon Cook. Apparently without thought of the likely consequences for himself was Deano, since he promptly inserted himself into the epicentre of the mayhem and thereby later found himself prominently in all the photographs of the incident. These looked like they were chosen for the action they captured and their newsworthiness, but also to deflect attention away from some others (on the Wolves staff) toward the Eagles riders as instigators. On this basis, you can see Deano apparently intervene with punches as well as with advanced street-fighting skills in wrestling and one-to-one combat. Events were very confused,

[1] When I spoke with Chris 'Geernob' Geer months later at the Brighton Bonanza, he recalled: "they started attacking Nicki Pedersen - I really like him - but when I saw the old man was hurt, I just got involved without thinking about it. They say the bloke was a giant but he seemed like a midget to me. I felt like killing him. I didn't feel a thing though my eye swelled where I got kicked and punched in the head and my shoulder popped out. When I was down only David [Norris] stood in for me. Afterwards I was in a daze 'cause I didn't know I was concussed or what I was doing really. Later Nicki sent me a nice text thanking me for standing in for him - as I say I like him - though I did it without thinking of any of the consequences. That's speedway though, all sorts goes on sometimes, like when the fans were spitting on David at Poole. You just have to try to ignore it, if you can, I just didn't that time".

but if ever you found yourself in such a situation then Deano would now definitely be the person you'd choose to have on your side. The idea that Geernob was dead or brain-damaged brought out volcanic anger and vociferous concern in Floppy who, like many people in the heat of the moment, thought he'd possibly been killed. Bad enough to witness, but worse if you're both a friend as well as the person who actually employed Geernob to be there that night in the first place. Caught up in the frantic thoughtlessness that overtook many in the few minutes of the drama, the responsibility weighed heavily on Floppy who initially intervened in the mass bundle and then chased the fleeing security man round the pits. To no avail but not for lack of trying. He was shouting like a man possessed and his face was contorted in rage and concern. He was also keen to find a policeman. Given that it is almost a cliché that speedway prides itself on the complete lack of a need for them to attend any meeting, it was always going to be highly unlikely that Floppy would manage to find one in his search.

I should stress at this point that many Wolves riders as well as other mechanics, staff and assorted personnel also got caught up in the melee but I'm unable to recognise them or properly describe their role at all accurately in the ensuing dramatic confrontation. Some were keen to defuse the situation and actively pursued that end. They shouldn't be tarred with the same brush as the security man. On the management front, Jon Cook was another of those immediately involved and, along with Floppy, one of the chasers of the surprisingly agile and fast-moving security man. Strangely, compared to my expectation, Peter Adams remained aloof and mostly kept his tinder dry, but was there throughout, unlike CVS who immediately retreated to watch events from behind the walls of his office. This didn't lend credibility to his unofficial but emollient description afterwards that it was very regrettable incident but only really handbags. If it were just that, I'd hate to see a real fight. The incredible hulk scarpered quicker than those who sought to chase him, which left Floppy in particular with an excess of adrenalin which he channelled into loud rhetorical exhortations to those around him about where the long arm of the law had temporarily got to and other philosophical questions. Mostly, he was keen to remind everyone of the truth of the old adage that there is never a policeman around when you want one. And, no doubt, they'd have been shockingly young looking if we'd have found one!

By the time Chris Durno had arrived from the eyrie of the referee's box to intervene in the pits the hurricane of violence had subsided to only susserating levels of seething undercurrents. Ultimately in his report on the night to the SCB, mainly because of the architectural lay out of the grandstand and the pits, Chris would be unable to provide an eyewitness account of the exact order of proceedings during the fracas since he was unsighted some distance away from it. He sensibly called an interval to allow all parties to calm down and for the concept that we were at a speedway meeting to regain its hold, rather than continue in the same vein as though it were some brutal battle that had been reconstructed from the English Civil War. Unfortunately, feelings among the Wolves faithful ran high and throughout proceedings they had bayed for justice and blood – mostly from Nicki whom they blamed absolutely for events – but in frustration they also turned their anger towards the small knots of Eagles fans that had made the bank holiday journey to the Black Country. This isn't the way to go on and doesn't reflect the warm welcome you invariably receive from this most knowledgeable of crowds. But, in the heat of the moment, these things are understandable. If they had been able to see all that I saw close at first hand, there would probably have been even more distemper in the crowd and it is lucky that this wasn't the case. Many Eagles fans then retreated to the grassy plot within the pits 'secured' area for their own safety. The numbers there indicated that, whatever people might claim in the future, there weren't hundreds of fans of the ornithological persuasion to witness these memorable acts of violence.

How various people reacted to the collective anger that seethed throughout the pits was instructive. Jon Cook retained a distant air and admitted, "I'm too old for this sort of thing anymore" (the implication I gathered afterwards, when I thought about it further, was that this once wasn't always the case). Nicki was as cool as the metaphorical salad ingredient, so he sat quietly in a corner and resumed his maintenance of his tear offs, used his impressive hairdryer style implement and generally kept focused on his races ahead, apparently oblivious of his own role as catalyst for the whole thing kicking off in the first place. As an unofficial exercise in team building it served both teams well and I observed that the Eagles did actually stick up for each other as 'a unit'. Peter Adams managed to shrewdly channel the anger and aggrieved outlook of his riders and their mechanical staff into a superb fight back on the track, where their actions would speak loudest. This was particularly impressive recovery in the light of the weakened nature of the Wolves team and speaks volumes for his tactical nous, motivational skills, and canniness under pressure. You can only but admire such an approach really.

After the enforced break of the early interval, the Wolves rode with a competitive spirit that enabled them to remain in close contact throughout the rest of the night, despite fielding a massively weakened side. Not that passion had deserted the Eagles side of the pits either. After they trailed in behind the Wolves riders to concede a 5-1, Deano and Davey Watt had an almighty barney on their return to the pits. Well, to be accurate, Deano massively got the hump, outlined Davey's shortcomings in colourful language and generally rearranged the organisation of any tools and equipment that was closely at hand. The mute response from the Australian only seemed to provoke his further ire. The violent storm that was Hurricane Deano was allowed to blow itself and, perhaps, the earlier adrenalin still coursed through his veins. His own score on the night, like the few previous meetings, wasn't at the level he'd expect nor would it satisfy the standards that he habitually sets himself. Even Steen outscored Deano with a three paid four haul of his own.

The meeting eventually came down to a last heat decider, held in a decidedly tense atmosphere that Nicki coolly ignored (as he had studiously done all night when sat calmly alone in his own section of the pits) to complete his five ride, 15-point maximum. He celebrated wildly to loud jeers from the Monmore faithful and replied to their unmistakeable gestures in reciprocal fashion. After a warmly serenaded victory parade for the Eagles from the Monmore faithful, they retreated to their dressing rooms for a lengthy team talk behind closed doors with Jon Cook.

The SCB had to order an extra large carpet under which to hide the results of its subsequent enquiry into the events of the night. No details were ever publicly released – though I understand both clubs received fines – and the speedway world continued in its orbit, just as it always had, in its own sweet way. The Matrix reasserted itself and the speedway press, the local media and the Internet forums buzzed with claim, counterclaim and outlandish supposition. Photos that incriminated both sides were published that showed conflicting images of the fracas, though some of these mysteriously and quickly disappeared. Wolverhampton and Eastbourne promised their full co-operation with the authorities.

The Wolves official website commented:

> "Tempers boiled over following a first bend tangle between Lindgren and Nicki Pedersen in Heat 9, with representatives from both clubs involved in some unsavory scenes. Referee Chris Durno called an early interval and restored order, and the action which followed was out of the top drawer."

Whereas the Eagles official website noted with a firmly pointed finger:

> "We will cooperate fully with any investigation and would like to place on record our support for the actions of the match referee in difficult circumstances. We would like to state our shock and outrage at the actions of a member of the Wolverhampton speedway security team and trust that the appropriate actions will be taken by his employer… The catalyst to the whole incident, a Wolverhampton Speedway Mechanic, was dealt with by the Referee on the night, and we trust that once Wolverhampton speedway have acted against their Security steward, both teams can move on and enjoy successful seasons"

If this were *Dixon of Dock Green*, as soon as was seemly after the denouement, Jack Warner always appeared just before the screen fades to black to wrap up and then say "good night all". Though, significantly in a break with tradition, for once he wouldn't update us on what happened to the so-called culprits. Again idle speculation about what has or hasn't happened is no basis for further comment on my part. In my previous account of these events in my book *Showered in Shale* Jon Cook asked a rhetorical question for which the answer is thankfully, most of the time, "speedway". The question was, "in what other sport could participants be assaulted by the staff employed by the home team and the police not become involved?"

2nd May Wolves v. Eastbourne (ELA) 46-47

Another different chapter about this fixture appears in my book *Showered in Shale*.

Taxi Waiting?

7th May

At this time of year, the country roads that lead to Arlington are lined with thick carpets of brightly coloured bluebells that remind me of the springtime glades in the woods of my Hampshire childhood. If they're this thick and beautiful on the verges of the road, I can only imagine what they're like deep inside the National Trust owned woods that are lovingly preserved in this part of Sussex. The area that surrounds the Arlington Stadium is famous among ramblers for its country walks and, as I think about it, the many flowers suggest how the renowned vintage Bluebell Railway received its distinctive name.

I wait a while in the pits to meet with the very helpful Dave Fairbrother from the *Speedway Star*, a great big bear of a man who is kindly going to take the time to explain the mysterious world of track shops throughout the country so that I can better sell my speedway book *Showered in Shale* when it comes out. He doesn't arrive at the time we've arranged and, since we've never met, it doesn't help that I have no idea what he looks like. Dave Mitchell, one of the Eastbourne machine examiners, advises that I look out for "a big bloke with cameras". There are quite a few big blokes among the fans who stand idly in the pits, but none that fits the description there with cameras. As the pits lane soon closes to non-authorised personnel and there's still no sign of Dave, I make my way round to the track shop to look at the Eastbourne replica tops that have finally arrived. They're brightly coloured, accurate replicas of the team uniform but if anything they seem to be constructed of even thinner, more synthetic material than replica football tops. While I'm there Kevin 'KC' Coombes tries over the tannoy to drum up and reignite the interest level among the fans in the stadium by calling them "summer tops", as he promotes an interestingly narrow range of sizes from "XL to XXL". He outlines all this in his distinctive cheery voice, though tonight he sounds slightly bored and his voice only runs a range of emotions from A to A.

There's been an action packed two-week break from activity at Arlington, though away from home there has been "the fight" at Wolverhampton and Floppy still continues to suffer from the effects of his fall at Swindon. Jon Cook covers some of these events in his programme notes, which pointedly mentions the "profound effect on us as a team" of the shenanigans at Wolves. Andrew Moore's form is mentioned with "delight" while JC also highlights, "you don't need to be an expert to know that the form of Adam and Dean is causing great concern". Ominously, if I was Steen Jensen, I'd notice that my own poor form wasn't even mentioned, which is a worry for the future given, putting it politely, how inconsistent he's been so far this season. As if to dispel these lingering doubts in the minds of the management and fans, Steen powers to a second place behind Davey Watt in his first race.

The flabber of the crowd continues to be gasted when the Shields–Barker duo shows a clean pair of back wheels to Swindon's star rider Leigh Adams. The moment at which they actually beat 'Mr Consistency' in the form of Leigh Adams, the man who's topped the averages for the whole season in the Elite League these last few years, it prompts a very good impression of Victor Meldrew from Dave Rice standing next to me. His mantra of "I don't believe it" continues when we get to witness a surprising but encouraging heat win for Mooro in heat 8. Before we get to see that happen, the heat before has Nicki Pedersen make absolutely no concession to anything so namby pamby as team riding with his weaker partner, when he soon leaves Steen to almost idle a considerable distance at the rear as the solitary star of his own one-man race. It's unfortunate for Steen's confidence that his number 6 position in the team ensures he is programmed to be paired with Nicki in his second and third races of any night. In heat 11, he repeats the earlier medicine and, once again, rides round at the back of the field some distance removed from the other riders, albeit that he looks the part on his bike. Next to me, Dave is too resigned to bother to comment harshly, though he does wistfully note the apparent lack of effort expended by Mr Jensen to close the apparently ever widening gulf between himself and all the other riders.

The half-time interview features JC questioned by the inimitable KC who instantly curries favour when he introduces the club's promoter as "the young Jon Cook". Who, quick as a flash, wryly replies, "you're trying for a pay rise". After a series of KC's trademark easy but facilitating questions, JC concludes the interview with a rallying call to the mass ranks of Eastbourne fans gathered tonight at Arlington, "we are a team, so get behind the team as you're part of the team!" The "team" in the crowd close by to me react with torpor and only truly become at all animated when the news comes through, announced by KC, that Floppy is "withdrawing from the meeting and is being rested on the paramedic's advice". It's not so much the sensible precaution taken, since he still suffers from the after-effects of his crash at Swindon, but more the realisation that he will have to be replaced by Steen in heat 13 that is the cause of the disconsolate groans.

Those who ultimately matter the most at any speedway club, the riders, immediately act upon JC's words of encouragement; well, at least those of the written variety in the programme! Davey Watt continues with his excellent form at reserve, while Deano has comparatively bucked himself up and continues with his best evening for some time in heat 12 with another second place to give him, by his recent standards, a humungous total of six paid eight from his four rides. However, Steen by virtue of his paid win in his initial race has, if I were a lawyer, technically also responded to Jon's call to arms but nonetheless still remains immune to a complete recovery of his undoubted potential. Predictably, his third consecutive ride with Nicki garners the same outcome as the two raced previously and, sure enough, Steen finishes comprehensively last. It's an unfortunate situation compounded by Leigh Adams who beats Nicki for the first time tonight and, since he rides as a tactical ride, his points are doubled — though the overall scores still retain a healthy margin in favour of the Eagles at 49-35.

Nonetheless, it's all too little too late for Swindon and normal service is resumed in heat 14 with another win for Watty and a third place from the resurgent Shieldsy to go along with his earlier three race victories. The meeting has shot by with lightning speed under the watchful guidance of referee Frank Ebdon and a drawn final heat leaves the final score at 56-40. The Eagles gain the bonus point and this will please Jon Cook immensely in his unofficial battle with his

Steen psychologically prepares but fails to notice his missing back wheel! [Not shown] © Jeff Scott

Margaret by Board 51 © Jeff Scott

Bob & Roy's tractors bask in pre-meeting sunshine © Jeff Scott counterpart, Alan Rossiter, another from the stable of the Terry Russell managed promoters. It's another baby step on the road in the ongoing campaign to emphasise to the eponymous Terry Russell the comparative superiority of all things Eastbourne Eagles when contrasted to that of the other Elite League speedway club he owns, the Rossiter-led Swindon Robins.

After I watched the Robins get mauled, on my subsequent journey back home down the nearby country lanes I see a couple of extremely confident foxes nonchalantly walk through a large bluebell glade on National Trust property. While I do, however, for once manage to travel to and from the speedway without any sign of limousines on the roads, I'm pretty sure we'll soon hear of the arrival of "a taxi for Mr Jensen" at Arlington.

7th May Eastbourne v. Swindon (ELA) 56-40

13th May

According to the veteran speedway reporter with the most exotic nomenclature in British Speedway, Edwin Overland, the passage to victory for the Panthers was "*eased*" by the absence of Steen Jensen (!), Nicki and Floppy. To be fair, based on his Elite League average of 0.67 Adam Allott won't adequately replace Steen who presently rides at 4.67. The joke practised on the public by the demands of the GP series had a much greater impact on the visitors than the home side, who had the luxury of racing with Peter Karlsson and both Drymls (Ales and Lukas) in superlative form. On the night only Deano and Watty took the chequered flag in pole position and only two Eagles managed to make double figures.

The ever wily Panthers team manager Trevor Swales, with half an eye on the Arlington crowd size for the return leg fixture, refuses to count his proverbial chickens and brandishes his military metaphors when he notes, "it was only half of a full battle". Jon Cook sings from a slightly different song sheet that echoes Norman Tebbit while it avoids Julie Andrews: "We need to get stuck in. We are not using words like 'struggle' or 'mountain to climb'. We are just focusing on the fact that we have a job and we can do a job".

13th May Peterborough v. Eastbourne (KO Cup, 1st leg) 56–37

Of Sawdust and Sky

16th May

The first Monday night meeting of the season doesn't appear likely to start because of the heavy rain we'd had throughout the day. The weather forecast is for more rain. Still, even though it's the sort of evening that you wouldn't expect to see racing, you also know that with the presence of the Sky Sports cameras and equipment at Arlington they will try everything possible to allow the meeting to proceed. The fact that it's promised in the television schedules and the rumoured but probably exaggerated £125,000 cost of each outside broadcast is incentive enough for everyone to do everything they can to ensure that the meeting is held. The fact that it might be slightly unsafe on the track, despite the oft repeated canard that "the safety of the riders is always our main priority", disregarding that it won't be very exciting to watch for those at the track or at home, probably won't enter the new speedway reality equation of 'safety and entertainment' out = 'money and TV' in.

At the season-ticket holders' entrance at the turnstiles, the lack of a queue means that the lugubrious Dave Prodger is comparatively chatty tonight. He's the brother of Roy Prodger, the taciturn Senior Clerk of the Course who's often part of the Arlington formation tractor-driving team led, as ever, with considerable élan, panache but few words by Bob Dugard. Dave has watched the racing since 1946, although he stresses that nowadays it's mostly "only attending the meetings not watching them". His work on the turnstile and in the office afterwards on race night means that he rarely gets to stand trackside. Not that he gives the impression that he is that displeased at this situation, "it's all changed – now you just make the start and it's over". If this doesn't lead to processional racing then, "there's such a difference in the machines between the top riders and the others that some just don't have a chance". And he doesn't only mean Steen. Along with the deterioration in the quality of the racing, Dave feels the sports atmosphere has suffered from the time when he first began to watch, something he can still vividly recall, namely "all the dust and the cinders" of the early days. He's not hopeful that there will be a meeting tonight and seems much more animated when he discusses his forthcoming knee operation.

I've come along very early to the proceedings to again try to meet with Dave Fairbrother, the elusive Lord Lucan figure from the *Speedway Star*. Sensibly, he's decided that the threat of poor weather makes it pointless to journey to Arlington, although I don't learn this until the next day. It seems he'd rung Deano to check on the likelihood of a race being held and, based on what he'd heard, then decided not to attend; but since I don't know Deano, I wasn't able to guess this or find out his change of plan when I stood around in the pouring rain by the pits entrance looking for a "big bloke with cameras".

Inside the stadium, there's an extremely sparse bordering on a very meagre crowd tonight, which you'd expect to find on a televised racing night anyway, but with the poor weather, it would almost be as quick tonight to introduce the members of the crowd to the riders. When you watch a live meeting organised by the television people to suit their weekly schedules and their concomitant need for frequent commercial breaks, you find that the flow of the meeting is totally disrupted. You get an even more exaggerated stop–start effect, where intense activity (usually four races) is then followed by a pronounced lull (for a commercial break and for the personality presenters to air their opinions) rather than the usual continuous flow of races. But, then, who pays the piper calls the tune in most walks of life and this meeting jerkiness appears to be one of the prices of televisual fame for the speedway fraternity. Everyone in authority or anyone who owns an Elite speedway club professes complete and absolute delight at the situation. There are no dissenting voices at all. Officially, the line is that the exposure and the professionalism of the product presentation outweighs the low crowds and the severe discontent with the iniquity of the Sky Sports inspired introduction of the play-off system to decide/engineer the ultimate League Champions. In this respect, speedway has become more and more like soccer, its Sky Sports counterpart sport. The needs and opinions of the paying fans have rapidly become an irrelevance, except to provide brief local colour or as the backdrop for lip service about their loyalty and fervour etc. during the play-offs. There's not much doubt that it's much more comfortable to watch a televised meeting at home – albeit for many people it loses all its innate charm, the atmosphere as well as most of the thrills – rather than find yourself shortchanged at the actual live meeting by television's demands. As with most other fans that subscribe to Sky satellite television ("those posh enough and lucky

The Sky Crane est arrivé. © Jeff Scott

The Deserted Arlington Turnstiles. © Jeff Scott

Keen Ipswich fans brave the elements. © Jeff Scott

enough to have Sky" as Kevin 'KC' Coombes subtly puts it when he implicitly acknowledges the notoriously extortionate monthly fees) I'm taping tonight's programme. This is partly to see behind the scenes – runaway the best aspect of Sky's work, yet even this insight can be akin to being tortured sometimes with its facile questions and turgid *longueurs* – but, more likely, to disagree with the banality and hyperventilating nature of the commentary and expert analysis. But also, to fall prey to vanity, so it's partly to see myself on television ("hello mum") – which isn't that hard to do with the limited numbers of people who actually bother to attend tonight.

Whatever, the merits of the situation, and in the speedway world there are strong advocates of both possible perspectives albeit only one set of opinions with any financial clout or authority, there's a large Sky Sports outside broadcast team presence inside and outside the Arlington stadium this evening. The large vans already parked and occupy a huge area of the car park by the entrance gates; the distinctive black-and-silver Sky interview booth is already in place, located on the stock-car track by the pits area, ready in anticipation of tonight's 'insightful' opinions and interviews from Kelvin Tatum and Jonathan Green. And, of course, there are all the cameras dotted throughout the stadium grounds, including a camera suspended high atop a lengthy crane arm that provides a bird's eye view of the track and the surrounding countryside. It is a countryside that reveals a skyline heavy with black clouds and the absolute certainty of rain.

By 6.45 p.m. the promised heavy rain has materialised and whether you're a rider, track staff, a fan or with Sky Sports, pretty soon we all feel pretty soggy. The riders and the Sky people look particularly morose as it appears very unlikely that the racing will be held, but because it's a live broadcast, the show will definitely have to go on, albeit with no action to speak of[1]. The production manager runs about in the rain under his massive umbrella that isn't well suited to the narrow confines of the pit lane. Jonathan and Kelvin go through some last-minute rehearsals in their special booth. This mainly involves synching themselves with prepared pictures on the monitor and practising that certain speech register that shouts 'I'm reading from a cue card' to the audience watching at home on the sofa. The importance of the Sky Sports team – for providing the much-needed television exposure that drives the increased level of commercial sponsorship revenues rather than their support of the sport *per se* – has even enabled them to commandeer a sheltered space for themselves in the pits during this deluge and there are lots of self-important individuals who stand around to take full advantage of it. A truly important person, the owner of the Eastbourne licence and the original broker of the Sky Sports deal within the sport, Terry Russell, is also there. The talk of the terraces is that he always attends at his clubs when there's the opportunity of an appearance on the telly. He's always dapperly dressed as if ready for a business presentation or an after-dinner speech at the club. The financial size of the Sky Sports deal he brokered has inevitably led to allegations and gossip about significant commission as a finder's fee for him. Jealously, bitter and unfounded rumours are a fact of life everywhere and the confined world of speedway is no different fuelled, no doubt, in Terry's case by resentment at his apparent success in a wide range of

[1] Even during a rain off, track-grading delay or rider injury – this behind-the-scenes aspect of the Sky coverage is a real strength when it occasionally gets beyond the boringly predictable and standard questions they love to ask as they investigate the obvious with puffballs like: "how will you do today?" "How did that feel?" "Is it going to be a tough match?" and so on.

speedway-related businesses, but which his nearby top of the range Daimler or Bentley (I'm not sure which, it's definitely not a Rolls or a Jaguar) with personalised number plates doesn't exactly dispel. But then I imagine he was already a successful businessman anyway before his involvement in speedway, so such ostentation is probably mandatory and, anyway, goes with the territory. He must have a love of speedway, though, doubtless inevitably deep seated and lifelong, since it's not usually the road to untold riches and he's invested to become the owner of a few tracks in recent years, even if you ignore that he has arguably become the most influential figure in the British speedway.

As I stand around with other bedraggled members of the public, I can't help but overhear the Eastbourne promoter and co-team manager, Jon Cook say to his boss Terry Russell, "when it stops raining, it goes ahead – we'll be racing". This sounds like incredible optimism as the rain continues to fall very steadily. Also sheltering in the pits is Sky's roving commentator, Sophie Blake, who provides a bit of glamour along with her reporting throughout the season. With disappointment, I notice that she smokes and I can mentally imagine what my mum would say about how cigarettes don't enhance the looks of an attractive woman. While I become totally soaked, I bump into some local characters in the form of the Strudwicks with who, by happenstance, I used to stand with on the terraces. In this case John and his son Niall (unusually pronounced Neil), who looks incredibly grown up compared to the enthusiastic young child I can remember from a few years back. He was always mad keen for speedway and I knew he spent many hours on the small but respected practice training track that they have at Arlington. Niall's father John has now given up his work as a raker with the track staff in order to concentrate on the mechanical side of the sport in order to help his son to fulfil his dreams and ambitions to succeed at the sport as a rider. It's a lot of travel and preparation with all the maintaining and cleaning of the bike. "It's costing around £300 per month presently with *no* earnings" John notes as he stresses the word "no" very heavily. For the young men who try to find their way in speedway, the earning prospects are very limited and the costs high to exorbitant for the majority of riders. Apart from those lucky enough to have wealthy parents, lucrative sponsors, trade connections or those gifted with exceptional talents. John tells me that Edward Kennett was rumoured to have only been paid £400 for winning the recent Under-21 Championship, as the prestige of victory supposedly outweighs the size of the prize the BSPA is prepared to offer. The costs of such a meeting must be met but, given how well attended the meeting at Rye House was, this does seem a very small prize in comparison to its prestige or the earnings at the stadium on the night. Nonetheless, riders like to race and pride stalks all walks of life. Speedway is no different so, whatever the financial rewards, the value to your esteem and self-worth in victory is comparatively incalculable. John glows with pride and Niall has taken on a newfound teenage confidence that has replaced his childhood shyness[2].

Niall appears positively energised with the speedway life. As I talk with him you get a small sense of how hard the life is and what the rider's gradual apprenticeship might involve. Both could talk at great length as if it were a sunny day, oblivious to the rain that drenches us. Eventually I surrender to the elements, but not before I learn more of the intricacies of bike maintenance, the continued and notable progress of cousin Lee Strudwick at Wimbledon, and the "hard" transition that there is from excelling on a 250 cc bike to a fully-fledged 500 cc machine. It's life affirming to observe John's joy and pride in his son's activities, gradual improvement and maturity. I resolve to watch Niall race in as many second halves at Arlington and elsewhere as I can this and following seasons.

It's still raining, but even harder than before. The few people who are exceptionally keen enough to have bothered to attend the meeting have sought shelter from the storm. The friendly but always wry Martin Dadswell, at the track shop, resorts to ostentatiously tidying the stock to pass the time, while he patiently waits for customers and the appearance of the franchise owner, Nick Barber, "who owns most shops in the South"[3]. Next to me, an affectionate but very bedraggled young couple closely studies the stock but, after some lengthy consideration, they decide not to buy anything. I talk to them. He's only just started to attend again, though he came as a child with his granddad. He can vividly recall the thrill of the speed and the noise. They are based in Hastings and feel it's "good to have a local team". As she watches the rain begin to slow, she seems slightly less convinced about speedway, and though she enjoyed her first ever meeting a few weeks ago "this one seems a bit different". It's touching that they're even here, especially with the rain and the fixture on the telly, but I put it down to love, the impetuousness of youth and the chance to snog at length in the rain. To smooth the path of true love and to encourage their future speedway attendance, I helpfully explain the rules that surround the re-use of their tickets if the meeting is abandoned before heat 6.

Even when the rain finally stops at 7.30 p.m., it looks likely the meeting won't happen. But like madness, depression or alcoholism in the

[2] By the next season I would see Niall confidently stride around Arlington, hand in hand with his girlfriend, as well as making further strides towards his speedway dreams.
[3] 2005 was to be last season that Nick Barber owned the franchise since this is now run on its own behalf by the Eastbourne Eagles with Martin Dadswell in sole charge of this part of the Arlington empire. Nonetheless, the key supplier of the shop remains Nick, who now has to only content himself with the role and profits of a distributor without the headaches of the management that Martin now has inherited.

family, the secret that dares not speak its name is that Sky Sports need to keep the home audience pinned on the sofa, watching nothing[4]. The track staff have the awful task to spread out the piles of sawdust that have been enthusiastically thrown onto the track by Martin Dugard from the huge plastic covered bales precariously balanced on the back of his quad bike. He loves the quad bike, which, since he retired, he treats as a new toy cum surrogate four-wheeled speedway bike as he always appears to drive it round at great speed on a race night. The sawdust they spread is totally ineffective to absorb the water on the track and King Canute-like in its futility. In the crowd we suffer, well those stupid enough to stand and watch like myself, from severe dust inhalation as the moderate breeze covers us in a thick film of sawdust that sticks to our wet clothing. Though it's a change from being showered in shale that would always be preferable. It's as though the track staff management thought they could only convince us of their earnest intentions to hold the meeting if they coat us all in wood dust. The sawdust they manage to apply to the track forms a gooey mush instantly. It will damage the racing surface of the track for weeks, even with the ever-resourceful and vigilant Bob Dugard in charge of track TLC, and it doesn't even manage to achieve its intended purpose to improve the track condition. Still, as they say on stage and at the circus, the show must go on.

With the track totally gunked up, nearly an hour after the rain stopped, the riders for the first race tentatively approach the line. The visiting Ipswich riders cope very well with the conditions as Hans Andersen sweeps to an easy win while Karol Baran, looking at ease in the difficult conditions, moves past Adam Shields just before the finish to record a 1-5 race result. The Eastbourne pair could best be described as riding with extreme caution. The fixture is then held up for an emergency track inspection by referee, Ronnie Allen, before it's abandoned with track conditions unsurprisingly judged as "unfit"[5]. 'What a charade!' could be a polite conclusion as the few fans that actually bothered to come along tonight make their way out to the very boggy conditions of the car park as the rain sets in heavily once again.

My journey home, after three soaking hours at the track, also becomes a nightmare after an accident in poor driving conditions by the A27 level crossing shuts the most direct road home to Brighton. When I finally got back six hours after I originally left, I then discovered that I wouldn't be watching all the chatter with the riders and managers on my tape of the Sky programme. A last-minute change of channel from the one advertised, an extremely irksome last-minute but not infrequent decision, meant that there was nothing to watch. Trying to tape the later highlights programme was even more frustrating as Sky Sports, in their wisdom, chose not to show anything they'd broadcast earlier[6] but instead they show a re-run of their pet speedway project, the most recent Grand Prix. This demonstrates the contempt that Sky Sports holds for the fans that actually attend the televised meetings. The spectacle is messed up at the meeting for the convenience of the home audience and you return to find that you can't luxuriate in the banality of the rain delay coverage but instead have to endure another re-run of the relentlessly lauded, and more commercially significant for Sky, Benfield Sports International run Grand Prix series. Oh well, such are the perils of actually turning up to regularly watch meetings in the flesh.

[7]It's amazing the perspective you can get from nearly 200 miles away on your sofa! Interestingly, in this instance, it's a case of like father like son. Chris Louis, who was also not in attendance at the track due to injury, but had reportedly texted the wonderfully named Ipswich Witches team manager Mike Smillie to note he had "ridden in similar wet conditions at Arlington, and that it would make it better than normal". All this informed comment only confirmed my disappointment at missing the actual broadcast.

16th May Eastbourne v. Ipswich (ELB) 1-5 abandoned

---

[4] The task to fill the time and airwaves with insightful chatter or comment usually falls to Jonathan and Kelvin. They struggle manfully to be entertaining at the best of times when there is actually some racing going on, so inclement weather that hasn't yet forced a cancellation is always a challenge for them.

[5] To pander even more to the perceived need and exigencies of the contract with Sky Sports, by 2006 the decision to race or abandon the meeting is no longer the final decision of the match referee, even after consultation with those who will have to risk themselves on the track – the riders. The final decision rests elsewhere than the match referee with someone called a Meeting Steward, who is allegedly paid 20 times more than the referee for this 'responsibility'.

[6] Which further confirms the widely held view on the entertainment level and quality of these ramblings in the rain, since even Sky Sports views it as not sufficiently watchable television to even repeat!

[7] Luckily, John Louis, the Ipswich promoter was able to watch the match on his television safe and dry at home in Ipswich. Taking a bizarrely surreal perspective in the *Speedway Star* a few days later, he suspects that Eastbourne influenced the abandonment decision for their own unstated ends after the first race defeat. He's trenchant in his criticism of the abandonment. John is quoted as observing, "I have been involved in dozens of meetings when conditions looked more dangerous and risky than they did in the only race we saw". Interestingly Jon Cook mentioned to me a few days later that he wished he sent out Deano in the first race, a rider replacement ride taken by Adam Shields, as he would have rode in a manner that would have convinced fellow closely watching riders in the pits that conditions were just about rideable. Thereby enabling a few more races for everyone to possibly acclimatise to the difficult conditions.

From One Extreme to Another

21st May

It's an afternoon and evening of huge contrasts as I manage to experience a unique combination of events within a few miles of each other in the Sussex countryside. As you drive on the winding, hilly road that is the A27 between Lewes and Eastbourne you're very aware of the small villages, the rural environment and the beautiful countryside. Close by the turn off onto the country lanes that takes you over the unmanned railway line towards the Arlington Stadium, you can easily see the Long Man of Wilmington etched in giant form on the chalky hillside. It always fascinates when seen in the distance from the passing road, whether you're the driver or just a passenger and therefore able to study it at greater leisure. Before you even get to this point on the A27 you have to negotiate a short stretch which features a winding section of road with sharp corners and undulating blind hills. It's the sort of road that makes you simultaneously relax and accelerate. It's also a notorious accident black spot that claims its share of deaths every year, as regular as clockwork. Those involved are often locals who know the road well, and visitors too, as well as the inevitable innocent victims who try to edge their cars out of the hugely dangerous junction that leads back to civilisation out of a narrow lane from Charleston. The A27 is a dangerous road at the best of times that has famously claimed the lives of many including that of 'Q' from the James Bond films who you'd expect to have had a gadget to stop this very eventuality. But at this particular section of the road close to Charleston, the accident and death rates are so high that the council has plastered the road in both directions for miles with bright red tarmac to warn blasé drivers of the impending difficulties ahead, accompanied with lots of dramatic signs that urge extreme caution and control of your speed. An unexpected benefit of the highway authorities colouring these roads in a dramatic red for safety reasons is that any unfortunate bloodstains aren't quite so obvious.

It's to Charleston that I head before the Knockout Cup encounter with Peterborough, a meeting that will bring Peter Karlsson back to the track for his first appearance since his recent display of dangerous petulance. Interestingly, despite the historic strength and importance of Eastern Europe as a region that over the years has provided a steady stream of gifted speedway riders, this rich seam of recruitment has slowed though Peterborough still have a pair of brothers who ride for them who come from what we now know as the Czech Republic. As a teenager, my first close encounters with almost any foreigners was through speedway, since these meetings had a varied mix of nationalities in comparison to, say, the then more limited exoticism of football. There was a glamour, hardiness and rarity value to the speedway teams that used to often visit from Poland, Czechoslovakia or Russia. It turns out, in retrospect, that this was the high water mark of those generations of gifted riders that come from that region. Nowadays, the vibrant speedway culture that still prevails in Poland enjoys the same fanaticism among the fans, but has become diluted through the impact of the legions of gifted foreigners that now conversely ply their trade in *their* leagues. At least that is how it appears viewed from this country, where a prolonged bout of insularity has affected the appeal of the various levels of British speedway for all but the most brilliant and ambitious of the most recent generation of Polish riders. It's partly the demands of the travel, the poorer levels of pay compared to home (a reversal of the historic norm) and because of the ever-changing imperatives of the points structure that underpins our team composition but we've really lost something when it comes to regularly seeing Eastern European riders ride in our leagues. Riders from Scandinavian countries are still very well represented in Britain, as are the Aussies and the Yanks and after that every other country only features to a lesser extent, including the nearby Eastern European and Nordic countries. You hesitate to link this decline in the supply of riders to British speedway from those regions to the impact of the recent economic resurgence as well as the change in the political make up of Eastern Europe sped up by the decline and eventual collapse of the Soviet Union. But it appears that speedway, despite itself, must have some connection with contemporary historical events and the subsequent greater emergence of the free trade or open market economy.

To investigate this further prior to the meeting, I drive up a narrow single-track road that takes me to the famous farmhouse in Charleston that was the country home of the influential cultural phenomenon of the Bloomsbury Group. A loose association of influential artists, writers and thinkers dating back to the first half of the 20th century (so called because of the part of London they lived in) they used to escape from what they viewed as the narrow restriction of bourgeois, upper middle class life in the city to the freedom of the

countryside. It was a time of free love and freethinking well before the swinging 60s. The impact of their brilliant, challenging and modernist work endures to this day in art, philosophy and politics, but is often unnoticed since so many of their ideas have now been incorporated into what would be considered the mainstream. Anyway, it's a beautiful idyllic location, surrounded by hills, woods, unspoilt country walks and rivers. I park on a narrow chalky lane close by the cottage, still decorated throughout with the artifacts of the Bloomsbury Group and, more interestingly, their bizarre murals or paintwork that adorn every room in the house, created in an age when home decoration, especially weirdo artist decoration, wasn't an activity pursued by the middle classes but only by their servants under strict instruction to ensure conformity and normality. Sadly, I don't get to visit the house itself – so I don't find out if Virginia Woolf had a room of her own there – since the talk I will attend is held in a tent in a garden large enough to accommodate quite a crowd. It's a huge white billowing affair, the kind you imagine they might erect at the more popular village fayres in the summer, and it's already crowded with comfortable and prosperous looking people who sit on the rows of school hall chairs that have been laid out before the slightly raised podium.

The average age group of the audience would be considered old even by the standards of speedway crowds, as the median age seems to be well into the mid to late 60s. The absence of children and families is noticeable. Sitting next to me I have a famous London television and Sunday newspaper journalist who carries a pile of books and a deliberately understated but battered leather briefcase chosen to proclaim his credentials as a busy man of ideas and letters. His wife or partner is even more ostentatiously bohemian; she flamboyantly wears 'casual clothes' and make up that appears to have no regard for the sensual contours of her sleek figure. Her physical appearance provides a sharp counterpoint to her consciously dishevelled man of letters too busy to care about his appearance, demeanour or paunch. She has a brown leather jacket that you can only describe as beautiful, the sort of article of clothing that asks to be smelled or stroked. Her handbag is small but magnificent in its craftsmanship and the one time I glance inside it, I notice that it's filled with exotic and expensive feminine utensils. They seem completely happy and isolated, in the crowd but not of the crowd, although the tent is conspicuously full. She plays with her glossy and elegantly cut long dark hair throughout, and frequently takes her Alice band off and on or just fiddles with her plain but expensive rings. Both of them don't wear socks. It's a sunny day and since they wear deck shoes you can maybe excuse or understand it. Though there's quite a breeze that causes the sides of the tent to flap alarmingly at times and there is a chill when you're out of the sunshine. They seem oblivious but everything about them is carefully chosen and slightly affected, as he scribbles notes with a Mont Blanc pen into a moleskine™ notebook, and she dangles her shoes in carefree fashion off her painted toes. Needless to say, they don't say hello.

So what's all this got to do with speedway? Nothing really apart from the huge contrast I encounter an hour or so after the talk by Eric Hobsbawm ends. Actually, I lie. Born in Vienna in 1918, Hobsbawm is a historian of the Left now in his late 80s who speaks with an intensity and perspective that enthralls his audience. He recounts his impressions and experiences of many important historical and political events, as well as great individuals and artists. From the rise of Hitler, the optimism, decline and fall of the communist system, the swinging 60s, American foreign policy since the war, the rise of Europe, damage to the environment and so many other topics. His knowledge is polymathic and he shores his memories and incisive insights with some style and fluency. He's alive to his past and alive to his present, and despite the frailties of his body his mind retains a brilliance and sharpness that illuminates the tent. Given his background, experiences and predilections, despite the historic lip service paid to the importance of the proletariat on the Left, you know that he doesn't attend speedway regularly. Though Hobsbawm has written widely on jazz and its wider social context, it would have been illuminating if he had similarly interested in the shale and applied his brilliant mind to an analysis of the speedway!

However as a historian, his life has been spent witnessing or explicating human history and, in an era of rapid amnesia and short attention spans, he is an enduring reminder of a significant and important past. Speedway, in my experience, also has its fair share of men and women who've devoted themselves to the sport through eras of boom and bust, through thick and thin, with memories triggered by the racing, key figures of the past, or just evoked by sounds and smells that continue to allow the sport's history to live on in the collective memory and affect the sport today. In a society that sometimes fails to value the aged, infirm and dispossessed, speedway appears old fashioned in its links with the past, but still welcomes all comers into its broad church. I don't want to romanticise this too much, but these slightly 'retro' values of consideration, respect and memory definitely apply to the fans, helpers and track staff at Arlington as well as everywhere else throughout the UK, but it's an attitude and ethic that applies equally to most of the riders and their families. Some of them are superstars who travel the world and get paid superstar wages. Yet they still seem somehow approachable and comparatively normal, a boy-next-door type although obviously a somewhat deranged one who's ready to risk life and limb in a dangerous, high-speed activity. While, you can admire them for the risks they take or the bravery they show, you can't help but notice too that in order to ride at any level you must have extreme dedication to hard work. The demands of the sport are such that, as a competitor, you must regularly expose your vulnerabilities by continually racing and proving yourself over again, almost every night throughout the season. It's this basic but heightened work ethic and, the straightforward and uncomplicated nature of the competition that inspires the loyal devotion of speedway fans. These are same attributes of competition, hard work and a deep desire for success that Eric Hobsbawm enthrallingly describes, delineates and outlines as the engine of history at Charleston that afternoon. These valorised qualities are inevitably found at the more mundane everyday level of the local community with its hobbies, sports and obsessions. In the crowd at Arlington we all play our small part in this tiny version of human history. Nothing too grand, it won't change the world but it is important and it is history nonetheless.

It's hard to tear myself away from an enthralling talk in a billowing tent in beautiful country garden but close by, in equally idyllic countryside, the lure of speedway calls as strongly as ever. When I arrive, just after the pits area has closed, I stumble across Lee Strudwick and his father, Ian, people whom I stood by for years on the home straight at Arlington. Lee has just started to ride in the Conference League for Wimbledon and you can see by the determined look on his face that the chance to fulfil his dream to ride competitively affects him profoundly. He looks completely alive, but simultaneously affects that teenage pose that claims it's nothing too special. He is studiously polite and a credit to his parents, as ever. You can see by the delight and pride on his father Ian's face that it really is something special, particularly as Lee has begun to show real skill, potential and aptitude according to many accounts. This independent verification of his ability, not just the understandable bias of a parent, bodes well for the future. Lee, along with his cousin Niall (and his dad John), always attended the races at Arlington and the lad's always wanted to ride. They seemed to be extremely well informed and to know who was in and who was out as well as the composition of both teams. Niall used to bring his own immaculately pre-prepared scorecard as well as small stepladder to stand on so he could comfortably see over the safety fence. It was a time when we could stand right next to the track, before Health and Safety regulations dictated that we move a few metres back. We were so close you could almost touch the riders as they went past. When Niall stood on his mini-steps, he often did touch the riders' hands in congratulation as they held them out for the adulation of the crowd as they passed on their victory laps of celebration or before the pre-meeting parade. I'll definitely go to Wimbledon to watch him a few times this season and I tell Lee that I really look forward to seeing him ride well there. In fact, I'll feel completely proud on my own behalf, just like I do when Niall rides in the second halves at Arlington. The idea that the young children who stood close by me at home meetings so recently have now turned their dreams into reality; that both have graduated to riding properly, never mind that Lee has already progressed to make an impact in "league racing" makes me feel simultaneously proud and terribly old.

I can't stay to chat too long as I still have to meet the mysterious Dave Fairbrother who attends as the Eastbourne and *Speedway Star's* occasional photographer, that's when he's not being the magazine's subscription manager and – now that we've finally met – a generally all round decent chap. He's a mine of information, gossip and insight, seems excited by the idea of my book *Showered in Shale* and promises to help with information on the country's track-shop owners, although I have started to compile my own list as I go round the tracks as these shops will be vital to the sales of my book when it's published. Because he works for the *Speedway Star* and is a fan,

Dave weaves himself in the warp and the woof of the speedway fraternity throughout the year. He's involved intensely during the season, and he has the special good fortune to travel regularly to every major speedway meeting throughout Europe – mostly Elite League, Internationals and the Benfield GP series – as part of his work, and he also has an ongoing brief to closely watch on/off track comings and goings throughout the winter. He witnesses many of the intrigues, machinations, power plays among the complex variety of personalities intimately involved in the sport without the distorting lens of the heavily sanitised report of these events that's produced for public consumption in the magazine that employs him. Some things just aren't reported. But Dave has the advantage to witness events as they unfold, while he's paid for the privilege to do so. It's a position looked on with some envy by the ordinary fan, although I quickly gather that Dave remains an ordinary fan and down-to-earth person who just happens to have wonderful access to all the sports characters and behind the scenes. He's very discreet though and determined not to unnecessarily shatter any illusions that I might hold. One aspect of the sport he does express himself strongly on, however, is the large number of foreign riders that compete in modern British speedway. It's a situation so common and ordinary that even a bastion of Britishness like Arlington has succumbed to the dictates of remaining competitive. Dave recalls, "there was a time when Eastbourne never had a foreign rider or dreamed of getting one". It's a modern necessity, but one that he decries, "I blame the promoters who are not interested in British riders or giving them time to develop".

After he steps briefly onto his soapbox, Dave has to step off to prepare for the evening ahead as one of the photographers on the centre green. His photos often appear in next week's Eastbourne programme so he has to go off to position himself, but not before he promises to try to help with the book when it's published. Round at my usual place by the start line, thankfully completely dry this evening, the terrace chatter is filled with rumours that Nicki Pedersen was adamant that he didn't want to risk riding last Monday night versus Ipswich in case it jeopardised his fitness for riding in Sweden on Tuesday night. This seems just completely unfounded tittle-tattle, especially since none of the people who claim this were even present on Monday to see the poor conditions first hand, when the track really did look unconducive to racing if not downright dangerous. Nor did they have access to the conversations in the pits (I didn't either) or a hotline to Nicki's mobile. It's amazing how these stories take on a life of their own. Equally I didn't see the 'highlights' of the rain off as reported on Sky Sports so have no idea what was said there or misconstrued from the endless piffle that they have to come up with just to fill all the time when there's nothing happening. Whether these reported comments are true or not, which I doubt, we must live with the fact that a skilful rider like Nicki will always be in demand in all the major speedway leagues and meetings and so, doubtless, this story will be resurrected again after the next 'contentious' rain off decision[1]. So, inevitably, he has to be mindful of his own safety, schedules and a complex set of financial imperatives rather than just give blind undying loyalty to Eastbourne, much as we'd welcome that as fans of the club.

In the programme, Jon Cook reveals that Floppy had taken a few more weeks to recover from his concussion than initially expected. It's a sensible and pragmatic decision, despite Floppy's "patience wearing thin" at the additional delay. Now that Floppy has been pronounced fit to line up for the team tonight, he might be able to channel his frustration into some wonderful riding against Peterborough. Apart from comments on how rough and unusually grippy the track looks, the terrace chatter mostly revolves around the surprise appointment of Dean Barker as Team Captain as a replacement for Floppy. The decision is confirmed a few minutes later by KC who announces Deano as the "new skipper". With this out of the way, KC again repeats his Monday night mantra – listened to with studied indifference by the small crowd then – that he has "big news about the Cardiff Grand Prix that I can't tell you just yet, though I can say that it's big and exciting". While we wait for our heart rates to return to normal after this incredible excitement, we learn from KC that a small aspect of modern fashion has finally arrived at Arlington in the form of some state-of-the-art "speedway wristbands which are available for £2 in the track shop". Demand for the wristbands appears to be restrained, at least among the unfashionable types that surround me, and interest levels remain studiously catatonic regarding the mysterious "big news".

Before the first race of the night Floppy is loudly cheered to the start line. Peter Karlsson is roundly booed in memory of his previous appearance at Arlington, when he dangerously parked his bike on the first bend in a fit of pique. Floppy wins easily to establish an early lead, which Deano extends further in heat 3, when he casually assumes the mantle of team captain with a comfortable third place finish in his first ride in the new role. Heat 4 features the much-anticipated clash of Nicki with his vehement arch-critic Sam Ermolenko, who is very loudly booed throughout. It's a race between two ex-World Champions with supposedly added spice and significance, since Ermolenko had been specifically identified earlier in the week by Jon Cook as a persistent critic of Pedersen in particular but an inconsistent critic of so-called "hard riding" by other riders in his commentary on television. This might or might not be hypocrisy, though the reality is that as Ermolenko's writing and television career takes off, his successful riding career will wind down, and the nature of his position requires that he takes or manufactures 'strong opinions' on contemporary matters of note within the sport. His comments on Nicki are just part of his work and are probably sincerely held, rather than just a convenient affectation to further advance the visibility of his fledgling media career, though they also suit this purpose[2]. Just as you'd expect, Nicki doesn't have to try at all hard to easily beat the declining force that is the ageing Ermolenko nor, for that matter, does his partner Davey Watt. It's anti-climactic for the partisan home crowd who had risen to the defence of their adopted hero with some sustained jeering of Ermolenko and some pointed applause for his team mate, Peterborough's last-placed Richie Hawkins. Dave Rice next to me says that he isn't surprised to see young Richie start to ride at the Elite League level since he's carries on a family tradition and follows in the tyre tracks of his father, Kevin, who was "always a steady rider for Ipswich" (I seem to recall it was Peterborough, Nottingham and Coventry, but the memory plays tricks).

Heat 5 sees Deano appear to have one of those special engine failures that often occur for speedway riders when they trail badly in the race, in this case accompanied with the usual ritual of frequent downward quizzical glances at the machine, before Deano slowly pulls off the track onto the centre green while the race continues. Exactly what you'd expect to happen after a genuine failure but the crowd around me reacts as if they suspect that Deano has affected the canny professionalism of a phantom engine failure. Near by, Jane leaves Deano in no doubt as to her thoughts when she shouts, "you rode like a freaking woman, Barker!" to the oblivious rider as he departs slowly back to the pits. At Arlington like many sporting arenas, it seems the crowd always likes to have something or someone to vent their real or imagined dissatisfaction upon, even though the score line is already a comfortable 19-11. This increases further when tonight's Public

---

[1] Sadly, early in the 2006, the final decision about whether a track is rideable or not at a televised meeting has now been devolved from the riders, although they will apparently "be consulted" and their opinions given due weight. The reasons behind this mid-season change are rumoured to be linked to a number of live televised debacles on Sky Sports, the 2006 ELRC in particular. It is a decision that represents a greater assertion of the natural commercial imperatives of promoters with an understandably keen desire to get a meeting run once they actually have a (large) crowd inside the stadium. Even if you ignore the school of thought that says 'we used to ride in much worse conditions years ago', this change doesn't appear to have common sense on it side, nor is it a step forward and, irrespective of assurances to the contrary, does appear to neatly coincide with contractual interests of the exclusive broadcast rights holder. For the record, the decision to commence racing will, after due consultation with the riders, be taken between the SCB Official Meeting Steward and a nominated 'TV Coordinator'. These TV Coordinators will be mysteriously chosen for their fixtures, most likely by the geographic location of the meeting in question, and drawn from a panel that includes Terry Russell, Alan Ham, Graham Reeve, Colin Meredith and A.N. Other. While they are all responsible people and are to be trusted; it is also fair to say that the ultimate arbiters of whether a meeting will now go ahead will not only be non-riders but will often involve also those with more than one decision-making hat to wear. Interestingly the first time this approach came into force for a televised fixture at Brandon, the riders appeared reluctant to ride but still spoke about them "to put on a show". I always had the impression speedway proudly claimed to be a sport, not a pantomime or circus? Whatever the real reasons behind this change, it nonetheless appears to be another example of the BSPA's famous 'legislation on the hoof' and is indicative of the powerlessness of the riders and the toothlessness of the riders' trade union, the Speedway Riders Association. Ultimately, it doesn't smack of independent or authoritative decision-making, while it also simultaneously undermines the authority of the referee and the riders, plus the oft-repeated canard that rider safety is always a priority will have less force as a consequence.

[2] The close ties that bind the Grand Prix series, Sky Sports and BSI have bound even tighter in 2006 with Sam's appointment to the newly founded and "revolutionary position" of Sporting Director at the BSI-owned and renamed Reading Bulldogs (though they appear on the official BSI website as "BSI Reading"). It's an opportunity for Sam to bring his expertise to bear behind the scenes, to 'professionalise' the Bulldogs riders, equipment preparation and planning as well as part of the often foreshadowed but inconsistently implemented John Postlethwaite campaign to selectively transplant Formula 1 concepts and approaches into British speedway. A jarring note, however, is Sam's repeated valorisation of his role and his Bulldogs colleagues when he commentates during Sky Sports coverage of the Elite League or the GP series. It's hardly an independent perspective but the combination of his undoubted expertise/insight allied to cookie-cutter Americanisms must have appeal to both sets of his employers and, hopefully, the television audience! Though, like many areas of speedway, exact details are scant and independent research or verification non-existent.

Enemy Number 1 elect, Sam Ermolenko, falls and is excluded from the re-run, which Floppy and Watty win easily from Hawkins. It certainly appears that the Eagles have adapted quicker and with greater aplomb than the visiting Panthers to the rare Arlington experience of an unusually rough track; conditions which will invariably result after all the sawdust it received earlier in the week during the abortive attempt to run the Ipswich TV meeting for the Sky Sports television people. It's just a shame that it's only a KO Cup encounter rather than a League meeting. Things are going so badly for the Panthers that Steen Jensen even gains a point in the next race to ecstatic but ironic cheers from the crowd. KC again takes the chance to remind us that he has some pending "big news about Cardiff". He's so excited you begin to wonder if Prince William will make a special appearance on a bike at the meeting. Still the interval isn't far away so we'll only have to wait with bated breath and fevered anticipation a short while longer.

Enthusiastic cheers are the order of the night from Jane. She greets Davey Watt's third place in heat 10 as if the point ensured that he became World Champion, rather than it just further extended the huge lead for the Eagles. During the break, I bump into Jon Cook who scuttles along in the darkening evening behind the home-straight grandstand en route to the referee's box. He puts the ease of the impending victory down to "the rough track suited us more" as well as, "consistent riding from Nicki and David".

The next minute the earth barely remains constant in it's orbit as we learn from an almost hyperventilating KC that he's not to get married to a princess but it's almost the next best thing besides, "I am honoured to announce that I have been selected to be the announcer at the Cardiff Grand Prix in June and I feel privileged to have been chosen!" The crowd concertedly chats among themselves about other more mundane matters in celebration of the "big news". It's the sort of petty, narrow-mindedness that inevitably greets the hard-won success of others in their chosen careers. I won't attend this year's GP and the audience at home who watch on the television won't hear a single word throughout, but I'm sure that KC will rally the huge crowd and inject some of his razzmatazz, hyperbole and élan into the proceedings. He is a unique and gifted announcer in a sport of distinctive voices. He remains a firm favourite of mine, is always entertaining and the standards he sets remains the litmus test against which I judge the commentary standards achieved by other announcers during my travels around the country.

After the "big news" KC is then emotionally spent and comparatively subdued for the rest of the evening, so thereby manages not to get too carried away with the size, regularity or ease of the Eastbourne victory. It's as if tonight's one swallow has made his summer and his infectious hyperbole chip has been temporarily disabled. Despite it only being the KO Cup, Jane nearby indulges her common but often disconcerting ritual of actually praying before a couple of the significant heats. In tonight's case, it's heats 13 and 15 that receive help from a Higher Authority. She does pretty well everything but kneel in supplication during these rather intense personal moments of silent prayer, often for around a minute. God moves in a mysterious ways, His wonders to perform. In this case, He bedevils Ermolenko with a tape exclusion in heat 13 before PK races away to victory in the re-run. Following a further appeal to another dimension by Jane, Ales Dryml suffers an exclusion that results in the last race being awarded. It's an easy victory in which Steen manages to avoid the unwanted mantle of the lowest scoring rider from tonight's meeting when his solitary, single point easily outclasses the three ride zero of the diminutive Conference League rider Jon Armstrong.

21st May Eastbourne v. Peterborough (KO Cup) 59-36

23rd May

Nicki's reputation went before him and the back wheel of his bike announced his arrival once again. Consequently, he was excluded in his first race after Scott Nicholls was launched into the fence. While Scott's bike was a write off, it upset the Dane's equilibrium sufficiently for him to take no further part in the meeting after heat 9. Not that he was the only one in the wars; the Bees ended the night with their treatment table occupied by Morten Risager's broken ankle, while the unlucky Rory Schlein went straight to hospital with suspected vertebrae damage after he was thrown over his handlebars. Steen takes up the slack, rides in an assured at the back of the field in each race and so fails to trouble the scorer in all four of his outings.

23rd May Coventry v. Eastbourne (ELA) 52–41

Were You There That Night?

25th May

In years to come this will be another one of those fixtures where people ask in a breathless tone: "Were you there the night Steen won a race at Arena Essex Speedway?" Even people who were in reality miles away will in the future claim that they helped swell the crowd, just so they can relive the stunning events of that night to their grandchildren. Luckily, I was actually there!

Arena Essex appeared to have run over the proverbial black cat even this early in the season and had already endured a campaign that would be acceptable only if it were the quick-quick-slow-slow rhythms of dance. But it was speedway, and it had already proved unacceptable to the often swift to grumble but long-suffering Hammers fans. The club promoter Ronnie Russell was prompt, as ever, to hold his hands up where he was at fault and to work tirelessly behind the scenes to try to book the best available guest riders to replace the injured Mark Loram. The season had started so promisingly with some thumping wins and had even included an away victory at Oxford. However, with the injury to Mark Loram added to the brief arrival and departure of speedway World Champion Tony Rickardsson on a short-term one- month contract, the Hammers now found themselves becalmed and the fans had begun to snarl on the Internet message boards and forums. Ronnie hasn't taken to this aspect of modern life, particularly as it gives undue prominence to those so-called supporters that deliberately, or otherwise, try to damage the aims and prestige of his club. If the squeaky wheel gets the oil, then the World Wide Web amplifies minor squeaks to a crescendo that alienates potential sponsors and the stay-away fans. Even the forum on the club's own official website had, bizarrely, become infected with this will-to-doom mood among a small subsection of the quick-fingered typists who lurked there.

All this should have meant that tonight was an ideal time for the Eagles to visit in search of some valuable early season Elite League points gained away from home. Most weeks, Ronnie would have already heard every excuse possible from any of the top riders that he had tried to book as a guest. In the programme, Ronnie complains that his "mobile phone bill has gone through the roof". And we all know how expensive those overseas calls can be! Alternatively, he has often been frustrated by the "8 Day Rule". On top of that, it appears that at many fixtures that often end in defeat, the final scoreline doesn't reflect the "true story" of the meeting from Ronnie's point of view. However, tonight he had engineered a coup by getting Jason Crump as guest – a chance that arrived when his average dropped by a vital fraction

when the "new Green Sheets" were issued – though as the Hammers already knew to their cost "one swallow doesn't make a summer" and speedway is, at the end of the day, a team sport. Still, the very news on the grapevine of Crumpie's appearance would normally encourage valuable numbers of additional fickle, stay-away fans through the turnstiles to watch him race and witness the contests with Nicki Pedersen. Unfortunately, the Eagles were without Nicki Pedersen tonight and had gone out and signed another Belle Vue rider as a guest, in this case Jason Lyons, and so almost makes this unofficially appear as a triangular team tournament tonight.

The chance to barrack Deano would also draw some additional fans to the Arena Essex Raceway and the Eagles had Floppy in the squad who had already shown a real feel for the circuit when he rode for the Hammers as a guest against Coventry. How he would perform was an imponderable, as time and circumstance had painfully intervened since that night when Floppy had successfully dashed around the Thurrock raceway as a guest rider for Arena, in the form of the head injury he sustained at Swindon.

In another continuation of a parallel injury jinx, the Hammers would have to ride tonight without the services of Roman Povazhny who had damaged his foot in Sweden the night before. The operation of rider replacement would place an additional strain on the already beleaguered and weakened home squad. In fact by the time Crump came out onto the track for the first time of this evening, the Eagles had already roared into the lead thanks to the Shieldsy–Deano pairing in heat 3. A good race from Dean always attracts ribald comment and jeers from the terraces here and tonight was no exception. It is a state of affairs that Deano handles with equanimity. He comments diplomatically: "Nothing against Arena Essex – it just caught me in one of those years [2004] when I was there. The fans and everyone was superb but being back at Eastbourne is like being back home again. I am well happy."

In reports afterwards, it was claimed as a somewhat tenuous justification that the 'new' Thurrock track surface worked against the home riders and favoured the opposition. This wasn't at all evident from the vantage point of the terraces, nor was it really reflected in the scores that remained close until heat 14. Apparently an unsettled "top surface" unsettled the Hammers! Though to a lay observer like myself, the track appeared as smooth and free of dirt as is usual on race nights round here. That said, every Eagles rider did record at least one race victory with the exception of Mooro who failed to score all night. Perhaps, with someone else in the team obviously not coping with conditions and apparently riding as poorly as he often manages, this lifted a metaphorical and psychological weight from Steen's slight 20 year-old shoulders. Whatever the reason, not only did Steen get a point for a third in his first outing but, in heat 6, he got another one to match it when he kept Gary "ex-World Champion" Havelock at the back of the race throughout. This was due to a mixture of factors that included a poor gate initially by Havvy who then found himself unable to find a line to actually pass the young Dane. Afterwards, Trevor Geer definitely felt that Steen's slightly eccentric and erratic progress for four laps round the circuit was a significant factor in this win, "although to be fair, Havelock couldn't get past him as he was all over the place and he didn't know which way Steen was going to go!"

Still, "a point is a point" as they say and the comparatively huge boost to Steen's fragile confidence that this provided had the Eagles actually choose to bring him in for a reserve replacement ride. It was a shrewd move that saw him fly from the tapes and, though we didn't know it at the time, this resulted in Steen's only away heat victory of the season! He managed to easily beat two riders who really do know their way around the tight confines of the Thurrock circuit – Paul Hurry and Josh Larsen. It would have got even better for Steen who, with his dander well and truly up – was then only robbed of another victory by over confidence and bad luck when he pirouetted in exuberant style on the fourth lap, while extremely close to the finish line. It appeared much harder to execute the 360-degree turn that he did and still almost remain unscathed on his bike than it did to finish. Though he had another pointless ride later in the contest, for a couple of heats his confidence and talent finally burned brightly in the Eagles colours and this was to turn out to be as good as it got for him all season on an away track! Indeed, his five points from five rides could have been much, much more. Life is full of ifs, ands and buts. But if, that night, his confidence had received the boost of another race victory to follow so soon after the earlier one, who can say if he would have gone on to live up to the hyperbole and early season expectations that his undoubted talent on a bike had created? As it was, Steen was to continue to remain tentative whenever other riders pulled alongside him. He was invariably fine with room all around him – this can always be guaranteed at the rear of the field – and the track ahead to race towards; but with riders alongside he was soon and always too easily passed.

The race of the night was still to come between Floppy and Jason Crump in heat 11, where Floppy led at great speed until he was passed superbly through the proverbial gap the size of the eye of the needle. Though he rode to a five-ride maximum, Crumpie was only really offered any effective level of support from his fellow countryman Josh Larsen. The Eagles' star rider of the night was Adam Shields, though Floppy also rode with some brio and confidence in a manner that approximated his true self, while Deano gave the Hammers faithful glimpses of the skill that they hadn't often witnessed last season when he had donned the patriotic red, white and blue colours of Arena Essex.

Jon Cook was wreathed in smiles afterwards, so quickly pronounced himself "delighted with the whole performance" and with what he viewed as an "excellent win at Arena where, in truth, the scoreline flattered the home side". He went on to note that "youthful exuberance" had cost Steen points and that Floppy had done especially well "because it has not been easy to ride through his injury as he has done". Overall, Jon felt "pretty excited" and could look forward to the season's campaign with some degree of anticipation and expectation: "it is starting to come together quite nicely. We have three away wins on board and we have the potential to get more".

25th May Arena Essex v. Eastbourne (ELA) 43–47

Another different chapter appears about this fixture in my book *Showered in Shale*.

Gary 'Easy Rider' Havelock. © Jeff Scott

Davey leads the pack. © Jeff Scott

Alan casually studies the form. © Jeff Scott

June

DAVID NORRIS

"He's got Nicki Pedersen – the most ruthless rider on the planet – behind him"

4th June

Ever the psychologist, Matt Ford claimed, "the last time we went to Eastbourne luck was on our side". Jon Cook's concerns are more prosaic, since he aims for a "small change" to "strengthen the reserves" before he then pointedly mentions Steen's "youthful exuberance" in despatches. This knack of allowing points to slip away has caused Mr Jensen's average to fall to 3.10 prior to this match. The freefall of his progression and average continued unabated against the Pirates with another three ride zero that effectively again saw him MIA. This led Jon Cook to consider his options and announce that, though still in the throes of recovering from injury, Sheffield's Richard Hall would 'double up' (in place of Adam Allott) with Steen in future. Another candidate, Ulrich Ostergaard, would have also been considered but for "moving house in Denmark". With masterly understatement, JC noted, "Steen has found the going a little tough of late", though he offered the always sensible advice that, "he needs to sort out his gating and find a bit more consistency".

In the event, Poole provided the majority of heat winners and led until heat 11. The Eagles won the last race and secured the points, but only after Antonio Lindback was controversially excluded after he came to grief in deep shale. Even at the end of a night's racing, quite how Bob had allowed these deposits to gather on his invariably pristine Arlington track surface beggars the imagination!

4th June Eastbourne v. Poole (ELB) 46–44

Steen Triumphs

June 18th

It feels like we've wandered into our own speedway version of *Groundhog Day* with yet another meeting with local rivals from around the M25. The visit of Arena Essex attracts a large crowd dressed in summer clothing to Arlington. It's a very warm and bright evening that, when combined with his own sunny disposition, Arlington's very own maestro on the microphone and Master of Ceremonies, Kevin Coombes, is keen to celebrate. He enthusiastically reminds us all that we're "officially welcomed to the summer!" Sadly, I'd been absent from the Cardiff GP meeting where, by all accounts, KC excelled. Well, actually, he excelled in his own account and memory of Cardiff[1], something about which he almost immediately informed us all after his perfunctorily quick run through the team line-ups. To be exact, he did initially broach the subject by enquiring rhetorically as to how many of the crowd had been to Cardiff. His questions were quick and direct but didn't require us to answer. "Wasn't it something else? Wasn't it a fantastic atmosphere? Wasn't it great to see our very own Floppy in action?" By all independent accounts, he worked the large but extremely diverse Cardiff GP crowd into a frenzy though, sadly, none of his masterly control of the crowd was audible or featured in my recording of the Sky Sports broadcast. Those who saw him perform at Cardiff said that KC was like a man possessed of even greater energy levels than his usual Tigger-like approach.

Throughout the evening, KC repeatedly welcomes "the big summer crowd here this evening" and is almost breathless in his anticipation of the racing, although I can't recall any recent close encounters at Arlington against "local rivals" Arena Essex. I believe that everyone would agree that you can only really have one true local rival – in Eastbourne's case that is Poole. But maybe there's a distinction to be drawn between a geographically local rival (Arena) and a psychological rival (Poole)? One handy measure of actual rivalry could be whom do you support when Poole races against Arena? Another key test would most probably be whether or not you glory when either of them suffers defeat or unexpected misfortune. On this basis, you'd still have to say our natural rivals are still Poole, although the last few years would have been particularly pleasurable if Arena had really been our "local rivals".

KC welcomes "Mr 'Fast Fingers' Frank Ebdon" to the referee's box perched in the bright sunshine above the start line and then claims that Frank is, "enjoying the luxury of race control this evening, it's like a greenhouse in here tonight – phew!" It is definitely a sweltering evening. With two Russians riding for Arena, KC is dying to use his pre-prepared phrase 'From Russia with Love', but he just about manages to control himself and hang onto this *bon mot* until they find themselves on track together in heat 8. Heat 1 does however have KC come over all geographically informed, with relative distances between Australia (Shieldsy) and what KC calls Russia (Serge Darkin) – though it's actually Uzbekistan – mentioned as the riders head to the start line. The exoticism of travel doesn't have any enduring fascination for KC since he omits to mention that Floppy travels in from the nearby wilds of Hailsham or, for that matter, that Havvy journeys to Arlington from yet another typically English rural idyll, in this case Yarm in North Yorkshire, the beloved village home of many wealthy footballers. The arrival of Roman Povazhny at the tapes for heat 2 lets KC lamely riff with a juxtaposition on a geography and film theme: "from Russia with a bit of attitude". Given our accepted cultural clichés regarding Russia with its frontier spirit, vodka drinking, distinctive headgear and the prevalence of the criminal fraternity, KC seems to unconsciously allude to uncharacteristic level of wussiness exhibited by Povazhny. Perhaps it's the influence of his Christian name, Roman. This race sees a real rarity with a true collector's item in the form of an actual Steen Jensen victory, who powers away from the start to actually win an Elite League race! In fact, it was to turn out to be his ONLY home race win of the season, although his final tally for the season was to be double that amount since he had also already gained another, delightfully matching, Elite League race win away at Arena Essex. Nonetheless, it's so shocking that

---

[1] Actually KC is one of country's leading speedway MCs. Given his easy facility on the microphone and the larger-than-life personality he projects, KC is surprisingly modest to the point of shy when you chat with him in person. I genuinely believe that he would make an excellent contribution to live commentary at the speedway fixtures shown on Sky Sports television. When I have observed him first hand, he definitely has the insight, the personality, can paint pictures with words, connect with people and do all this while effortlessly multi-tasking in the referee's booth at Arlington – even with loud distracting voices constantly ringing in his ears from his headphones. KC should apply for a screen test (sound test?) forthwith and accompany his application with his own version of the commentary for any Sky meeting. Maybe, Eastbourne fans should petition Sky Sports for him to be given this chance?

the crowd is stunned into silence and KC seems temporarily lost for words. Jon Cook had in fact presciently noted in his programme column that our "Achilles Heel" at reserve had shown signs of possible rejuvenation; mainly this was because Andrew Moore had started to ride well in that position. But since Steen was also no longer "under the weather" and could re-welcome the help of his regular mechanic to the pits "to prepare his machines"; an aspect of his performance that Jon darkly but accurately noted, "is an area in which he struggles". This sort of subtly nuanced, almost schoolmasterish report would be lost on Steen for whom English is, at best, his third language. You would, however, hope that he'd start to show a bit more application and oomph that his talent should clearly deliver. Even a win for Steen can't really stir the crowd from the apathy and torpor towards his performances that his rides usually provoke except, of course, when he stimulates severe rage in the other Eagles fans around me by the start line.

KC's keen sense of occasion and geography continues with heat 3 as Deano arrives on the track billed as "one of the famous Eastbourne boys". Although Deano hails from London and Eastbourne's other long-time favourite son, Floppy, comes from Hailsham – in Australian terms of distance they're both next door, so we'll just have to nod along with KC's description. Deano suffers throughout tonight's meeting a result of the combination of sweltering temperatures and the lack of "lining" in his kevlars that caused him to ride this meeting, with an eye on adaptability and fashion, "in thermals and a big roll neck". Shortly afterwards a closely fought race between Nicki and Roman Povazhny provokes Dave next to me to exclaim, "that was bloody brilliant – fantastic racing!" An accurate comment, but not one that would let him challenge the silver-tongued KC who contents himself by repeating, "Wow!" over and over. With some more attention to the track and the second outing for the bowser to water the circuit, KC indulges in his specialty – confirming the evidence of our own eyes – when he assures us that the bowser is out "just making sure the track is in tip-top condition". KC then goes all technical on us, and elegantly combines horticulture, geography and physics, when he muses that this will be the last outing for the bowser as, "we don't have to worry about evaporation problems when the sun goes down". Because it's close to the longest day of the year, this seems a trifle optimistic but, as the sun gradually sets, it turns out to be completely accurate. A different career in horticulture awaits KC if he ever tires of all things Arlington and, recently, Cardiff.

Ever in search of a pun or *bon mot*, KC refers wittily to the visitor's sponsors – Husqvarna, the proud manufacturers of the world's biggest lawnmower – intermittently as "husk-banana". When this doesn't even raise even a titter, KC decides to don his metaphorical doctor's white coat when he interviews team captain Deano during the interval. They quickly rehearse all the traditional platitudes about Arena being a tough team, not to be underestimated and so on, before Deano takes great pleasure in the "performance of the lads so far" etc. Soon they move onto the vexed question of David Norris's health or, more specifically, his inconsistent recovery from the concussion and continuing neck injury he suffered at Swindon in April. KC starts the ball rolling and observes, "when he's not on a speedway bike the neck injury is fine". From the way Deano describes the sensation of riding a speedway bike, it's enough to put you off completely since you soon gather that the intense vibration you actually feel is akin to riding a pneumatic road drill. Those not of a technical disposition should look away now: "the machines are very light, so there's a lot of vibration or torque when you get on the bike, setting the nerves off in David's neck". It all sounds very painful and if that's what Floppy has to endure at each meeting no wonder Gary Havelock and Sergei Darkin unexpectedly beat him so easily in the opening race of the fixture. The industrial injury caused by excessive use of a pneumatic drill is known as 'white finger' and Floppy appears to temporarily have the speedway equivalent – 'white neck'. As if the risk of damaging yourself racing speedway isn't great enough already every time you race, Floppy appears to literally put his neck on the line every time he rides. Help, sorry about that, I worry I've now begun to unconsciously borrow from the KC lexicon of humour.

Despite Deano's fears of a close match, the meeting meanders to its foregone conclusion, although not before a painful end to the evening for Arena's American rider Josh Larsen in heat 12. He tangled with Deano, who had fallen himself when chasing Povazhny, "I went in a little bit harder than Roman did. We had just had an interval and they had graded the track. It was a little 'icy' and there was nothing to hold me up. Roman went in a bit slower than I anticipated and I had to park it up and drop the bike. I feel a bit sorry for Josh because he laid it down to miss me and then got hit from behind." The quick-thinking Josh was, unfortunately, struck heavily from behind by Steen Jensen, who was inevitably already trailing by some distance. Josh was, like many speedway riders, already riding through the pain barrier to race in this meeting, after he had previously sustained a back injury riding for his country in the World Team Cup qualifier over in Latvia. So breaking his collarbone in four places was further bad luck. He lay prostrate on the track for some considerable time before he manfully walked back to the pits in excruciating pain without the help of a short trip in the available ambulance. This kind of bravery is legendarily common among the riders but, in this case, Josh had decided to walk back to the pits to spare his already overdue and heavily pregnant wife, Kim, any undue, additional stress. What a gent! Sadly, this meant that all the Larsen family would be going to hospital at some point that week – Josh to undergo surgery and Kim to have their baby.

Shortly thereafter we almost witness a unique heat 14. Whether it's a combination of weak opposition or a newfound confidence from now having reliable mechanical help in the pits, Steen Jensen is having his best ever meeting at Arlington for Eastbourne. Well, actually, his mammoth tally of seven points from four rides is due to his excellent heat 2 followed by a catalogue of misfortunes that affected the riders in all his other races. It seems Steen only has to join a race tonight for someone to fall off and get excluded, or get badly injured when he runs them over. Although he's been replaced by fellow reserve Mooro in the penultimate heat 14, we're treated to the sight of three Eastbourne riders attempting to join the Arena riders already at the tapes. After a few hand signals from the pits and Start Marshal Alan Rolfe, Steen heads back off again. KC wittily notes, "we're so keen to win this one that we have three riders out for the race!" To again confirm the evidence of our own eyes aurally, KC interviews Jon Cook before the last race of the night. JC is delighted at the widely expected win, but is even more chuffed at the "two fantastic crowds at the last two meetings". With another win for Nicki Pedersen to complete an immaculate 15 point maximum, the Eagles portion of the crowd funnels away from the stadium car park in buoyant mood.

18th June Eastbourne v. Arena Essex (ELA) 52-42

Passions Run High at Wimbourne Road

22nd June

The South Coast derby fixtures with the 'old enemy', the Poole Pirates always produces an additional frisson of tension among the supporters of both sides. In recent years the anticipation has remained the same for the Eagles fans, but the results haven't exactly boosted our bragging rights with our erstwhile competitors. In fact, while the rewards of their continued success have flooded into the Wimborne Road trophy cabinet over recent years, ours has remained mostly empty. To make matters worse on the trophy front, one of the rare gilt-edged chances that we have had in recent years, now receding to the dim and distant past, ended in tears as we were robbed of the Elite League crown through the introduction that year of the play-off system!

The fact that the Eagles haven't gained the results we would have liked them to when they have rode at Poole recently has, along with their own annual expectation of more trophies, continued to delight the Pirates supporters. We have tended to struggle to exert any real sustained pressure on the home riders, and the make up of our squad for this latest trip on a hot summer's day in June doesn't promise to end the disappointing run of defeats there, despite my intuition that the Pirates squad is beginning to show the telltale signs of weakness that might presage a year without any trophies for them. The recent 'B' fixture had seen the Eagles originally win by two points, though "Mike and Matt" in their programme notes nurse an aggrieved tone about their recollections of the events surrounding that particular fixture at Arlington. There is quite a litany that includes the "saga concerning the missing Matej Ferjan" as well as "Antonio's exclusion" that apparently has been "debated over, and over, and over again" in Pirates circles. So much so that "while everyone has their own views on the rights and wrongs", the promotional partnership prefer to raise philosophical and methodological questions not actually covered by the 2005 rule book, notably "whether Antonio was given enough room to race, even if there was no contact between the riders". Magnanimously, they agree it is for the referee "to decide" but imply he dropped a bollock.

On the subject of Ferjan, the rulebook is again consulted, this time by the Eagles who protest to the SCB afterwards about the use of rider replacement for the missing Pirate. This protest is upheld by the SCB and the deduction of the four points 'scored' led to the 44–46 defeat for the Pirates now being 'officially' amended to a more resounding 46–40 victory for the Eagles. This rankles so much in Poole with its management that they draw deeply on the lessons of history: "past meetings between the Pirates and the Eagles have been highly-charged affairs, with the odd bit of controversy thrown in for good measure" and this leads the two promotional M's, Matt and Mike, to believe that the events of the first leg 'B' fixture "can only spice up tonight's fixture even further and spur on the Pirates".

Wherever a fixture features Nicki Pedersen, it is safe to say that it rarely needs spicing up for either the riders or the fans. Maybe spicing down would be advisable, if there was such a thing, even without the later events tonight of heat 9. Before a wheel has turned I have had a fantastic behind-the-scenes introduction to everything Poole speedway by the club's gifted press officer, perpetually avuncular, charming and perennially modest, Gordie Day. I quickly learnt that the club clearly had many knowledgeable and committed staff everywhere you looked with a genuine, shared belief in the values of their club and whoever donned the skull-and-crossbones race bib.

All this behind-the-scenes access had the brilliant result that during the meeting I was able to stand on the fourth bend with the riders of both sides and to observe all that went on in the pits. Well, at least, on the Poole side of the pits as well as the shared commonway areas that led out onto the track from the Eastbourne side of the pits, intersected by the Poole access point and the short stretch of distance over the tarpaulined cover to the track. Before the pre-meeting parade the riders from both teams mingle very amiably with Deano in particular simultaneously the centre of attention and the witty glue that informally binds the protagonists together tonight while they wait to fulfil their publicly allotted roles and behaviours. There is much smiling and flashes of teeth on both sides. The Pirates have a star-studded team: Krzysztof Kasprzak, Antonio Lindback, Ryan Sullivan, Bjarne Pedersen and Matej Ferjan. All of them mix amiably with the Eagles. On our side Shieldsy appears reticent, Mooro shyly detached as is (strangely enough) Nicki who stands on the periphery of this group and wears his only-really-ever-cool-in-Eastern Europe style sunglasses. "Dave" Watt, as the programme race card christens him (as it does "Dave" Norris), is affable but slightly to the edge of the group and Floppy is noticeably anxious and slightly frenetic during this brief respite before the rider parade. They are surrounded by various officials that signal their authority with caps, fluorescent jackets, official jackets of the suit or anorak variety as well as a men in bright overalls that have benefited from the latest biological washing powders. Deano is in his element – jovial, self-deprecating, witty and slightly (self-)consciously, strenuously on-message as a geezerish "good feller". If it's an affectation, it is a clever one as Deano's contemporaries clearly respect him. The respect of your peers and contemporaries is an accolade you can't win in a single night, claim as your right or have delivered after a specific competition. It is bestowed and derives from a thousand little instances – those insignificant moments in a lengthy career that invariably highlight your 'true' character in a rich panoply of speedway locations – in the pits, on the track, in the van, on the dance floor or in bars. Those myriad social interactions build over time to burnish your reputation but, if ever lost, it is always irrevocably so and never recoverable. Many of the riders that surround him are probably confident that they can beat the 2005 version of Deano more times than he beats them, but he is definitely not taken for granted. Nor does he fail to briefly bask in the professionalism of his flippancy and, through happenstance, perhaps the shrewdest decision of the season (or many seasons) taken by JC was to recognise his real importance to the team and team spirit with the recognition of the Eagles captaincy.

The first couple of heats are an exchange of 5–1s. One to the Pirates with Floppy trailed off third and Shieldsy a re-mounted faller but distant finisher. This is followed by a difficult-to-anticipate romp from Mooro and Cameron Woodward, the latest rider to assume the mantle of the problematic, possibly jinxed, No. 7 slot. What really stands out as noticeable from my vantage point is the sheer urgency of the whole of the Pirates pits – how they all work together on the bikes of "their team", all the mutual coaching of each other and the apparent absence of hierarchy that means you automatically help out your team mates. It is a level of effort and teamwork that doesn't deliver the goods immediately since the Eagles toy with their supporters in the stadium by apparently promising a possible night to remember with successive heat advantages. The Poole side provide a peculiar mix of signals – they aren't quite firing on all cylinders and also aren't quite lacklustre, though they hint of better things to come.

They struggle back onto level terms by the end of the seventh heat only for their trump card of Lindback, riding at 2, being wasted in unceremonious fashion with an exclusion for a fall. I get to observe first hand his frustrated almost violent reaction to this turn of events as he strumps along the track back to the pits. This petulance shows his age – something he mostly masks with his studiously 'cool' demeanour and, more relevantly, with his mature riding ability and flowing style – but it also communicates a desire to win that the Eagles collectively don't muster. It is an emotional and attitudinal difference that Nicki inadvertently manages to crystallise in the Pirates riders and galvanise in the pits staff, Poole officials and crowd in one typically combative, but slightly misjudged manoeuvre, when he comprehensively plants Matej Ferjan into the inflatable safety equipment after he spills him from his bike and enables him to have bounce off the track surface for good measure. It is harsh enough to automatically result in Nicki's exclusion by Barry Richardson, the SCB official on duty tonight. The crowd and the Pirates riders react with vehemence and ill-suppressed anger. Even the scoreboard operator throws aside all vestige of impartiality with the addition of "dirty bastard" to the information about this decision regarding Nicki's exclusion. They say sticks and stones are more injurious than opinions, but the reaction to this incident says all you need to know about the real tenor of this contest. It is about pride and bragging rights, but somehow runs deeper. The most spectacular reaction to the incident comes from the diminutive Poole captain, Ryan Sullivan, who doesn't stand on ceremony or decorum in his rush to confront Nicki while he is still on the track. Ryan draws himself to his full height, which temporarily seemed appreciably taller, to bellow, "I'll freaking have you any time!" Phew. This is top-drawer, massively pent-up frustration exploding over the place like jet-propelled volcanic magma – corrosive, ferocious but weirdly disproportionate as though Ryan has harboured resentments against Nicki, his own continuing 'spotty' to poor form in the skull-and-crossbones colours, and a convenient focus for every incidence of bullying at school, comments about his stature, and everyone who has ever cut him off in his high-end black BMW. In short it was noticeably over-blown and definitely not a reaction guaranteed to restore calm on the terraces or in the pits. Davey Watt intercedes to try to calm the inflamed Sullivan. As for the riders themselves, it could easily and self-righteously be pointed out that the blue touchpaper had been lit by Nicki, though any spark tonight would probably have had an incendiary effect albeit not such an explosively dramatic one. It is never dull where Nicki is involved.

A major barney threatens but managed to contain itself as a skirmish, where words and gestures outweigh physical reactions though there is still a good degree of clasping of fists and interceding on others' behalfs for a few minutes among the riders at the pit gate and the 'neutral' shared access points. Confusion and temper reign. By now I know from past experience, but can't see to confirm this, that Nicki will be calm and retreat quickly to his part of the pits, but it is much more a question of how the Eagles will channel their heightened tempers and nerve. The same question of how this will be channelled applies to the Pirates riders but they not only have the 'moral' high ground that Nicki's actions and subsequent exclusion assure them but also take full advantage to ram home a 5–1 in the re-

run. This happens after the referee brings forward the interval to allow Matej time to recover and fire up his second bike. It is a perfect and brave reply after the rider has spent some time prone on the track to receive the ministrations of the St. John Ambulance medical team. The Pirates repeat the dose in the next race through a very fired up Ryan Sullivan and a slightly less so Antonio. Psychologically this is game, set, and match. The only question remaining is how much strength in adversity the Eagles can collectively counter or the extent to which the wheels will come off the wagon.

There is still much generalised seething and there are a number of other flash points. A small section of the home supporters have gathered, as they do every week, by some fencing that separates them from the pits but that leaves them close enough to almost be part of the comings and goings on both sides of the pits. Along with Ryan, they have taken severe umbrage with Nicki, but they are also keen to share this ire around evenly. They say never judge a book by its appearances – except this one, of course, if you think it looks nice – and the appearance of one of the most conspicuously voluble of the Pirates fans is no exception to this rule. He wears the kind of clothes that indicates that he has come straight from his sweaty-bottomed middle-management office job. The only concession he has made to being at the speedway on a hot night is to have removed his tie and to keep the setting of his language at industrial. He loudly peppers the air with obscenities along with lurid observations about genitalia and family relationships experienced by Eagles riders and their fans on a daily basis. It is a partisan rant that would be best ignored, but one that ineluctably draws the attention of both Floppy and Jon Cook at different moments over the remainder of the fixture. It is hard to ignore and difficult not to object to, but the raw emotion generated means that this critic will definitely not listen to reason. Neither will the fans that also surround him who, in their anger, push extremely hard at the fence as though they have been caged and continue to press against it with a violence that suddenly makes it appear very flimsy. After the meeting there is talk of a "distasteful spitting incident" (aren't they always?) directed at Floppy but exact circumstances are difficult to corroborate and the usual speedway veil of silence quickly descends. What is certain on the night is that in his own exchange with this critic Jon Cook doesn't manage to assuage the anger or vitriol nor does he manage to engage in any real level of debate, but I'm sure he feels slightly better for his valiant but always doomed attempt to do so.

Floppy gets so wound up that he tries to channel his anger into taking to the track on his bike extremely early for heat 13. A heat that, by this late point on the meeting, represents the last real throw of the dice for the Eagles to recover the situation and overcome the six-point deficit that has now built up against the visitors. He is so early to the gate and keen to get going that the tractor has yet to finish grading the track and, quite correctly, a member of the track staff in the garish red boiler suit that they sport as a uniform at Wimborne Road refuses to open the gate when sharply requested to do so. This display of intransigence (or basic safety rules, depending on your point of view) is not at all well received by Floppy who reacts badly and brings his helmet menacingly close to this man's face so that he can share his thoughts more clearly. Eventually, when it is clear that quite a wait still remains the order of the day, Floppy about-tails in high dudgeon and races back at frighteningly high speed from the narrow confines of the Poole pits exit back to his own spot in the Eagles area of the pits. It is enough stress on its own to cause a recurrence of the concussion-like symptoms he has continued to suffer since late April. The warnings plastered about any pits area always say how dangerous it is for any notoriously fragile humans that stray there. Gordie Day looks on at the pulsating area of anger and emotion that is the pits area tonight, smiles, rubs his hands together and notes approvingly: "This is speedway!"

When Floppy eventually takes to the track for heat 13, he has psychologically already upset himself too much to provide an effective opposition. He fails to make the gate and finishes last. It's a placing that along with Nicki's second ends all chance of a win and only leaves a draw as an outside possibility. Ryan Sullivan, whose performance on the night can be split into pre- and post-incident levels of application, wins the race. Before Matej found the fence, he had only exhibited the middling level of form that has typified his effort levels and so frustrated himself as well as the Pirates fans, particularly when compared to his undoubted abilities and arrival in the squad as the No.1 rider and replacement for Tony Rickardsson To be fair, this was an unenviable task for anyone put in that position. A contributory factor to his recent performance has been the trapped nerves he has suffered in his neck and back. Afterwards, he brushes aside the niggles of various ailments and has been transformed by the Ferjan incident into a motivational club captain that not only leads by example with two exhilarating wins but does so in a manner that once rightly gained him the "Flyin' Ryan" nickname. The fixture stutters to a predictable conclusion with a win for the Pirates that in the final analysis is a straightforward 50–40. When I speak with Ryan afterwards he uses the practised language of the blandly anodyne interview, a technique many riders have rehearsed so many times over the years. Among the many platitudes are sound bites such as, "our team spirit showed through", "we dug deep", "we lifted it a notch when we had too", "your nationality is irrelevant in this team" and "it's not the individual scores but the team score that counts". Ryan also rails at length against what he characterises as Nicki's deliberate manner of aggression on the track and what he still maintains is a consciously executed fencing of Matej by Nicki (which afterwards Nicki strenuously denied). "We fully expected it to be 'tough' but not so 'hard'" closely followed by "it's part and parcel of the sport but we're lucky no-one got injured". For once the affectation that "you have to have an affinity with everywhere you ride" rings true through the commitment of actions on the track rather than words correctly said but not really tasted.

Phil Chard writes afterwards in the *Speedway Star*, "talk about explosive. This meeting had everything. Spills, thrills [and] a feisty on-track confrontation". In other reports afterwards, Ferjan and Sullivan both press their claims for the immediate introduction of the presently fashionable but probably unworkable concept of a 'red and yellow card' disciplinary system to curb aggressive riding behaviour on the track. Ferjan notes, "I am just lucky that I got up without any injuries after that crash. How can he say it was my fault? I was in front of him and I couldn't see him. He always does the same thing. He did it to me two years ago and now again. But he does it to everyone".

Nicki doesn't see the incident at all similarly to Matej and adopts the aggrieved and harshly treated tone of someone served with an ASBO for dropping their sandwich wrapper in the street: "All I can say is watch it on the video. I do ride hard, but I don't want anyone to get hurt. You have to be honest when you do something wrong. And if I was wrong in this incident I was would say that I was, but I wasn't". The luxury of the modern facilities provided at Wimborne Road Stadium are such that the fans have already had the opportunity to review the incident many times on the array of television monitors that are dotted throughout the rather deluxe facilities that comprise the main grandstand. They have not been shaken in their firmly expressed, vehement opinions and are unlikely to change their minds on mature reflection with the DVD in the privacy of their own homes.

The flame-haired Neil 'Middlo' Middleditch is keen to laud the win and the bonus point they gained on aggregate, but goes out of his way to praise Matej, who "showed great character to get back on his [second] bike" after his original one had been written off. Especially as "some riders would have called it a day after hitting the fence as hard as he did".

The Eagles squad break down their bikes and load their equipment onto their vans with a speed and alacrity that indicate that they must all collectively be on a promise. A large gauntlet of Pirates fans has swollen the departure committee by the back gates of the pits and the foul mouthed smartly dressed man has taken his place among them and continues to share his strong opinions with all and sundry. In the Eagles team, only Deano isn't going to rush off like a thief in the night. Instead he is drawn to the glass-fronted grandstand bar by the thought of possibly convivial company, the thump of the music from the disco and the swirl of its brightly coloured spotlights. An old Irish proverb used by W.B. Yeats has it that "strife is better than loneliness", so while Nicki prefers one course of action, Deano prefers another.

22nd June Poole v. Eastbourne (ELB) 50–40

Another different chapter about this fixture appears in my book *Showered in Shale*.

23rd June

The always delightful A12 traffic temporarily held up the referee Phil Griffin who the SCB had originally nominated for this fixture, but the last-minute local replacement – Paul Carrington who had turned just expecting to spectate – soon had the Foxhall faithful on his side and baying at the rider the opposition fans love to hate, the Eagles very own Nicki P. If this was a cheesy detective soap opera, the Dane would admit he was "bang to rights" after he helped Hans Andersen into a compromised position that enabled a close inspection of the safety fence. Hans picked himself up, dusted himself off and then went on to enjoy his own fairy tale evening that saw no opposition rider head him all evening.

In a weird moment of synchronicity, a short while later after the combative (or just plain wild, depending on your allegiance) Kim Jansson was excluded after Nicki found the dirt with a thump in the same spot during his next ride in front of the delighted and jeering Foxhall hordes.

The award for the best exhibition of 'Hand-to-Hand Combat with a Speedway Bike (Freestyle Class)' went to Robert Miskowiak for a virtuoso display of this rare art within moments of the tapes going up.

23rd June Ipswich v. Eastbourne (ELB) 55–38

Lessons in Medicine and Etiquette

27th June

A Monday night meeting in the summer with the Skybet Elite League's bookies' favourite and many people's Champions Elect will be a compelling prospect, despite the severe disruption that a Sky Sports television broadcast will invariably cause. It still remains worthwhile to attend when you bear in mind that Nicki Pedersen and Jason Crump will compete against each other. Since they produced the race of the season at Arlington in the corresponding fixture between these two sides in 2004, we can only hope that we will witness a similar contest. It's a warm and sunny summer's evening, but to judge from the car park, few spectators actually seem prepared to show up. Sky Sports are there in their full glory with the large outside broadcast vans that dominate the car park with a tall overhead camera on a crane in place for those standard panoramic shots of the track and surrounding countryside. The woods, fields and villages around Arlington look lush and splendidly green. The signs for the local villages, Upper Dicker and Lower Dicker, might bring a smile to the lips of the unwary visitor but it's the kind of early summer's evening that pleasantly raises everyone's mood.

To watch speedway meetings for any length of time amounts to a crash course for riders (literally) and the fans (metaphorically) in the ways and mysteries of the human body. More specifically, the study of the catalogue of injuries sustained by riders around the leagues soon gives you a complex insight into the many bones that form the human skeleton as well as the physiology of the body's organs. It's a kind of *ad hoc* anatomy course provided for free by the speedway authorities. This is a rarity indeed – a free gift from the speedway authorities and they say the only 'free' cheese is found in a mousetrap – but, for once, a definite but unexpected benefit to the fans, if not the riders, though it is the result of the law of unintended consequences. As an Eastbourne Eagles fan, my anatomy and physiology education has now extended into more recondite areas of medical knowledge as I follow the intermittent recovery of Floppy from his concussion, neck injury and subsequent upset to his nerves. This week the saga finds Floppy absent from the side and JC, once more, dressed in his white doctor's coat with the funny headband with the disk-shaped attachment and the reassuring bedside manner for this week's programme notes. Dr Cook's considered diagnosis is "David's health is still causing concern" while his prognosis remains cautiously optimistic "it should not be too long before normal service is resumed". Overall, with masterly understatement given his importance to the team in a vital part of the season, Cooky notes, "it is very frustrating for both club and rider". The notes also have some news on the bad luck that afflicts one of the Reserve positions. Steen Jensen, after 17 drinks at the Last Chance Saloon, has now become *persona non grata*, while his possible replacement, Richard Hall, is injured. This allows Joel Parsons the chance to shine for the team and appear on national television too; though fortunately for the rider he hasn't been jinxed or pressured by the traditional and usually exaggerated claims that he's an "outstanding young rider for the future".

The terrace gossip mostly concerns the comparative weakness of the Eagles at reserve and the inadequate performance of the riders who try to replace Floppy. The appearance on the track of Nicki Pedersen's sternest and most vocal critic, Sam Ermolenko, at the start line for a short filmed piece to camera on the relative condition of tonight's track for the Sky viewers at home, is a welcome distraction from this tale of woe and causes some casual booing as well as a few shouted, uncomplimentary comments about his parentage, abnormal genitalia and mental capacities. Sam has taken it upon himself to occupy an unelected position in the written and broadcast media to excoriate unnecessary aggression of certain riders, a 'campaign' which thereby provides a handy excuse to characterise and critique Nicki's approach to riding as "dangerous". This outlook is routinely presented as 'fair comment' by an experienced and ostensibly concerned rider, albeit one with considerable access to the oxygen of publicity, and motivated by the need to ensure an agreed level of rider health and safety when 'safely' racing. When one considers that this sincerely held concern might be more effectively presented by campaigning collectively via the riders' trade union, the Speedway Riders Association, there's a widespread consensus among the Eastbourne fans that Sam is very selective in his criticism. For example, tonight Jason Crump rides for Belle Vue. Often during the GP series, Jason frequently rides with great determination, single-mindedness and with some aggression. Sam and his co-commentators always laud this approach on Sky Sports as 'good hard riding', while any almost identical manoeuvre from Nicki attracts opprobrium and accusations of 'dirty riding'. Whatever the merits of these different opinions, Sam affects to ignore the abuse and criticism of the Eagles fans as he walks from the track, through the crowd, and up the stairs to the Referee's box and commentary booth perched above the start

line.

The stop and start nature of the televised meeting is as extreme as usual; it either gives no time at all between races or stretches the time between them so much that during them you can almost catch a nap or get some serious reading done. Heat 2 has an extremely close finish for the three riders who trail Simon Stead by a long way. They raced so closely together for the last two laps you could have covered them all with a bike cover or you could have "thrown the proverbial blanket over them" according to Kevin 'KC' Coombes. The first meeting between Pedersen and Crump is an easy win for Jason before he amazes the often easily amazed KC, stood in the pits area, to watch as Jason then immediately does his own bike maintenance. "That's what makes our sport so great, the winner and current World Champion gets straight off his bike, changing gearings and carburetors, getting his hands dirty and giving it that personal touch although he looked comfortable in winning that race". These sentences spill easily from KC's mouth almost without breath or pause, some offer insight, but mostly fill the time as he capably says everything and nothing with panache. He really is such an institution at Arlington. Tonight we need him more than ever as he whiles away the enforced *longueurs* of the night brought on by Sky and we forgive him when he repeatedly dares to ask the predictable question. KC is unafraid to offer a rider a compliment or ready-made excuse for their latest shortcoming, and they always agree with him. It passes the time divertingly.

Eastbourne spend the early part of the meeting easing into a good lead, while the ever-present danger from Belle Vue only consists of Jason Crump. After two wins in two races, Crump's evening ends with a whimper and an anguished yelp of pain when the violent jolt from an immediate halt caused by a broken chain in heat 9, badly damages his right wrist. He has to withdraw from the meeting and without him, the objective for Belle Vue for the evening becomes damage control, as they are now led by Eastbourne-owned Joe Screen, who competes on his trademark zebra striped bike. From this point on, Nicki Pedersen and Davey Watt score with impunity as they dominate the opposition riders. Between them they account for 33 of Eastbourne's 53 points and they almost score as many points as the entire visiting team who score 37.

With the departure of Crump, it's effectively all over. Luckily, the interval sees KC give a further masterclass in speedway lore when he asks one of his famous open questions of Weymouth's Daniel Giffard. Daniel lives locally and is an Eastbourne asset, so it's not a total shock that he's available for interview, but KC bigs up the exclusivity of "the chance of a brief chat with Danny". Posing like he's revealing an eternal mystery from an unexplored distant universe, KC opens with "Is Conference League a good product?" It's a question that's both rhetorical and familiar, one that enables "Danny" to ride a number of his favoured hobby-horses. Namely history, money, ambition and xenophobia, which he masterfully manages to include all in one sound bite: "the Conference League was a training league but now we get good crowds; earn a bit of money; while waiting for opportunities in the Premier League, though these are not usually for English riders". KC affects to be informed and enthralled by this before he moves on to discuss the Conference League's most exciting, young future prospect *du jour*, Bexhill's 15-year-old Lewis Bridger. "Danny" knows Lewis very well as a team mate and because they sometimes hang out at his dad's shop together. So there's a potent mixture of respect, banter and a modicum of envy in the reply, "Lewis

Bridger mechaniced for me last season when he should have been at school".

You can, of course, entertain yourself during the various interval breaks. I also catch up with Dean Saunders, not the ex-footballer but the proud sponsor of the resurgent Davey Watt. Dean has decided to accompany Davey to the World Cup in Sweden and Poland where he'll ride for his country, Australia. It's the first time Davey has been selected, a well-deserved honour merited by his exceptional early season form that has carried on from reserve into the main body of the team. Dean relishes the trip – as a sponsor keen to bask in the reflected glory, as a student of speedway and motorbikes in general as well as a recent friend. He's so excited you'd think *he* will ride in the World Cup. To help Davey succeed in the "biggest event he'll ride in all year", Dean has decided to spend 4000 Euros on "building a special engine" just for this competition, though he's keen to stress that it'll help the Eagles afterwards when Davey continues to use this 'special' engine in the Elite League. Apart from this news, Dean quickly moans about Poole "being a funny place", mainly because his sponsorship of Davey still wouldn't gain him the entry he expected into their pits area. "When I queried it and said I spent £8000 sponsoring Davey, a bearded chap said some people sponsor Rickardsson for £25,000 and they don't expect to come in the pits".

The resumption after the interval quickly reveals that the club suffers from a start-line tapes shortage. Only a single cord stands between tradition and a televised green-light start procedure in heat 11. This race includes quite a bit of confusion as it's announced that Belle Vue have replaced Smith with Stead before another announcement informs us that there's a delay as Belle Vue deny they are replacing Smith. After some further delay Stead does finally replace Smith as originally announced. As they stand on the terraces, the fans in the Arlington stadium aren't privy to the behind-the-scenes drama that the television viewers at home get to witness. As I've always maintained, the uniformity of the camera angles doesn't capture the full spectacle or atmosphere of an actual race as you see it in the flesh. However, what television does capture, though, are behind-the-scenes reactions and dramas as they eventfully unfold. Luckily as there hasn't been an unexpected last-minute switch of channel by Sky, I can later watch Belle Vue manager Ian Thomas in the full swing of a gloriously angry dispute with SCB match official Chris Gay. The basis for the dispute was whether the Clerk of the Course, Malcolm Cole – who is, after all, the official licensed by the SCB for these very communications - had correctly informed the referee that Ian Thomas has requested to change Smith for Stead. It would be a strange thing for Malcolm Cole to decide independently or to make up on his own accord, and the referee took the view that this had been the 'official request' of Ian Thomas. When, Ian Thomas questioned this decision, saying he'd "never declared an official change", the referee stood by the information passed on by the Clerk of the Course. Ian Thomas was then apoplectic that "his word" hadn't the status he thought it should have with the match official. His anger, on live television, quickly escalated and led him to infer, without any real evidence, that the referee had insinuated that he was a liar. The questions "are you calling me a liar?", "are you saying I'm a liar?" or the observation "I don't tell lies" wasn't ever really going to help resolve the confusion but allowed Ian to vent his considerable ire and frustration. Particularly when the referee Chris Gay, who remained studiously polite and non-confrontational throughout, by his very calmness only provoked more verbal aggression and petulance from Ian Thomas. The home audience witnessed Thomas's slightly sensitive and volcanic reaction although, in his defence, it was all said in the heat of the moment and, at least, you can't doubt his passion, commitment and determination to do everything to succeed as the manager of the Belle Vue club![1] After the meeting, of all those involved, only Ian was interviewed on the incident by the *Speedway Star*. An apology wasn't offered and remained very noticeable by its absence, though the report later that week quoted Thomas as saying: "I don't know if the Clerk of the Course picked something up from that conversation but the fact is that I never declared an official change. The referee refused to accept my word about what had happened so, as far I am concerned, he was calling me a liar and I don't tell lies. The Clerk of the Course might as well run the away team, if things like this are going to happen because there didn't seem much point in me being there. Decisions like this make speedway a joke."

Despite the magic he makes away from the track as a magician, Ian Thomas was unable to put the referee under his spell or to have sufficient material with which to conjure up a response from his team on the Arlington track. Meanwhile, back in the crowd, we remained completely ignorant of his unique but entertaining approach to conflict resolution and diplomacy. Instead we knew that the result isn't in doubt after the withdrawal of Crump. One of the many delays between races enables KC to interview Jon Cook. He outlines his straightforward philosophy when it comes to David Norris's fight back to fitness: "as long as he felt safe on the bike, I was happy to have

---

[1] Nearly a year later Ian gleefully tells me, "just make sure that you get in that I called a VAT man a 'liar' – he is a VAT man that one, you know – I called him a freakin liar. It's not often you can get away with calling them anything let alone a freakin liar! And on live television to boot, so looking back on it now, I'm pleased I had the chance and took it!" This is a form of double-talk as, at the time, Ian claimed on television that the referee had called him a 'liar' (though he hadn't). Such are the tricks of memory. Interestingly, after this chat, I heard that Andy 'Smudger' Smith was overheard loudly complaining around that time that night that he'd expected to take part in the disputed race and was miffed not to do so. Whatever went on it was all played out in its full confusion live on national television though later, as ever with those compelling but controversial moments during speedway live coverage on Sky Sports, it had been airbrushed away and edited out of the repeat version of the meeting. The referees decision always remains final and was definitively so that night.

The warm up fascinates as ever. © Jeff Scott

Crumpie does his own thing as Sky pundit Sam Ermolenko looks on © Jeff Scott

The reserves race - Stead, Parsons, Harrison, Moore © Jeff Scott

him". He also took the chance to comment pointedly on the recent consistent performances of Mooro after a slow start to the season as he recovered from the lingering effects of his broken leg. "All those know-it-alls – very few of them Eastbourne fans who are very knowledgeable – who wondered why we kept him, he's been superb!" After he'd got that off his chest, albeit not quite in Thomas-esque fashion, JC is, as ever, supportive of his team, "we've got a great little team and we'll keep plugging away". That's definitely what everyone hopes to hear and the ease of this victory raises local confidence levels astronomically. The "very knowledgeable" fans, near by me, take the chance for a quick bask in the glory of an easy win against the fancied opposition, though only recently when stood on the same spot I have encountered some of the self-same Eastbourne fans in their less well-informed incarnation that Jon pointedly complained about.

27th June Eastbourne v. Belle Vue (ELA) 53-37

29th June

Just the announcement of this fixture is enough to signal a wet weather alert in the Peterborough area. There was enough rainfall to gladden the hearts of the local gardeners and help their plants, though it came late enough to irk the assembled riders who had again gathered in the pits with the full intention of zooming masterfully round the vast expanse of the EoES circuit. Sadly, the torrential downpour at 6 p.m. had waterlogged the track surface within 45 minutes and led many to suspect that a thick layer of clay must lie a few inches below its surface.

29th June Peterborough v. Eastbourne (ELA) – postponed: rain

JONATHAN GREEN

"David Norris is wearing his new trainers for us"

Anarchy Nearly Breaks Out

1st July

It is said that rules are rules and when the rule of law is broken then anarchy takes permanent hold. Well, this is the sort of thing said in the papers when something they don't like happens. Since I've arrived early to Brandon Stadium I had the chance to choose my ideal parking spot and enjoy the opportunity to while away a few hours as I wait for the entrance gates to open. Little did I know that it would be an evening when a challenge to the rule of law, well speedway law, would nearly cause the Coventry Speedway Club to disappear in a bizarre dispute over the sports regulations.

Even a few hours before the meeting, there's quite a crowd of people already parked and ready for the fixture that pits Coventry against Eastbourne. The kind of people that arrive early and wait aimlessly for a couple of hours are usually the more dedicated fans; those who set off well in advance to avoid the Friday night rush-hour traffic or those that have travelled from a long distance away. They're predominantly senior citizens, in pairs or sitting alone in their cars, though sometimes with the odd family. There's an outbreak of sandwiches, newspapers and flasks of hot drink. Bonhomie is kept to a minimum, as the weather threatens with intermittent drizzle and a cool wind. There's also a lot of people playing Radio 2 loudly, not because they're being selfish or wish to show off their extra powerful speakers, but because they can't hear well. I also settle in for a read of my paper, a few sandwiches and a chance to watch the world go by. But the world doesn't go by much in a mostly deserted speedway stadium car park.

I had called the speedway office a few days ago and eventually spoken with Colin Pratt who'd brusquely and firmly informed me that he wouldn't be able to find the time to meet with me or answer any questions, even if I turned up really early, as he'd be "too busy". He also hadn't seen the introductory letter from Peter Toogood and, understandably, since it's the one race night Coventry have each week, there would be lots for him to do to occupy his time. We decide that my research interview will have to wait until another more convenient time. It's definitely a shame not to be able to speak with Colin, since he's always been someone I'd admired from a distance, not least because of his rather gruff, pragmatic and down-to-earth approach to his job. There is a new owner at the club nowadays, West Midlands businessman Avatar Sandhu, who has by all accounts (after some initial suspicion with regard to his intentions for the land around the Brandon Stadium) invested heavily in the stadium infrastructure and the team itself. Mr Sandhu had also taken the unusual decision during the previous season, to appoint a co-team manager, the experienced but sometimes waspish Peter Oakes, to help out the Bees who had spent the previous season disastrously locked at the bottom of the league. So a lot of new brooms were sweeping clean at the club, consequently the supporters were gradually overcoming their natural scepticism and their real fears that the land would be sold for executive housing by Avatar had almost completely receded. Colin Pratt, who'd been widely expected to feel 'crowded' and usurped in a similar manner as Lady Diana famously did in her marriage to Prince Charles, ostensibly thrived sharing various responsibilities with Peter Oakes. During the close season, the club had invested for the future when it bought the services of one of the country's most gifted young riders, Scott Nicholls, though in typical speedway fashion the level of the fee took a tribunal to arbitrate and the protracted payment terms debacle still rumbled on midway through the present season. In fact the sum of £36,000 was still outstanding as I sat in the car park and tried not to question my own state of mind, for having arrived so early with nothing to do but sit and wait. So I turned the music up like everyone else …

I decide to pass the time and practise my detective skills, in this case my powers of observation. The first sign of excitement is the arrival just after 5 p.m. of Coventry rider, Chris 'Bomber' Harris, driving at a breakneck speed in his large white van. I know it's definitely him because of the large sign on the side of the van that proclaims 'Chris Harris – International Speedway Rider'. I'm sure that he hadn't ridden for the senior British team at the point the sign was commissioned for his van, although he has just been included in the squad for the forthcoming World Team Cup fixtures later in the summer. Neither the sign nor the van looks newly painted, but given he's already ridden for his country at a junior level, it's easy to understand his large lettered patriotic pride and delight in that achievement. So far this season though, he has ridden exceptionally well. If he translates this form to an international level, he'll become an instant

hero to the wider British speedway public as well as the Coventry fans. I continue my stakeout as a wannabe detective from the comfort of my car, and ten minutes later I watch the surprisingly early arrival of the Eagles very own roué, Dean Barker. He doesn't drive his own van but it's clearly him. A couple of things give this away. Firstly he wears his distinctive trademark woolly hat, a beanie hat I believe they're called among the younger set that Deano still mixes with. They are hats without a bobble on top and worn for reasons of fashion rather than practicality or warmth, particularly since it's now July. I also know it's him because it says 'Dean Barker' on the side of his van, though I don't notice whether it confirms his employment as a 'speedway rider', international or otherwise. That's already enough practice for my observational skills; so I decide to strike up a conversation with anyone else nearby who is prepared to talk and foolhardy enough to leave their car to brave the strong breeze and the drizzle.

I assume they'll be well informed, mainly on the basis that if they're here already, they must surely be committed fans. The lady close by has her car festooned in Coventry Bees stickers and scarves. She believes that the club has "gone downhill" and doesn't have much time for Avatar Sandhu, the new owner, as he's "just a businessman". She takes some reassurance that the existing covenants on the land ensure that it presently can't be sold for housing or other commercial developments because it has to be used for recreational purposes, especially reassuring since she strongly suspected that these were his intentions. She tells me that the team has been held back by "lots of crashes and injuries this season", notably to Morten Risager and Rory Schlein. Risager has already resumed riding while Schlein intends to return by August. The lady feels that Schlein should wait to fully recover and not ride again until next year. She wants to know "why don't his parents stop him?" before she answers her own rhetorical question, "they're like all sportsmen, and they just want to compete". She reserves particular scorn for Andreas Jonsson "who never seems to want to ride – there's always an excuse why he's away, whether it's his stomach, some other illness or a broken foot". A broken foot sounds a serious enough reason to my mind, but clearly what applies to Rory doesn't apply to Andreas in this lady's eyes. She's full of her own rhetorical questions, and the recent careless talk and brinkmanship by the Coventry management, along the lines that they might not proceed with the purchase of Scott Nicholls after all, also disturbs her equilibrium. "How does Scotty feel now they say that they don't want to sign him?" she asked querulously in a broad Midlands accent. Before I can even begin to think of an answer, the heavier drizzle drives us back to the comfort of our cars.

A few hardier souls, many of who are of an age old enough to have survived the Second World War, never mind a bit of rain, already queue by the side of the stadium, and wait for the gates to open as usual at 6.30 p.m. Strangely though, the gates don't open then and the queue in the rain just keeps getting longer and longer, but everyone remains patient in that stoical archetypically English way – i.e. with many grumbles and outlandish surmises. No one really seems to know the exact reason for the delay. I overhear someone say, "nothing surprises me nowadays!" but I fail to learn why they aren't surprised. The consensus among the bedraggled fans when the entrance gates still aren't open at 7 p.m. is that a protracted dispute now rages inside the stadium between the two teams as well as between the Coventry management and the BSPA. The bone of contention apparently concerns whether Joonas Kylmakorpi will ride for Coventry tonight, but that is linked to many other outstanding issues and an alleged wider dissatisfaction Avatar Sandhu feels at his treatment by the sport's governing authorities. There's even some wild speculation that the Coventry Speedway Club might actually close for good this evening. No sooner do I think to myself how amazing it is that a short, unexpected delay can be interpreted through so many mouths into an immediate threat to cease trading, than we all gradually learn from the Coventry staff that wander the length of the increasingly impatient queue, that this might actually happen! Well!

As we slowly start to file into the stadium at 7.10 p.m., it's clear that the threat of dissolution has temporarily abated. The mere threat of such an action is a clear indication of intense frustration and anger on behalf of Coventry's management but, also, a disturbing sign of perhaps a less than serious attitude towards your responsibility and obligations towards the history and fans of the club[1]. The chatter throughout the stadium concentrates on this rather shocking news and possibility. Just inside the gates, I meet off duty referee Chris Durno and his son Tom, resplendent in his Manchester United replica top, as they come out of the track shop. As an inveterate fan of the sport Chris likes to watch as many meetings a season as he can and his work allows. Many of these are in his official capacity as a referee but he also enjoys the races with his son whenever he can find the time. Tom appears shy initially, but becomes much more animated when he discusses his local heroes, such as Scotty Nicholls, who rides at the Brandon Stadium. At eight he's just slightly too young to appreciate how fantastically lucky he is to have a father who is so closely involved in the warp and the woof of the sport. Chris is surprised by the threat of closure, but says that there's been trouble brewing for some time over many issues including financial transparency, transfers and averages among many others. There is also the perception at Coventry that not all speedway teams are treated equally or consistently by the governing body of the sport. When I ask whether or not there's merit or not in these perceptions, he only shrugs and chooses to keep his own counsel.

There's been a general rush by the fans to the pits area, most likely to check if every rider is there and to see if it all looks as normal. It doesn't seem any different except for the large crowd of curious spectators. We can see Peter Oakes, who chats animatedly with Jon Cook. They are having a long conversation but, apart from that, the pits is full of riders and mechanics who studiously work on their bikes or warm them up in preparation for the meeting. The track surface itself looks exceptionally well watered, soaked by the rain we had for the hours while everyone waited or queued patiently outside.

As I climb the steep steps of the main grandstand and vainly look for a seat not covered in a thick film of red dust, the vastly experienced announcer and ex-promoter Peter York gives a brief summary of the events that led to the delay in the entrance gates opening. He speaks in an earnest, serious tone that wouldn't be out of place at a funeral or maybe at a coroner's office when they announce the results of an autopsy. We learn everything and nothing at the same time. "This meeting has only gone ahead as an Elite League fixture as a result of Jon Cook taking what he described as the 'hardest speedway decision of my life'". The fans are thanked for their patience queuing outside and Jon is thanked again for his decision to "put fans and speedway first". We're also told that, "Coventry announced they'll be meeting the BSPA at their offices next week with their management team to iron out their differences". The practical upshot of the agreement is that Joonas Kylmakorpi will be allowed to ride this evening, but not in the return fixture tomorrow night. This is as a result of a special dispensation suggested by BSPA Chairman Peter Toogood after many hours of tense negotiation and agreed by JC for pragmatic and altruistic reasons, even although technically under the rules that govern the sport, Kylmakorpi really shouldn't be able to ride.

With little further ado, nearly 15 minutes late, military marches blare excessively loudly through the tannoy system. It's played at such a volume that you'd suspect that the operative has recently trained and honed their skills on the prisoners at Guantanamo Bay. The track staff and St. John Ambulance volunteers march out to this stirring din followed by the announcer Peter York. Immediately afterwards riders emerge onto the covered dog track for their pre-meeting parade and their individual introductions to the crowd. All the Eastbourne riders are greeted with polite applause from the Coventry fans except for Nicki, who is loudly booed. The Bees crowd cheers the home team loudly and with affection.

The vehemently contested presence of the rider at the centre of the dispute, Joonas Kylmakorpi, soon appears. He takes to the track in the first heat and rides home third for a single, potentially valuable, point. Billy Janniro wins easily and celebrates with a wheelie loudly serenaded with a quick burst of Springsteen's *Born in the USA*. The Coventry riders ignore the light rain that now falls steadily and race

---

[1] I later learn that, in fact, Mr Sandhu's continuing horror and frustration at the unprofessional approach to the administration and running of the BSPA and SCB plus the often *ad hoc* implementation of its rules, regulations and procedures had bothered him from the outset of his control of the club since it contrasted so sharply with his usual experiences and expectations of governance, equality and transparency in his life as a successful businessman. The Kylmakorpi straw didn't quite break the camel's back but brought things to a convenient head. I expect Mr Sandhu will retain his ability to pose difficult questions to the BSPA in the future.

away to win by some distance from the trailing Eastbourne pair. We're treated to the sounds of a speedway track favourite, especially so in the mid 1970s and early 1980s but still showing some signs of life in the present day, Emerson Lake and Palmer's *Fanfare for the Common Man*. The persistent drizzle now becomes a light rain and the Coventry pairings continue to excel in these conditions, as they again easily win. There's just enough time before the next heat for the initial team of the by now rather damp and bedraggled start line girls to be exchanged with a new and dry lot. They needn't have rushed out onto the centre green since the chance of any further glory for the start girls or the riders now ends, after some delay for a track inspection in the rain, with the abandonment of the evening's racing due to deteriorating track conditions. Given that the rain now falls heavily it's hardly a surprise, although it's unlucky for Coventry who lead easily 14-4 in a fixture expected by many observers to be close and much more competitive. Even if the meeting had started promptly at the advertised start time of 8 p.m., there wouldn't have been sufficient races to declare the fixture completed.

With many moans and groans, the disgruntled crowd slowly disperses. I also leave, disconsolate and dissatisfied with the refund procedures at Coventry stadium. These ridiculous terms and conditions of refund after entry are similarly self-serving among most speedway clubs, though they remain somewhat antediluvian and do not encourage the regular fan or the mythical "new supporters" that the clubs claim that they are so keen to attract to the sport. It's a definite disincentive for the sport to unfortunately find yourself at a meeting considerably delayed by arcane wrangling where you have to pay £15 to only see three races. I'm a long distance from home and yet the club will not refund my entrance ticket since it remains valid for the next three meetings. It is not a compelling prospect to travel on a Friday to Coventry – a round trip for me through rush-hour traffic of over 300 miles – to take advantage of these readmission regulations or, for that matter, to wait for the same fixture when it's rearranged at some unspecified future date[2]. It's definitely a poor substitute for a refund and an obstacle to retain customer goodwill but, let's be fair, it's more reasonably likely that you would return to the rematch of this fixture against Eastbourne if you are fortunate enough to have unlimited holidays and money for yet more travel. Given the present demographic and income profile of the sport, this appears highly unlikely to be the case for the majority of fans.

The nearly terminal nature of the stand off between Coventry speedway and the BSPA subsequently dominates the speedway forums and is reported at length in the next week's *Speedway Star*. Avatar Sandhu feels strongly about the situation his club found itself in and, as the owner, acted in the confrontational manner he felt to be the best response to that situation. JC is reported as saying, "after much to-ing and fro-ing, I was left with the decision to either run, or not run and possibly close Coventry Speedway down. I put speedway first and made the decision for the fans". And the clubs, he might add, since the absence of

[2] The fixture would be eventually rearranged for much later in the season and is then a televised encounter broadcast live on Sky Sports, thus Coventry's best offer is for me to pay for another 300 plus mile round trip to watch a meeting that will be disrupted to satisfy the always disruptive requirements of a television company that weren't in attendance at the original fixture. It's difficult to see how the increasing rare species at a speedway meeting, the out-of-town fan, benefits from this experience or would wish to repeat it! Still, Coventry Speedway club, like any other, could solace in the fact that those are the rules and regulations that apply throughout the sport. A slightly disingenuous position, especially since they delayed this particular meeting by appealing against the strictures that don't suit their own sense of fair play. Still rules are rules and set in stone – unless the BSPA management agrees by a majority vote to change them, which it regularly does on pressing matters of recent concern for the promoters.

Coventry as a club would severely affect every club's revenues and deprive the sport of one of its last remaining premium stadium facilities. The *Speedway Star* when it pointedly commented on the "stand-off" noted darkly, "there are some Elite League clubs who feel Coventry are employing bully-boy tactics and holding the sport to ransom". It was clearly a complicated situation, but this determined response by the Coventry Bees is not needed or repeated in any other of the country's other professional sports and, as a consequence, this further diminishes the reduced standing of speedway outside the charmed circle of its dwindling band of devotees. Speedway definitely suffers from the comparison and, luckily but hardly a cause for celebration, the sports reputation in the wider community is only saved from further damage by its severely diminished media profile[3].

1st July Coventry v. Eastbourne (ELB) 14-4 (abandoned)

Badly Stung by the Bees

July 2nd

The severe disputes of the previous evening's fixture still rumble along among the Eagles fans as the clubs immediately face each other again in the return fixture. As part of the agreement to allow the racing to proceed and to avoid the immediate dissolution of Coventry Speedway Joonas Kylmakorpi will not ride tonight. Because he's very familiar with the Arlington racetrack, this has to count as a potential positive for the home team's prospects of victory. Apart from the "special dispensation" guest Henning Bager who will ride in Kylmakorpi's place, the sides remain unchanged from the previous evening. This leaves Eastbourne weakened by their use of rider replacement for the often talismanic but still injured David Norris. Coventry have the considerable tactical advantage of the very much on-form Chris 'Bomber' Harris who rides at reserve and thereby, according to the regulations, will be able to have as many as seven rides throughout the evening. It's completely unlikely that Coventry will choose to continue to dispute the applicability of this particular aspect of the sport's regulations this evening, especially as it's so clearly to their advantage! The need for a victory is a frequent topic among the waiting crowd in the build up to the start of the meeting. Most people hadn't been at Brandon, but if you listen to them talk you'd have thought Eastbourne had taken a support of hundreds of fans.

JC's programme notes, which were written before the Coventry away meeting, bill the visitors as "Play-Off Rivals" and he rather presciently notes, "the Bees have certainly found their form of late". For once, the notes make absolutely no mention of Steen Jensen, which I'd interpret as another ominous sign, if I were him. Statistically at least, his performance last night at Coventry was his best yet in Eagles club colours as he finished second top scorer albeit with one point. Admittedly the meeting was abandoned after three races. Nicki Pedersen did not ride and four other riders scored zero. Instead Jon concentrates on a nightmare journey to Ipswich for a 55-38 hammering. "Our visit to Ipswich is best forgotten, as so often has been the case with our trips to Suffolk". It is, however, a trip that will linger and live on in the minds of the riders for some considerable time since it took them an average of six hours to "reach the track after the main road to Ipswich was shut". I'm grateful that I'd missed the memorable joy of this experience.

In addition to this insight into the often hidden but laborious travel side of a modern speedway rider, we learn yet more about the ongoing medical saga that is David Norris's campaign to try to regain complete fitness. He's been to "Goring Hall Hospital", which was

[3] When you look back on it with the benefit of hindsight at the end of the season, this decision to allow Coventry "special dispensation" to sign Klymakorpi on loan to ride for the Bees was a pivotal aspect of their late season burst of form that allowed them to snatch their first league title since 1988, via the play-offs system. Allegedly the legal advisors hired by Avatar Sandhu apparently ran rings round the poorly drafted and vaguely worded SCB regulations as well as drove a coach and horses through the similarly otiose BSPA directives, thereby contributing to this decision to allow the "dispensation". So, you could perhaps argue that Mr. Sandhu's bluff or intransigence was, ultimately, a significant factor in the determination of the whereabouts of the 2005 title crown.

The open pits policy attracts interest. © Jeff Scott

Nicki with admirers. © Jeff Scott

Steen greets his public. © Jeff Scott

previously unknown to me as a speedway injury centre of excellence, where he underwent more scans than luggage in a terrorist alert at the airport. With the results of a consultation with a specialist pending, Floppy will certainly have had a fine opportunity to contemplate the slow road to recovery or, at the very least, a post-speedway career in one of the medical professions.

In one of those quirks that illustrate the accessibility of speedway riders to the fans that follow the sport, just prior to the meeting I get a rare chance to speak to Nicki Pedersen in the Arlington stadium gents' public lavatory. He's yet to change from his civilian clothing of a sweatshirt with his own name as a logo, some Doc Martens type shoes and some pleasantly recherché and unfashionable stone-washed effect jeans. It's good to note that he's a hygienic chap, as he spends quite some time washing and drying his hands extremely thoroughly and fastidiously. I wish him luck for the evening ahead. In terms of this book, this is about as much of an interview as I get with Nicki, when he smiles broadly and appears to genuinely mean what he says to me, in this case, "thank you, I hope you really enjoy it this evening".

Nicki leaves, gets changed and rides very well throughout the evening. Sadly, the same can't be said for the rest of the team. Steen powers to another three-ride zero in sharp contrast to his opposite number 'Bomber' Harris who scores 11 hard-earned and vital points from six rides. His German teammate, Martin Smolinski, whose opinion about 'Bomber's' nickname we don't learn, or even know if he understands its true derivation, scores comparatively poorly. This is irrelevant in the context of a good all-round team performance from the Bees, who easily sting the Eagles into submission. It all started so promisingly when KC welcomed the crowd to "a slightly sun-kissed Arlington".

The Eagles started with all the urgency of a torpid coelacanth and by the end of the fourth heat we're already 8-16 behind. We pull back the difference to only four points after the next heat, but that's as close as it will get all evening. Even intensive watering of the track and lots of careful attention from the ever-cunning and resourceful Bob Dugard on his tractor can't stem the momentum of the Bees very confident and aggressive performance. Even moving lots of the shale near to the fence, "doing the track to suit Nicki" as the nearby Margaret Rice knowingly puts it, makes no difference.

In order to distract from the grief of watching the home team ride, KC throws himself into a series of lively interviews with the riders. First up is the reticent Adam Shields, who usually likes to restrict himself to as many words as the points he scores per meeting. Tonight, though, by his standards he's positively loquacious. Well, he answers the questions fully for once rather than his usual monosyllabic manner as if he's an anxious patient at the dentist. Most people charitably put his brevity down to his natural modesty, though he's definitely a man that makes the simple things simpler. The interview is just the sort of challenging, philosophical encounter KC relishes when he lets himself off the leash for a few brief moments. We're treated to a simultaneous insight into some of the economics of being a speedway rider, "to get a bike you can win races on in the Elite League you need £2,500". On this basis, Steen urgently needs another £2,499.99 towards the cost of his machine. Adam also offers some qualifying mechanical insight when he notes, "the engine is simple really but the equipment needed to work on them is very expensive and often more than the bike". We already know enough to pass a GCE in Applied Technology, or whatever they call metalwork nowadays, never mind that Adam has masterfully alerted the home crowd to the need for some riders to spend as long in the workshop, with the right equipment, as allegedly some of them do having fun in the bars and clubs.

Nicki P and Scotty N spend some fascinated but happy moments as they peer over the inflatable safety fence close to the pits, and studiously watch every pirouette of Bob Dugard's tractor. They try to fathom what fiendish effect his mazy circuits of the Arlington racetrack have upon riding conditions and possible racing lines. Dr KC, metaphorical stethoscope in hand continues to try to distract the crowd from thinking about the racing too much. In this case, with news of Floppy's "four concussions in a year" which should worry the most carefree of fans or parents, never mind the gruesome sounding "three bones out of alignment in the neck" that a "London specialist" has identified. The treatment prescribed is "total rest", which in the manner of a phantom pregnancy, we see that Steen has taken completely to his heart and Deano adopts intermittently. All the gory detail makes everyone's neck in the crowd feel suddenly dodgy. Unable to hear beneath his helmet and therefore unable to be temporarily distracted by these descriptions, we're treated to some impressively aggressive riding that lets a determined Bomber pass Deano. It's a confident passing manoeuvre and so daring that it seems as though achieving third place was absolutely vital to him. It was vital, of course, but only really for the badly trailing Eagles and not the up-for-it Bees.

Claims that Nicki Pedersen always rides with reckless abandon and with a level of calculated aggression that puts his opponents at risk are finally disproved in heat 10. On the third bend of the first lap we're treated to an exhibition of strange team riding where Nicki guides his own teammate Adam Shields from his bike, into the fence, and enables him to get a fleeting taste of the Sussex shale. This evenhandedness surely gives the lie to the slander that Nicki deliberately targets his opponents. The ladies in my group protest loudly at this tactical approach, while Dave Rice asks with faux naïveté, "he didn't hit him, did he?"

All that's left of the evening is for KC to repeatedly clutch the patriotic straw that the winning pairings we now have so often seen from the visiting Bee's this evening feature "young English riders". They say that the appeal to xenophobia is the sign of a bankruptcy of ideas and intellect, in politics this holds true, but at speedway we all applaud along at some wins for what KC terms "the Great Britain Corporation". There's no doubt that the rider of the night is Chris 'Bomber' Harris, who spent the evening blasting from the back past the Eastbourne riders. My neighbour Judy Hazelden blames the lack of skill in our performance because the Eagles don't ride regularly enough together as a team and, everyone's favourite reason this season, "we're very weak at reserve". Coventry ecstatically ride round on a victory parade, whereas you can imagine that our lot look like they've lost a tenner and found a penny. The mostly disappointed crowd still applauds the visitors warmly all their way round the circuit.

Some people head for the car park, maybe to rush home to drown their sorrows or to go to somewhere slightly more scenic to appreciate the beauty of the crimson sunset sky. The only red that stands out in the pits are the faces of the riders, hopefully, where KC collars promoter JC for a quick insight into his mood that follows a comprehensive 42-51 home defeat. Not mincing his words, Jon agrees with the majority, "we were bloody awful, there's no excuses and our riders have been riding the track long enough". After reiterating the lack of excuses, he forecasts that there will be quite a crowd round the full length mirror in the changing rooms as "we've all got to take a long hard look at ourselves, we can't afford to slip up". As usual and eager to find the positives that dictates his outlook when he has his promotional duties in mind, JC trots out that hardy perennial of a claim that, "we've got a lot of excitement to come". But more from the school of factual observation, rather than of excuses, he then notes that the Eagles need to start winning matches away "being realistic, we're not going to win without David, our season is dependent on David coming back".

The crowd that remains behind for the second half are treated to the chance to see the potential future stars of British speedway during their apprenticeship. Sussex style, at least, with the Under-21 Championship for the county and some additional Youth races. There is lots to interest the impartial observer and myself. I'm delighted to see that the Strudwick cousins are both racing – Lee in the Under-21's and Niall in the Youth races. There's also a strong field of riders entered for the Championship that, unfortunately, is cut back to five rather than the scheduled ten races.

The widely fancied rider who is strongly tipped for future success, Lewis Bridger, suffers a last bend engine failure that robs him of victory and any chance in the Championship. Although he's only 10 yards from the finish line, in sheer frustration he starts to push his bike home to the pits rather than across the line for a consolation point as Lee Strudwick had fallen. KC who, when he does them, always sounds as if he's more relaxed and that he loves the second-half commentary since these races feature the raw youngsters for the future. He really comes into his own, fluently mixing wit and sincerity, but tonight comes over all teacherly when 15-year-old Lewis

ignores the chance of an easy point, "that's inexperience for you, he'll learn from that". Luckily Lewis can't hear him, as he doesn't look in the mood for meaningful lessons as he strops back towards the pits.

In heat 2 we see a rare appearance by Adam Filmer, wearing Dean Barker's old race suit, to race against his sister's boyfriend, the Weymouth rider Dan Giffard. Only two riders manage to finish this race and Adam strikes the fence with some force on the last bend of the penultimate lap. KC makes the race winner, Dan Giffard, sound like a cross between Ironside and Superman as he catalogues his recent injuries, "it's great to see him back after horrific injuries in 2004 when he had two broken legs and found himself in a wheelchair". Lewis doesn't make the start in the next race, which is won easily by Matthew Wright. The next race witnesses another fall for Lee Strudwick while Adam Filmer suffers the ignominy of being lapped by the remaining riders. Another contest between Dan Giffard and Mark Baseby in the final qualifying race has them both qualify to then race each other again in the final. Mark has looked very comfortable in both his races but he falls when he tries too hard when it matters most in the last race of the night. Dan Giffard manages to win his third race of the night and greets his victory with a delight that wouldn't be out of place if he'd won the World Championships. Throughout the Under-21 Sussex Championship, we've also been treated to some fine racing from the Under-15 youth riders. There are maximums for a couple of riders – the wanted version for James Walker who wins every race and an unwanted three-race series of resolute, determined but nonetheless still last places for Niall Strudwick. Given how enthusiastic the Strudwick cousins and their fathers are about their speedway riding, I'm sure that it'll be viewed as another helpful experience in their ongoing apprenticeship for both of them. As the still healthy crowd departs the Arlington Stadium grounds, we can't deny that watching the second half racing has got us back to basics and has lifted the earlier general gloomy mood of the terraces.

2nd July Eastbourne v. Coventry (ELA) 42-51

Of Puddles and Psychology

4th July

The lure of a trip to the perpetually rain swept East of England Showground is too hard to resist on American Independence Day. As has been the recent norm with fixtures between the Eagles and the Panthers, both sides have driven to the rather exposed pits area adjacent to one of the largest tracks in the country to prepare to finally race this oft postponed meeting.

It's a truism within speedway circles that if the riders perform well it is down to them and if things don't go so well, then there are a litany of other excuses to explain this away. One traditional suspect to blame is the track itself, though there is another speedway saying that correctly has it that speedway riders actually race on bikes (the bit they're in control of), not tracks (the bit they're not in control of). The EoES track has long been a traditional cause of concern to many visiting riders. Mostly it is the sheer length and speed of the thing that invariably makes the task of bike set-ups very hard to manage successfully. Another frequent moan is the state of the track surface itself which has attracted epithets like "rough", "deep", "difficult" and "dangerous to race upon". It is safe to say that some riders are beaten before they even pull up in their van and others arrive with the approach and psychology of losers. Even for the home riders, the track has been a source of concern that has often garnered comment. Recently, thanks to the expert care and thoughtful ministrations of trackman Julian Pettican, less mental space and time has been expended on this hardy chronic worry. But then a winning team that rides with confidence praises itself and its own performances rather than seeks other explanations. An exception to this rule is the present Panthers squad who would have gone out of their way to praise Julian to his face as well as to buy a crate of beer for him as a sign of their appreciation.

One glance at the track is enough to convince Deano and the rest of the Eagles team to utter the equivalent of "Houston – we have a problem". In his role as captain and team spokesman, Dean is swift to corner the taciturn Panthers team manager, Trevor Swales, to express some incredulity as he waves his arm towards the safety fence and the 'deep' surface of the track that lies beyond it, "as a captain I have to ask – what is that out there?" Trevor affects magnificent ignorance that anything is out of the norm, but Deano persists with his theme with some humour and a claim that it would be better suited to other motorcycle disciplines and different equipment. In this case, most likely moto-cross bikes rather than the finely calibrated machines that are the vehicles of choice for speedway riders. With a smile and great equanimity, Trevor offers to lend Deano a moto-cross bike from his van. After some more banter and discussions, Deano retreats back to the Eagles part of the pits compound and Trevor gleefully congratulates himself on this early and easy psychological victory over the experienced Deano: "the track'll definitely have him beaten now".

A few steps away, the outlook for the Eagles prospects are presently as dark and gloomy as the sky for Eastbourne promoter Jon Cook. There has been the on–off impact of the injury to Floppy, the blistering home defeat to Coventry at Arlington the previous weekend, and the vexed problem of Steen's continued lack of form at reserve, the sharpest of contrasts to optimistic but unfounded early season claims that he would be a "real prospect" after a short but necessary period of acclimatisation. All of this plus a healthy dose of poor luck has blighted prospects and soured the outlook, although Jon hasn't forgotten his trademark wry humour: "we're falling so fast we could disappear out of the league soon". Trevor Geer thoroughly rehearses the Steen issue with Jon and reviews the different tried and tested approaches he has so far employed without success. Mostly this involves understanding, kind words and an attempt to build up Steen's fragile confidence, though clearly both men already deep down feel that the high point in Steen's Elite League British Speedway career might have already been passed and that this particular cause is lost.

One of the models that economists like to promote is the 'Law of Diminishing Returns' and that might be where Steen finds himself now, on the downward side of the distribution curve. Not that Steen would have ridden according to Jon, even if the heavy rain had held off and the meeting had gone ahead: "Steen's been a big disappointment to himself and us; though luckily he declared himself unfit, otherwise I'd have had to!" It then rains so heavily there is a dash for cover by the riders and mechanics of both teams who shelter in

their respective bike-shed styled areas. Everyone on the Panthers side automatically congregates by the tea urn to philosophically watch the world wash by with a refreshing cuppa in hand. St Swithin eat your heart out!

4th July Peterborough v. Eastbourne (ELA) – postponed

Another different chapter about this fixture appears in my book *Showered in Shale.*

11th July

For once, probably because it was staged in Sussex, a meeting with the Panthers didn't signal that the umbrellas should be retrieved from under the stairs during a summer otherwise noted for its drought. With much of his stuff still unpacked in boxes at his new home in Denmark, Ulrich Ostergaard started his Eastbourne career with an imperious win in the reserves race in a way that signalled how he meant to carry on. But then thoughts that he may have accidentally left a gas ring alight on the cooker distracted him from further troubling the scorer.

Not that the meeting for the Sky cameras lacked entertainment on the track or off it, as Jonathan Green hammed up the excitement in trademark wooden style ably supported by his sidekick on malapropisms, Kelvin Tatum. Even though he has a proven record for serial exaggeration on live television, Kelvin forgot himself for a moment and genuinely appeared to mean it when he said that Deano's journey from last to first in heat 12 reminded him that he couldn't recall such an "exciting last lap". His memory was still sufficient enough for him to remember to glance in that slightly fey, self-aware way at the camera before all this talk of the riders being hidden on the finish line under the proverbial blanket again distracted him. Afterwards Deano admitted, "it was entertaining", before he severely reprimanded himself for some poor starts. It's an area that he's set himself extra homework, though he then went on to congratulate himself on a smart technical breakthrough: "I changed a bit of stuff on the engine today". Nicki dropped a solitary point in six rides, while Steen maintained his average through the effective and simple device of not actually riding.

Promotional activities had boosted crowd numbers for a Monday night Sky meeting and caused Jon to gleefully note, "the last Monday crowd was up on what we had previously had on a Monday". However, he accidentally failed to mention that it had rained that night, which is weather much more suitable to any fixture against the Panthers at the EoES.

11th July Eastbourne v. Peterborough (ELB) 48–42

16th July

This season's notorious team of a thousand nationalities arrives at Arlington with yet another new-look squad riding under the Oxford Silver Machine team banner. No one could ever accuse promoter and team manager Nigel 'Waggy' Wagstaff of timidity when he wants to ring the changes to his team. It's an approach that either motivates the riders to fight for their places, or, more likely, they quickly descend into apathetic resignation when things don't quite go right for them. They're definitely only too painfully aware that another change, which probably involves them, will be just round the corner. Not that injuries have exactly helped team stability, but Waggy has shown quite an appetite for what Chairman Mao called "permanent revolution". You can imagine that any really keen Oxford fans would avoid having their favourite rider's name put onto their replica shirts. Well, it would be a safe bet to put McGowan, Hancock, Iversen or Hamill on your back, but apart from them any other rider's name would be too risky to contemplate. If the 1970s fashion of tattooing your admired riders' names on your body were still popular, any Oxford-based tattoo parlour would thrive.

Tonight the Sussex audience will be treated to the chance to watch Kroner (not yet replaced by the Euro), Gustafsson and Tomicek who guests in place of Gafurov. A quick glance in the programme confirms that Steen Jensen, the Eastbourne rider spiritually closest to an honorary Oxford rider, is still "unavailable through illness". What's not inside my programme, although there's still nearly an hour to the start time, is the market research questionnaire that the BSPA are using to survey the British speedway watching public. It's impressive that the BSPA has awoken to the modern reality that potential advertisers and sponsors need to understand the make up and constituency of the traditional speedway audience. Said advertisers and sponsors will definitely want to learn all about speedway's various market segments and stratifications before they'll potentially consider investing any serious amounts of dosh. We continually hear throughout the year of the urgent need for greater cash injections into the sport from local and national sponsors. If this survey will help that process, it deserves praise but unfortunately the utility and efficacy of the results appear to be handicapped by a number of small but significant flaws – specifically, the number of surveys provided as well as the content, structure and methodology of the questions. These problems will inevitably reduce the quality and accuracy of the results.

We all understand that a sample is what it says it is, namely a statistically relevant subset of the total population to be examined from which you can hopefully extrapolate meaningful conclusions. Sadly the majority of the crowd at Arlington arrived too late to get a copy, due to insufficient supplies. Or, it may be the correct number was supplied, who knows, it's all a mystery. We can safely say that if the surveys were only handed to the early arrivals, it would skew the survey towards only capturing data from the really committed supporter (who likes to arrive early, bagsy their favourite spot and leisurely visit the pits prior to the meeting), or those who've travelled the furthest distance and have allowed enough time for their journey to take into account unexpected delays. In fact, as I think about it, these careful journey planners might make ideal respondents. But ironically for a company named on the survey form as 'Influx Marketing', they've gone out of their way to manage to ensure they don't get an influx of completed questionnaires!

These comments aren't solely due to my bitterness at failing to get the chance to win any of the prizes offered, namely the chance to see a "BSPA Shared Event" – who would have any idea what that was unless they were already a speedway fan? Or to have the chance to win tickets to watch some more mysterious sounding events with interesting acronyms such as a "VIP Trip to the PLRC or ELRC" or tickets to a World Cup qualifying round. All of these are attractive enough incentives, if you don't already have your ticket to see the World Team Cup[1], if you're already a speedway fan well versed in the casual freemasonry of the sport's terminology. But they're probably not so hot to use if you're not familiar with this aspect of speedway's language.

But then a quick glance at the questions reveals that the authors assume that they'll mostly be preaching to the converted and the chance

[1] Those fans organised and keen enough to arrive early, might also book their tickets to such events similarly early!

Bob with hose in hand. © Jeff Scott

Shieldsy in the pits. © Jeff Scott

The perpetually smiling Greg Hancock by his toolbox. © Jeff Scott

of casual spectators taking the survey is as likely as the meeting itself being interrupted by a snowstorm. The questions themselves appear to lack little interpretative power beyond the narrow confines of the available answers you could give. Most notably they lack any obvious interpretative or formal grading/scoring system. Like, for example, the ones that you sometimes get when you travel by plane on holiday where you can rank 'the overall quality of the in-flight service' from 'very poor' through various gradations like 'average' to the highly unlikely 'excellent'. Many of these questions suffer from bad syntax, others make rather rigid assumptions that don't include the full range of possible answers or else seem pointlessly intrusive. Some questions manage to combine all three of these potential faults, a remarkable achievement for 20 questions on a double-sided piece of paper.

My favourite part, where the survey betrays its own point of view, were questions about the number of holidays you take per year and where you visit (seaside/Europe/Other parts of Britain/Other Overseas destinations). The question on qualifications ranged from 'None' to betraying the questioner's worldview and possible age by their selection of acronyms. After they ask if you bought the programme, they immediately then assume that you did since they follow up with a question about the programme. This extremely general question was a forlorn attempt to establish the effectiveness of the recognition of the many companies that advertise at that particular meeting ('Do you use the services advertised in the programme?'). This futile masquerade, an attempt to establish the level of brand recognition of advertisers among the attending spectators, but it's a question that I'm sure the promoters would prefer to remain shrouded in mystery; particularly as they will hope that their general reassurances about effectiveness of such adverts satisfies all concerned enquiries. I believe that programme adverts are often reliably ineffective in generating new business, except by sheer serendipity or from those who consciously wish to support their club's local sponsors. Many of the service offerings are uniquely local and extremely specific, so it's difficult to see how much new volume business they could generate.

As I travelled round the country, I've noted that the types of sponsorship and advertisers attracted to speedway vary from the specialist, to the local, to the obscure or unusual. As I casually glance at the Eastbourne programme for this meeting, I realise I do not intend to bet; hire a van; have some printing done; buy a toilet alerter; read *The Herald*; go to Buddies in Polegate; use an electrician or paint; get insured; record a CD; visit the Transport festival; hire a disco; start a website; fit out an exhibition; move, sweep up or hire a plant. And I've hardly begun to list all the possible services. Though I must say, on a personal note, that I'm delighted all these people sponsor the club and the riders, since we probably wouldn't enjoy the high quality racing that we do get see at Arlington otherwise. In fact, I'd always recommend all of them to my friends should they ever be in need of these services, and I wouldn't hesitate to allow myself to be influenced – consciously or subliminally – by their attractive, informative, and eye-catching space advertising. Marketing is an industry where they inevitably say that 50% of all advertising works: only they don't know which half.

The survey also assumes that none of the spectators at a speedway meeting read

[2] The *Metro* represents fastest growing and most attractive market segment to advertisers comprising a high number of 18-35s in its readership!

the *Daily Express*, *Independent*, *Metro*[2] or *Sport*. The most surprising omission, in light of the rich historical heritage that it has in its reporting on and in its sponsorship of speedway meetings is the *Daily Express*! Despite these omissions, at least the compilers did have the imagination to expect both sexes would attend as the survey asked for your Gender, Who you came with, and the number of people in your group. Maybe they hoped to try to send them all on holiday, once they had your name and address as well as your age and income details.

Overall, the questionnaire reeked of amateurism tarted up in a valiant attempt to appear to solicit information in such a way that, on a sunny day with the wind in the right direction, might influence a wavering potential sponsor that the speedway demographic would be ideal for their product. However, they say the number of fish you catch depends on the size of the holes in your net. This net had holes so large, it would struggle to catch a whale. It would have been more fun and only marginally less useful if they had asked more imaginative questions, for example: 'what colour is your goldfish?' 'What was the name of your first school?' 'Should the death penalty be introduced for unfair riding'; 'what is the make, model and mileage of your car?' 'Does your language let you down in important social situations?' or 'Would you consider an evening class in speedway bike maintenance that leads to an internationally recognised qualification?'

I had half a mind to write to Influx Marketing asking for a copy of the results under the Freedom of Information Act to learn the full details of their insight into this season's speedway spectators that this questionnaire generated. Or, once the devil was in me, to write to them to check their full compliance with Data Protection regulations, but decided that life was just too short to bother to do so[3].

After the crowd carefully observes a minute's silence for the passing of John Vincent, Eagles' fan and Chairman of Wealden District Council, the meeting itself began. It was never expected to be that competitive, but terrible luck and sudden injuries quickly had the Oxford side on the ropes. The meeting turned into a busy night for the medical staff. Indeed, it was an evening they'd have been advised to keep the engine running on the ambulance, they had so many stricken riders to remove from the track or to ferry to the local hospital. Mostly it was the Oxford riders who suffered and, by the end of the meeting, it was pretty well the case that anyone who could ride, did ride, for the visitors. Henrik Gustafsson withdrew after a crash in his first race of the evening that caused "his shoulder to pop out" as Kevin 'KC' Coombes delicately described such an excruciating experience. Billy Hamill then withdrew after two rides, as he felt very much "under the weather" from a recent tumble that seriously exacerbated the fragility of his recovery from his early season catalogue of horrendous injuries. This made an already difficult task impossible; Oxford were only able to track one rider in the often the often crucial heat 13 with the match already effectively over at 46-29.

In a meeting that challenged the skill and capabilities of the Oxford team manager and the St. John ambulance team in equal measure, heat 14 capped off quite an evening. The first attempt to run this meeting saw Lubos Tomicek "come together with Davey Watt" according to KC. It was an encounter that resulted in Lubos's immediate withdrawal from the meeting, a decision made easier for his team manager Waggy who told KC, "Lubos was stunned and didn't know where he was!" In the re-run, it appeared that Iversen didn't know where Watt was, when he appeared to spear him with his bike before he then fell heavily himself into the fence on the final corner of the first lap. After an extremely lengthy delay to load him into and take him away in the ambulance to Eastbourne General Hospital, we learnt that Watt had "luckily only suffered shoulder, chest and rib injuries", but otherwise was conscious and in "severe pain". The few riders that were left for Oxford managed to complete the final race of the night as the Eagles ran out easy victors 57-35. In the final analysis, the cost in injuries was high for both sides with Greg Hancock, the only visiting rider to offer any real resistance against a good all-round performance from the Eagles.

16th July Eastbourne v. Oxford (ELB) 57-35

18th July
Once again, Nicki was in the thick of the action at his old home track with a flawless 18-point maximum. Even the track record set by

[3] "All surveys are subject to several sources of error", the small print said. "These include: sampling error (because only a sample of a population is interviewed); measurement error due to question wording and/or question order, deliberately or unintentionally inaccurate responses, non-response (including refusals), interviewer effects (when live interviewers are used) and weighting. With one exception (sampling error) the magnitude of the errors that result cannot be estimated. There is, therefore, no way to calculate a finite 'margin of error' for any survey and the use of these words should be avoided. With pure probability samples, with 100% response rates, it is possible to calculate the probability that the sampling error (but not other sources of error) is not greater than some number. With a pure probability sample of 1016 adults one could say with a 95% probability that the overall results have a sampling error of +/- 3 percentage points. However, that does not take other sources of error into account". This is the small print that the renowned US market research company Harris (of America) disclosed to the National Council on Public Polls. Imagine how inaccurate the 'Influx Marketing' data must be given all the flaws it has? Source: Peter Preston, *Guardian* 14/8/06

Deano shares a joke with a departing Mooro. © Jeff Scott

Billy Hamill waves before the warm up. © Jeff Scott

Floppy on the last visit to Monmore Green was beaten (along with the Eagles) by 0.13 of a second by Mikael Max. One way to celebrate his own 400th appearance for Wolves. Though Eastbourne used rider replacement for Floppy and Joonas Kylmakorpi as a guest, it was weakness at reserve that proved crucial with Mooro and Hall gaining only two points whereas the Karlsson (M.)–Pecyna combination gained 14.

This time it wasn't Monday Night Fight Night among the riders and staff but, nonetheless, there was still much verbal passion. As is traditional much of this ire was directed at Nicki, though it again only served as a spur for him to further raise his performance. Vociferous abuse of Wolves David Howe, by one opinionated Black Country fan during the after-match interviews on the centre green, needled him enough to confront his tormentor on the terraces afterwards. Though he had again done his talking on the track with ten well earned points, Howe has consistently failed to win over the hard core Wolves faithful in the way that Adam Skornicki, the enigmatic rider he replaced, had. Maybe he should immediately grow a ponytail and smile a lot while he speaks with an impenetrable accent?

18th July Wolverhampton v Eastbourne (ELB) 49–41

21st July

Floppy didn't manage to return to Wiltshire, the scene of his innocuous early season accident. Medical advice is to take "strong muscle relaxants" as part of his recuperation, though he still has to endure the frustration of not knowing whether recovery is just around the corner or remains a mirage in the distance. With a furrowed brow, Jon Cook indulged in a rare nautical metaphor to describe the situation, "personally for David this is a nightmare and team-wise, we will have to knuckle down and weather the storm".

To win at Terry Russell's other club is delicious enough, but to do it on a big track that until the 2005 season rarely suited the Eagles delighted all concerned. Local *Speedway Star* reporter Marc Lyons noted that the Robins' unbeaten home record had been "blown away" by the Eagles who "swooped to grab victory" in a last-heat decider that he would probably have described as "stunning" if achieved by other local members of the bird kingdom. Not quite magnanimous in victory, JC said, "I think it is one of our top five victories – winning at a big track. We normally go to big tracks and try for damage limitation. This is what we said before the parade". At this thought all Eagles fans, as if they didn't know this already, double underlined their own existing mental note that to support the Eagles team away at some venues will, most likely, only produce victories once in a blue moon.

Usually of 'The Cup is Broken Never Mind Half Empty' school of thought, honed to a fine art as mine host behind the bar or during long hours on the congested roads in his lorry, Alun 'Rosco' Rossiter didn't hesitate to flourish his near by onion to great effect. Never one just to say "well done" to his opponents, he mined a particularly rich seam of excuses, which only served to further highlight the severe blow to the Robins' pride of this defeat. His mood had already probably been tempered by his 40th birthday and late news that in nearby Oxford

[1] Isn't "stupidity" a better epithet for putting petrol in a diesel tank?

Peter Ljung's van had been immobilised when it was filled with "the wrong type of fuel" and had thereby deprived the rider of "his own bikes". With only a brief glance through his detective's magnifying glass, Rosco was in no doubt: "it is fishy and I am not happy at all."[1] Seb Alden also chose this particular fixture to experiment with the use of an engine tuned by a blind man for smaller tracks, after the correctly tuned engine wasn't allowed on the plane from Sweden "due to the terrorist problems".

As if all this wasn't already enough, the parking Nazis from the "local authority" had also got in Rosco's hair about the design for the car park layout for the World Cup: "we have had to peg out extra car parking – and I spent half my birthday doing that".

21st July Swindon v. Eastbourne (ELB) 44–46

Havvy Mark II, and When KC Met Ronnie

23rd July

A break from Elite League action has the Eagles, once more, face their local rivals, the frequently under performing Arena Essex Hammers. This time it's a fixture in the Knockout Cup Semi-Final, a two-leg affair intended to maximise attendance and to create a fair overall aggregate result. With a full squad this meeting would be one that the Eagles should win easily against one of the country's weaker teams. However, without the injured David's – Norris and Watt – there's a much greater possibility that the cliché of the so-called "magic of the cup" could be a significant factor in the first leg of this contest. A shock result is unlikely but, at least, it's a possibility.

Eastbourne continue a season of speculative selections at reserve, and tonight have picked Premier League King's Lynn's reserve rider Trevor Harding. He already knows his way to Arlington, if not round Arlington, as he's already been in the pits most weekends when he works there as mechanic for fellow Australian Davey Watt. With his trademark shrewdness, Eastbourne's Jon Cook has also selected Joonas Kylmakorpi to guest in the place of the injured Davey Watt. Arguably the season's most controversial rider, Joonas (still an Eagles asset) knows the Sussex track very well; he's performed superbly round Arlington many times for Eastbourne, when he rode for us, and also often, against us. It's been a strange season so far for Joonas, as he's made headlines for all the wrong reasons, mostly off the track rather than on it. After he left Peterborough under a bitter and dark cloud and thereby probably crossing himself off their Christmas card list for life, he then received the mandatory 28-day ban for his trouble. A dispute between his next club, Coventry, and the sports governing body about the terms and timing of the end of this ban, nearly resulted in the demise of the Coventry when its owner has a bit of a hissy fit reaction and threatened the league with his own club's dissolution. It must finally be a relief for Joonas to do his talking on the track.

The Eastbourne faithful, as they patiently gather in reasonably large numbers on a bright, very sunny evening, certainly have high expectations about his performance. We're also well aware that it's likely to be completed in double quick time since tonight's match official is, once again, the legendarily speedy referee Frank Ebdon, who always runs his meetings as though he has a crucially important and pressing prior engagement to get to immediately afterwards. JC in his programme notes welcomes the crowd to what he terms as "the biggest meeting of the season so far". It's a statement that manages to be completely accurate and a necessary exaggeration all at the same time. Most of the crowd, obviously, hope the club will win as much silverware as possible, but have mainly set their sights on higher aspirations, namely the Elite League Championship. There's no doubt that the Eagles would rather race against Arena than Ipswich, who the formbook would have indicated would be the likelier semi-final opponent. It's a stroke of good fortune that delights our resident MC, the always ebullient Kevin 'KC' Coombes, who introduces the visiting team like a slightly demented Santa as "Essex who put out Ipswich, chortle, chortle, ho, ho!"

Heat 1 starts ominously for the Eagles when they find themselves racing against the more mercurial and resilient of the two possible Gary Havelocks that could turn up to race. The usual Gary Havelock – the one that has seen it all before, done it all before – performs acceptably but in an inconsistent, slightly careworn, and jaundiced manner. On these days, what you see is what you get, with the clear impression that it's just another payday that doesn't motivate him that much any more. Unluckily for Eastbourne, the "another day, another dollar" version isn't here; instead we have the "shining example to young riders and stunningly gifted ex-world champion" version that flies from the tapes. Of the three ex-World Champions here tonight, you would lay money beforehand that Gary would perform the least well. Still, Mark Loram's slow return to his usual fine racing form after his serious early season injuries would have raised some question marks and made him another possible candidate for this unwanted accolade. Whatever the reason, Havelock wins the initial heat by a country mile in a manner that would lead you to think he's still reigns as the world's number 1 rider.

Almost immediately, normality returns with a comprehensive win for the Eagles reserves in the next race with Mooro and Trevor Harding (one of a long line of Trevors – since his grandfather and father also share the same name) both showing a clear set of wheels to the opposition. The majority of the crowd is pleased to see Trevor Harding in the Eagle's body colour and not Steen Jensen as Mooro's partner in the team's Reserve berths. Although that said, not at all predictable and ever the surprising contrarian, JC's comments in his programme notes, somewhat strangely given Steen's recent and notorious poor form, appears to imply that Steen would actually have rode tonight but for a priority Premier League fixture for his home club, the Isle of Wight, at Workington. This would be a Lazarus-like resurrection in the club's confidence in his ability to perform well on the track after his meteoric decline over the early months of the season. Later, to confirm that we sometimes live in a mad world or, at least, that the job of promoter and team manager requires many pragmatic decisions, JC announces later, "Steen is our Arena specialist". This is definitely a case of the club's management skilfully making a virtue of a definite vice, in that the raceway at Thurrock is definitively the only track this season at which Steen has so far managed to look like a competent, professional speedway rider when he races in the distinctive Eagles race bib. Anyway, the ghost of Christmas Past is spurned in favour of the ghost of Christmas Present; Trevor Harding immediately plays his part to the full and is warmly cheered by the home crowd during his victory lap of celebration with Mooro.

KC hardly has time to note for the second time and subsequently thereafter with variations on a similar theme every time Harding appears by the pit gate, that "Harding mechanics for Davey Watt usually, so he knows how to set up the bike though it's Davey who's helping him in the pits tonight". The words are barely out of his mouth as the riders for the next race make their way round to the tapes. KC just about manages to exclaim that "fast fingers Frank is at it!" before Deano and Joonas Kylmakorpi race away for another easy victory. With the score already at 13-5, the chance of an Arena win already appears forlorn if not yet completely doomed although pride and the need to restrict the Eagles to a modest lead keeps them firmly in the saddle.

Arena are immediately helped by a rare Pedersen error when he accidentally falls though at the time he leads easily. After he quickly remounts, Nicki retires from the race after he considers the distance the other riders have travelled insurmountable and so allows Mark Loram to take the victory. Back where I stand on the terraces, a loud but apparently ignorant family continually disturbs the peace of the area with their four hyperactively boisterous kids. They look and act like they exist on a diet of junk food bolstered with 'E' numbers. The father is resplendent in an England shirt that fits very tightly over an impressively huge beer belly, the result of considerable time, work and investment on his behalf. Throughout he remains immune to the second eldest child who, despite its age, screams and screams throughout the whole meeting at a volume that nearly drowns out the roar of the bikes. The only thing that bothers either parent, particularly the father, is the lack of effort he perceives from the Arena riders. In definitely a case of do as I say rather than do as I do, since he'd probably break any bike he sat astride, nonetheless, he hectors the Arena team with a continuous stream of obscenities. His wife stands there unemotionally, while her only reaction to any outside stimulation is to harshly slap every tenth errant misdemeanor from any of her children or scold them with some vehemence and choice language for their continuously obnoxious behaviour. This nearby family drama makes it quite hard to concentrate on the racing but, once you stand somewhere regularly, your sense of ownership, propriety and stubbornness dictates that you usually refuse to move or show any reaction in a so-called stoically 'English' way, no matter how irksomely others behave. None of the regulars around me bother to comment to the family directly, so we content ourselves with raised eyebrows and our own valiant attempts to shout above them between the heats. We all realise that they're not your typical Arena Essex fans or, at least, we hope that Ronnie Russell's repeated and praiseworthy campaigns to raise awareness as well as support for his club hasn't backfired badly. Thank goodness it's Frank Ebdon who officiates here tonight as, accidents permitting, the heats are guaranteed to pass along quickly.

After Nicki has picked himself up from the shale and dusted down his kevlars, from then on it's Arena Essex that find themselves down in the metaphorical cinders. The only resistance to the onslaught of Eastbourne's outright successes is the odd drawn heat or yet another magnificent ride from the impressive Mark II version of Gary Havelock. This deluxe version takes to the track in the re-run of heat 8, after Mooro submits an excellent entry for "crash of the season" at Eastbourne in the initial attempt to run the race. All was going well for him until he disastrously attempted an overtaking manoeuvre on the outside in a space that only really existed in his imagination. There could only ever be one result from this somewhat foolhardy act of bravery – a heavy fall! However, it was a crash notable for the distance the bike then travelled *sans* rider as it somersaulted through the air before coming to rest a good way farther down the track. With Mooro straight to his feet, perhaps in cocktail fashion shaken, stirred but slightly embarrassed, the path was clear for Havvy on a tactical ride and ex-Eagles rider Paul Hurry to romp home for maximum points. This was the sum extent of the token resistance from the visitors for the rest of the evening. The confidence of the home fans was sufficient for some of the more voluble of them to loudly and disrespectfully shout out "who?" throughout the evening every time the not-quite-at-his-best Mark Loram's name was announced by KC. Nicki Pedersen fully recovered from his earlier fall at the front, and spent the rest of an untroubled night powering away from all-comers at the head of each race without ever looking like he had ever to exert himself too much. The most thrilling of the races that had Nicki miles away at the front in the lead was just before the interval, in heat 10, when his partner Adam Shields squeezed through another phantom gap to beat a rather surprised Roman Povazhny on the line.

The interval saw KC get good value from a discussion with the ever bluntly honest but slightly eccentric "team manager and entrepreneur" Ronnie Russell. Wearing the look of a man who has found the mini-bar of life completely empty, the always cheery Ronnie Russell shot from the hip and the heart throughout the interview, but initially took an onion from his pocket when he commented at length but without the violins that would be the ideal accompaniment for news on the declining attendances that have been grievously suffered at Thurrock this season. Since he fails to attach any blame or responsibility to himself for the reputedly inconsistent level of entertainment offered by his team during this season, RR prefers to concentrate on the capricious and fickle nature of the punters. "I commend the fans who are here, they're at home every week, but it's the ones we have lost that are casting a shadow over this club". As T.S. Eliot highlighted years ago, between the idea and the action falls the shadow, so it's definitely a shadow of financial pressure and comparative commercial failure against his own expectations that bugs Ronnie. "I can't even think about next season, it's been such a traumatic year on the track and off the track financially". It doesn't help the situation that the opportunity to ride for Arena doesn't appear to appeal to most riders, RR's door remains resolutely un-knocked down, despite this state of affairs Ronnie retains enough *joie de vivre* to relentlessly search for them throughout the season. To compound the difficulty of it all, life's inevitable inequalities have emerged with the rich getting richer and RR has found that he's unable to compete on a level playing field with the financial firepower of his more well-to-do rivals. "For every £1 that I have in my pocket, Coventry have £10" and many legal advisors, he might have added. It would be difficult to script a more depressed assessment of the club's prospects, particularly in a sport where the present generation of promoters' personalities have a default setting predisposed to hyperbole and permanently tuned a "hear no evil, see no evil" channel! Ronnie caps off a bravura review that would drive the less robust members among the club's supporters to queue for the exits or contemplate a trip to Beachy Head to end it all, when he observes that at the BSPA the promoters "make rules that even we ourselves don't even understand!"

In marked contrast, when JC is interviewed straight afterwards by KC, he's in a very upbeat mood brought on by a shock away win at Swindon earlier in the week. "It's always special when Eastbourne win away on a big track". It's left unsaid but many in the crowd imagine that it also pleases Jon to put one over on Alun Rossiter, his erstwhile rival-in-waiting and the team manager at Swindon. It would only be human nature if the owner of the promotional rights of both these Elite League clubs, Terry Russell (Ronnie's much less visible but more powerful and much more widely discussed brother) did make occasional comparisons. Eschewing any mention of Mr Rossiter and deliberately concentrating on the successful management and promotion his own team, JC refers to the fact that "we do seem to have plenty of heart among ourselves". He feels that the embarrassment of home defeat against Coventry delivered a welcome kick up the backside that has done wonders for the team morale, especially since then they've consciously tried to emulate the "spirit shown by Coventry". If JC was on the look out for lucky omens and charms, he's found it since tonight's guest "Joonas might spark things off like Gary Havelock did last season when he guested for us".

After he aims a curt broadside at critics unknown, who lurk on the Internet and spout disagreeable but also inaccurate doom-laden opinions, JC delights to note that "all the pundits on the Internet, those in 'the know', have been proved wrong". Just then the itchy fingers of Frank Ebdon sound the two-minute warning for the resumption of the meeting which thereby cuts short his castigation of his unseen critics, JC quickly takes the chance to praise his reserve riders, "Andy Moore has looked fantastic and Harding is just the sort of gutsy rider we want at Eastbourne". Before he gazes into his crystal ball to forecast "I can really see us doing the business".

It was a prediction that the Eagles form for the rest of the evening did nothing to dispel. Havelock would have top scored for the visitors but he suddenly ran a couple of unexpected lasts (or totally expected in normal circumstances), a surprise given his form on the night, in the always tough heats 13 and 15. Mark Loram demonstrated his innate class in both of these high-pressure races, though he lost out on both occasions to Nicki, but still ran him close enough without ever getting as close to beating him as he nearly did in heat 11. This resistance aside it was left to the Eastbourne team to illustrate their strength in depth. Deano showed particular skill and cunning when he shepherded home the less experienced and tentative Mooro in a superb example of the dying art of team riding. The "spirit" JC spoke highly of appeared to seize and move the riders and the crowd alike as well as the DJ who played a rousing selection of songs throughout, but closed with *St. Elmo's Fire* to serenade the riders on their victory parade. Hopefully, this is the meeting that starts the fire that will see the Eastbourne team fulfil their considerable but too often only latent promise!

23rd July Eastbourne v. Arena (KO Cup) 55-40

30th July

Whatever the July equivalent of the 'Ides of March' happen to be, they continued to gnaw at Alun 'Rosco' Rossiter. Luckily at Arlington his side were "almost as bad" as they were at Belle Vue where they were "just depressing to watch". Cut from a different cloth at the 'Motivational School for Promoter's Speeches', JC quietly smirked inwardly and was "full of praise" for his team.

Deano was on fire in his partnership with Shieldsy, who could win safely content in the knowledge his team mate wouldn't be far behind. Indeed, so far this season Deano has already strongly staked his claim as the 'Bonus Point King' of the Elite League. Rarely first, if this were *Romeo and Juliet*, Deano would be much more content to play the witty but supportive Mercutio and, to continue with this comparison, to follow others who lead the pack as Romeo. In plain speedway terms, he has a lot of seconds and thirds. By this stage in the season, the Eagles still hadn't satisfactorily resolved the problematic No. 7 reserve position and this week it was Trevor Harding's turn to drink from this jinxed chalice. Although from a family with a long line of Trevors, Harding could only manage two points.

This week the on-off return of Floppy was "on". He pronounced himself "relatively happy" with his comeback, and though he denied he was "race rusty" but instead admitted "I am just unfit". In fact off the track, Floppy like the rest of the Eastbourne Eagles were shocked and deeply saddened by the sudden death of Steve Heath, the Arlington Training Track guru, when he was at a motivational karting competition for Mildenhall riders and staff. A minute's silence was immaculately observed before the meeting and later an emotional Floppy dedicated his next race victory, in heat 8, to the memory of Steve Heath.

30th July Eastbourne v. Swindon (ELB) 55

August

TONY MILLARD
"You could describe Nicki Pedersen as a laxative rider"

8th August
On a rare Monday night fixture, Mooro continued his one-man campaign to maintain the "power riding" at reserve established earlier in the season by Davey Watt. The intractable problem provided by the other 'difficult' position still remained, though tonight Trevor Harding was able to continue his Elite League apprenticeship without fear over the possible loss of valuable points because of a widely expected easy win. Another five-race maximum for Nicki Pedersen was part of an all-round team effort and was complimented to great effect by Adam Shields. Deano festooned his performance with yet more bonus points to accompany the balloons that decorated his bike on the Isle of Wight the week before where he spent his 35th birthday riding in Ray Morton's testimonial.

It wasn't an evening to fill the Witches with anything other than gloom. It was characterised by Ipswich manager Mike Smillie as "a very disappointing performance and as early as heat 5 it was a damage limitation exercise". Unable to defend a 17-point lead, even the possible bonus point was frittered away, and for Hans Anderson, it was an under-par display that sounded the death knell for this season's league ambitions: "I think that's it for us".

8th August Eastbourne v. Ipswich (ELB) 58–38

A Tale of Elbows, Guests and Helmet Colours

12th August

A home meeting against Wolves is precisely the sort of fixture that the Eagles have to win if they are to seriously press for a place in the Elite League play-offs. It is our second Friday night fixture of the season, though the only truly proper one since the other was on a Bank Holiday. It's also about time that the Eagles asserted themselves against these particular visitors to Arlington, especially since it has been some time since the Wolves tasted defeat here. The fixture is given added piquancy by the events earlier in the season at Monmore Green, though a lot of the ire from this famous encounter has already been slaked in a 49-41 defeat there.

The Eagles will field a very much transformed team for tonight's fixture from the one that lined up for the home meeting with Ipswich four days previously. This was arguably the first time this season that we had fielded what could be deemed a full-strength squad, only for Jon Cook to learn by the Wednesday morning afterwards that he had by then lost the services of Floppy (out of action again with that troublesome injury, this time in Sweden), Shieldsy (broken collar bone), and Trevor Harding (scaphoid and collar bone). Nicki Pedersen has so far only dropped a single point in 16 races against his old club this season but, to the great disappointment of the Arlington faithful, will not appear in this evening's fixture. The dreaded GPs have raised their ugly, inconvenient head once again to effectively undermine the appeal of another one of our most exciting Elite League fixtures; a situation thrust upon the club "because of our need to run against this week's Grand Prix" as Jon Cook notes in the programme. Still, Mark Loram always does a good job in our race bib and is the best replacement for Nicki's high average we could hope for when all the other so-called 'superstars' that could possibly be booked as guests are engaged in the pursuit of personal GP glory elsewhere. And at one point mid-week it appeared that Mark's own injury battles might cause his late withdrawal. Mark is not the only guest, since Chris 'Bomber' Harris also lines up for the Eagles in place of Adam Shields. He is a shrewd choice by Jon Cook. Harris has been in spectacular form all season for the Bees, has demonstrated a real liking for the Arlington circuit on his previous visits, and is in the process of rightfully staking his claim to be regularly included in the Team GB squad for international fixtures. There would also be the additional excitement in the crowd brought on by another appearance by Steen Jensen, after his recent lengthy absence from the Eagles colours and a close study of the drawing board. The optimistic assumption in the crowd around where I stand is that he has been honing his skills elsewhere for the Isle of the Wight and has now sufficiently perfected them to merit a return to the team, though the results section of the *Speedway Star* doesn't indicate that this outlook is true. More likely, due to injuries like those sustained by Trevor Harding (along with the general unavailability of suitable replacement riders on the appropriate average), we have to re-blood Steen and vainly attempt to get him back up to Elite League 'speed'. We know that we will race tonight in the full knowledge that we are still desperately short of adequate manpower in the reserve slot not occupied by Mooro.

The Wolverhampton squad has a much more settled look about them and they track the team that they have used for the majority of the season. They have eschewed the need for a GP star to head their ranks in favour of their long-time favourite and stalwart performer, Michael Max, though tonight, since he is injured, they have booked the ideal guest replacement in the form of his brother – the softly spoken Swede (albeit with a strong Black Country accent) Peter Karlsson. They also have a couple of riders that would fall into the experienced-journeyman category, in the form of the much-travelled Steve 'Johno' Johnston and the incredibly diminutive Ronnie Correy, their small but perfectly formed American who is one of the oldest riders still plying their trade with the comparative youngsters at Elite League level. Then they say you are only as young as you feel, though it takes a special kind of 40ish male to don his kevlars and regularly race bikes without brakes! For whatever reasons, the Wolves haven't exactly set the world on fire resultswise this season, but remain formidable opposition at Arlington. It should be an enthralling contest with their side "arguably strengthened" and the Eagles "arguably weakened", but I'm sure most fans would instead actually welcome the chance to watch a full complement of their own 'regular' riders race tonight.

They say when the going gets tough the tough get going. After the start of heat 1, things haven't degenerated to 'tough' but Peter

Karlsson departs from the tapes in such a jet-propelled manner that Deano's attempt to clash elbows with him – from his inside gate 1 position – and thereby, hopefully, vaguely disrupt his smooth flow into the corner is a good plan only frustrated by the minor detail that Karlsson has already long since departed. Nonetheless, in as a rider replacement ride for Floppy, Deano still vainly flails out his strategic elbow, but it only wafts harmlessly into thin air. Indeed the start line is the only time that the Eagles riders get close to Karlsson for his first three rides until our guests 'Bomber' Harris and Mark Loram skilfully combine to relegate him to third place in heat 13.

Deano again rises to the responsibilities of captaincy and finds himself in the thick of the action all night. In his first programmed ride of the fixture, he starts a personal duel within a match battle with Steve Johnston, who looks likely to pass Deano after sterling work allows him to best Watty, but all this is only to lock up behind Deano and relegate himself to the minor placing. The resulting 5–1 allows the rather patched-up looking Eagles team to regain the overall lead after Steen's desire to impress and do well has sadly seen him burst through the tapes in the previous outing, the reserves race. The resultant 15-metre handicap for this exclusion would defeat even the most confident of on-form riders, never mind one so woefully bedraggled by results as him. Consequently in the re-run we see Ronnie Correy win by the proverbial mile and Steen distantly trail off at the back, albeit rather stylishly, in similar proverbial mile fashion.

Out for the third time in five races in heat 5, Deano entertains the crowd with a virtuoso and graceful display of advanced bike wrestling on the apex of the first bend of lap 1. In the manner of a circus lion tamer seeking to discipline a particularly recalcitrant big cat, Deano manfully tries to control the bucking beast before he admits defeat and retires. In the interval, mine host in the form of MC KC attempts to get to the bottom of this bizarre incident only for Deano to make light of his travails against his own bike with the nonchalant summary that doesn't capture the full glory of this visual experience: "I hit a bit of 'ice' and donutted three times". Not that Deano is the only rider to undertake spectacular manoeuvres with his equipment as Freddie Lindgren tries to outdo him in spectacular fashion on the final lap of heat 6. Freddie rears impressively at speed when in hot pursuit of 'Bomber' Harris, is thrown off into the path of the closely following Watty – who does exceptionally well to avoid him – while his bike merrily dambusters its own way in ducks and drakes fashion further down the back straight in pursuit of Harris, like one of the riderless horses you often see at the Grand National. Heat 7 sees the first of three successive drawn heats and showcases another cameo from Steen, who falls and remounts on the way to customarily bringing up the rear.

By the end of heat 10, the Eagles have drawn level on aggregate again thanks to a 5–1 from their guests Harris and Loram, so the situation looks poised for them to press on to try to gain the bonus point. Peter Karlsson hasn't read the script and wins heat 11 "In Memory of Steve Heath" and again this featured Steen finishing fourth to ride to yet another of his unwanted maximums – a perfect triple of completely defeated outings. When Deano and Johnston race the concluding leg of their own mini-duel, a Wolves rider again takes the chequered flag, but only after they have indulged the crowd with an aggressive, no-quarter given battle for the first two laps before another very combative passing manoeuvre by 'Johno' sees him establish the lead required to ride to ultimate

PK holds a maintenance masterclass. © Jeff Scott

Classic cars on parade. © Jeff Scott

Contemplative fans in the pits. © Jeff Scott

victory.

Heat 14 then finds itself mired in controversy and farce in equal measures and serves as the ideal example of why speedway as a sport loves to shoot itself in the foot. One of the ways it achieves this is by wreathing a simple proposition in rules so complex that they defy casual understanding by experienced practitioners of the sport, never mind the impossibility of providing a rational explanation to the fabled but elusive beast - the 'casual' lay punter – who just might (but rarely has) have happened to have accidentally strayed along to watch. Put simply, as the Wolves trail by 8 points they are able to attempt a last almost desperate throw of the dice under the present rules to gain the bonus point by fielding Peter Karlsson as a tactical substitute. This meant that he will start with a handicap of 15 metres from the start line and will wear the special black-and-white helmet that would double any points he gains. Wolves are unable to use him in the frequently derided role of a tactical replacement ride, since they are not the prerequisite 9 more points or more in arrears. The rules that govern this are exactly the same as above, except that the ride doesn't have a 15-metre handicap. So far, so complex!

Though handicapped, Karlsson still manages to catch up with and pass Mooro, but is unable to catch Davey Watt. Since his team mate David Howe then 'lets him pass' (another regular and unsatisfactory aspect that has resulted from the introduction of this regulation), Karlsson gains double points for his second place for a race score of 3–5 that would probably return the bonus point to Monmore Green, if the last race goes according to plan for them. However, we then suffer an inordinate delay before we learn that the meeting now borders on farce, as Karlsson is disqualified for not actually wearing the requisite black-and-white helmet cover.

Next to me by board number 51, John Hazelden had immediately pointed out that PK had erroneously appeared in the yellow helmet cover when he came round to the start line. On such tiny mistakes do championship campaigns flounder; ironic when earlier that evening the very wily Wolves team manager, Peter Adams, had explained to me that the chance to pit his wits, attention to detail, and speedway knowledge against his opponents and contemporaries was one of the primary appeals of his own position for him within the sport. The obvious and what is right in front of your nose can often elude you. But when the rule of law breaks down, the *Daily Mail* tells us we have "anarchy" and Barry Richardson isn't going to allow that to happen on his watch at Arlington as the SCB referee for tonight's fixture – so he (correctly) excludes Karlsson. This adds to the tension of the last race, as the Wolves now need a 2–4 to force a run-off for the bonus point and a 1–5 to win it outright. Anything less than that would see the Eagles win on the night and gain the much desired bonus point.

To my mind, this is where the GP Series has come back to spoil things again. Not only has it deprived us of the chance to see some of the most gifted riders of this generation of speedway exponents race, Pedersen and Max, but also it has compounded its effects when both of our guests line up for the Eagles in the nominated race. Not that I doubt the commitment and desire to win exhibited by Bomber Harris and Mark Loram, particularly Mark whom Jon Cook prefers to hire if he can in light of the many times he has excelled as a guest in the Eagles colours. But, these are not our own riders and, in these tense concluding races when vital points are at stake, you would have to fancy Nicki Pedersen to win the majority of them against practically any opposition, home or away, never mind when he's fired up against the Wolves. Predictably or surprisingly, depending on your point of view, Bomber trails in for his only last place of the night and Mark finishes second in a 2–4 result that will now require a race-off between PK and Mark Loram.

Given that PK has looked quick and on superlative form all night, hopes aren't high that Mark Loram will win this match race. As it happens, we don't get to see this race completed since after one lap of neck-and-neck racing with PK leading, Mark falls at the start of the second lap and is excluded by the referee as the "primary cause of the stoppage". Wolves triumph for the bonus point, the ranks of the Eagles fans around me are suitably deflated at this almost farcical conclusion, and so leave muttering about the iniquities of the GP series and darkly alluding to the dangers of guest riders. KC interviews JC who, in the context of the mid-week decimation of the team through injury, highlights the positives of a night when the Eagles gained two points he didn't really ought to expect, "I can't give them enough credit for how they've performed tonight". He reiterated this afterwards to local reporters: "I am absolutely delighted. That really shows that when we are down we are certainly not out and I cannot say enough about them". The view of the fans as they stream away isn't so forgiving or positive about this meeting, or what they feel that this implies for future play-off prospects for the club.

12th August Eastbourne v. Wolves (ELB) 49–41

Another different chapter appears about this fixture in my book *Showered in Shale*.

Two Superpowers Meet

20th August

When you push through the turnstiles for this important Elite League encounter, you immediately encounter one of the sports riding legends from the 1970s, Chris Morton MBE, standing by a table that displays copies of his recently published autobiography *Until the Can Ran Out*. He'd written the book with the prodigious serial speedway writer and journalist Brian Burford, but I learn from Chris that most unusually for this genre, he'd actually done much of the writing himself. I'd already heard that the book had done fantastically well at Belle Vue, as you'd expect, the club where he rode and still works. He remains hugely well regarded there and throughout the sport from his glory days. If the name Peter Collins is synonymous with Belle Vue and England competing successfully on the world speedway stage, it's impossible to think of the period without immediately recalling Chris Morton as well. With a wonderful title, the interest in his autobiography is bound to have tremendous appeal for fans of a certain age. Attending the Belle Vue away fixture with Eastbourne is also a shrewd book sales and marketing tactic. Even though Belle Vue presently run away with the league, it's a vital fixture for the Eagles to beat them if they're to continue their challenge to secure a place in the play-offs. They would be popular anyway but their team also features the added attraction of Jason Crump. The car park is packed and the stadium full, although, despite being positioned in a prime spot, there is strangely no queue or interest from the Eastbourne fans to buy an autographed book from Chris.

I'd already purchased a copy and didn't have it with me for an autograph because I didn't know Chris would be there. He's extremely pleasant, very down to earth and clearly delighted to have committed his life story and career to paper. It's quite a story, but I won't spoil it for those of you who'd like to read it for yourselves. From Chris's comments, I gather the history and speedway specialist publisher Tempus have put very little effort into promoting the book to the national press. Tempus have their own very good speedway contacts, but they don't try for greater sales with a slightly wider, but still sports-oriented, audience. Chris is also very concerned that Amazon UK, the online Internet bookseller, which undercuts him and sells copies of his book at a substantial discount. To overcome the lack of

national attention and the online undercutting, he tries to sells them directly (and profitably) at full price at as many tracks as he can around the country! Before I leave, I finally get his autograph, which I'll treasure, on a tiny piece of paper along with his email address. When I walk past and look over later during the evening, I notice that there's sometimes a small queue of potential purchasers or, most likely, ageing fans that want to reminisce with Chris about the glory days.

Tonight, however, the only focus for the Eagles and the large crowd is victory over Belle Vue to keep our unlikely hopes of title glory alive. Jon Cook doesn't mention this in his programme notes, but instead views this clash as an important practice for and a potential prelude to possibly more encounters in the Knockout Cup Final if both teams, as looks likely, qualify. Most unusually, Steen Jensen gets a magnanimous mention in JC's programme notes for his recent performance against Wolves, even though he is not selected for tonight's meeting. It was a meeting in which he rode to an apparently crucial zero points score. Something that wouldn't usually get praised by management or fans alike, especially when you consider it was actually part of the Eagles ultimate defeat. I just don't understand it; but, then again, many people play roles and make contributions that are vital but not all obvious to the fans stuck on the outside of team dynamics. Nonetheless, it's a mystery.

Having dished out the plaudits, Jon is much less generous in his comments on the performance of the match official. In fact Jon's very ticked off, and blames the official for inattention and then, as a consequence of that, for making a decision he considers a "sham". This poor decision ruins the meeting, "the referee, in my opinion, is ultimately responsible". These sorts of comments would get you a disrepute charge in soccer, but in speedway are all part of the rough and tumble. It's very clear that there's been lots of rough along with the tumble in speedway's past, so much so that Jon treats us to a brief summary of the some of the more underhand tactics and deliberate skullduggery of yesteryear. These were practices that could be also be commonly known, in every day parlance, as 'cheating'. For those not exactly *au fait* with these shenanigans, Jon then helpfully provides an extensive list of tactics he notes have historically caused a "fair share of controversy". These include "tyre tampering", along with managers and promoters knowingly operating the sports regulations "illegally", as well as also deliberately throwing races to gain strategic advantage. It's quite a catalogue of intrigue and manipulation, though heaven forefend that it still might happen here tonight or elsewhere during this 2005 season and presently sanitised contemporary version of the sport we watch each week. While in some manner, this still might happen, given the huge experience and lengthy involvement that many promoters and team managers have in the sport, it's definitely something not to ponder for too long, so I won't, just in case things aren't quite what they sometimes appear on the track.

There's no better way to immediately banish these suggestions than a quick listen to Kevin 'KC' Coombes as he introduces tonight's teams and ponders the impending spectacle. KC enthuses that we're about to witness an encounter between "speedway's two superpowers" though, to be strictly accurate, the table or recent championship triumphs doesn't bear out this grandiose assertion. The Eagles have David 'Floppy' Norris back in their midst once more, as he continues his season-long battle with his frustrating and recurringly debilitating neck injury. It's an appearance that KC wittily sums up as he introduces Floppy during the team parade as "the boomerang that is our number 1!" Given that Floppy is not fully recovered, the key encounters of the night are most likely to be between Nicki Pedersen and reigning World Champion Jason Crump. KC is optimistic that Nicki will be even more motivated, confident and on a high after he won his National Championship in Denmark last night. KC relives for us the basic details – namely that Nicki won all six of his races and then goes on to express delight on Nicki's behalf as well as being impressed by reports of the "very, very large crowd of 6,500" that the event reputedly attracted at Fjelstad.

It's an expectation of an exceptional performance that seems more of a forlorn hope after heat 4, when Pedersen leads throughout only to be overtaken on the last bend by Crump. Judy Hazelden, who stands next to me, is less than impressed and puts our collective dissatisfaction succinctly, "freaking hell, he done him on the line!" After she recovers from this upset and acknowledges Crump's excellent riding tactics, Judy still fails to appreciate the comparative rarity, almost a collector's item of a manoeuvre – to see a rider overtake Pedersen up the inside. "Nicki rode on his line throughout until the last bend and then came off slightly. You know, I could ride that bike better than them sometimes or at least be team manager!" Dissatisfaction levels in the crowd around me remains high, though the Eagles in fact lead (just), when Deano and Davey Watt immediately both try to occupy the same starting gate before the next heat. This definitely doesn't impress Judy either, "our bloody captain don't even know what gate he's going from". Deano then finishes last to much harrumphing from Judy.

The next few races are all nip and tuck as Eastbourne maintain a narrow lead. Between races KC takes the opportunity to interview Jason Crump who's in a reflective rather than a defensive mood. An outlook that many people claim is his default setting and has often in the past gained him the soubriquet "Jason Grump". Jason mostly contents himself with platitudes of the 'I'm just delighted for the team' type, consequently, we learn that there's a "lot of history" at Belle Vue, as if no other club has its own history, before Jase reveals that in the World Championship GP series next year "I'm going to give it a big go". This year's defence of the title, by implication, wasn't so big an effort, mostly because "life changes" after you become World Champion and he had a "tough time" dealing with it. Jason can't resist capitalising, however subtly, on the psychological advantage of an early win against his erstwhile GP rival Nicki Pedersen on his home track, "uncharacteristically he made a mistake and I was fortunately placed to take advantage of it". When he's interviewed almost immediately afterwards, just as any sports psychologist would instruct you, Nicki makes no mention of his loss to Jason. Instead he much prefers to accentuate the positive and so relives the glory of his victory at last night's Danish National Championship again. He's clearly delighted enough to struggle slightly with the elegance of his English conversation – for once a rare slip from someone with an easy fluency in our language – when in a slightly ungainly manner he reveals that victory was made all the sweeter since Fjelstad is "only 5 minutes from my living place".

David Norris falls in heat 10, which probably isn't good news for his continued recovery or his ongoing return to the side. Deano wins the race from the experienced Belle Vue pair of Joe Screen and Jason Lyons. It's a well-deserved second place for Screen, which we then all immediately admire more than we would usually, after KC lets us know that "Joe Screen's shoulder has popped out but he's popped it in again; how amazing is that?" It's definitely something that Joe Public wouldn't relish the experience of or view as 'normal' during a day's work. KC remains amazed throughout the entire incident, enough to detail his every move in the pits, "now he's getting back on his speedway bike: are they tough or are they crazy?" Straight after the interval we learn that the most likely answer is 'tough' since Screen storms to an easy win. Deano continues with the dramatically seesawing form that has characterised his season, when once again his reputation plummets from hero to zero by the simple action of running a last in this race.

The interval had passed in a blur of birthday announcements from KC who's delighted to carry on the tradition, instigated with Nicki earlier in the season, of Eastbourne riders compulsorily celebrating their birthdays on a race night. We learn that Floppy is 33 today and KC passes on many happy returns from the club, the crowd, and what I think I hear slightly muffled over the tannoy as "his wife Elle and two sons, Jack and Ashley". I doubt that there's a connection between the boys names and the famous deaf former Labour MP of the same name. Not that this is something KC stops to consider as he joyously also passes on birthday greetings to Glenn, Deano's friendly but taciturn mechanic, who shares the day with Floppy. What the astrological significance of two key staff members born on the cusp of Virgo but who are actually Leos remains unexplored. Floppy definitely doesn't roar from the start like a lion in the vital heat 13, but has sufficient tiger in his tank – his can hasn't run out – to gain an important point for third place ahead of Kenneth Bjerre. Heat 14 has two riders fall in separate incidents, on bends 1 and 3. The referee Robbie Perks makes what intuitively, and from a common sense point of view, appears to be completely the wrong decision when he excludes both riders, Andy Smith for falling on bend 1 and Davey Watt for 'not being under power' when he falls on bend 3, though most in the crowd around me felt that the race should already have been stopped by then. Still, we don't have our fingers on the buzzers and there's nothing like some controversy to get the blood flowing through the veins of the crowd who, as one, become quite animated and voluble in the referee's direction. Nearby, Judy rather mildly

adjudges the actual decision to be "silly" and, to put it politely, upbraids the referee for his ignorance of the rules and his lack of the mental capabilities to administer them. Fortunately, Mooro – with the help of team physio Jayne – is able to conquer his raging migraine sufficiently to beat Jason Lyons.

Though they lead by three points, a smooth progress to a play-off berth for the Eagles primarily depends on the last heat with another mini-contest cum duel between Crump and Pedersen. Though finely balanced at one race win apiece, it ends in anti-climax with an easy win for Nicki with Crump third. The only drama in the race is provided by Floppy who falls on his birthday again before he remounts his machine only to retire from the race in severe frustration. Floppy limps back to the pits so slowly that it's unlikely that a cake with 33 burning candles awaits him there, though his wish would probably at this point be for the season to end.

20th August Eastbourne v. Belle Vue (ELB) 46-43

TV Stardom Beckons for Many People

22nd August

In a season when Belle Vue have dominated the Elite League and swept all before them at home, except for a bizarre loss to Arena Essex (!), the combination of this record along with Eastbourne's reputation as being notoriously poor travellers when it comes to trips to Kirkmanshulme Lane, doesn't promise much from an Eagles fan's perspective.

I had the fantastic privilege to be able to watch the encounter from anywhere I liked in the stadium, just so long as I "didn't get in the way". I was told this by one of contemporary speedway's most memorable and larger-than-life characters, Belle Vue promoter Ian Thomas. He is literally quite a showman, as away from his promotional responsibilities, as he gets quite a lot of bookings as a magician-entertainer, mostly on the after-dinner and corporate events circuit. This year at the speedway, Belle Vue had brushed aside everyone before them, but the most prestigious trophy, the Elite League Championship, is now decided by the capricious method of the play-off system. A mechanism reputedly invented at the behest of Sky Sports television in one of those instances where the gilded media tail wags the speedway dog. On the TV, Ian projects a larger-than-life persona that manages to create the impression for the armchair viewer that he fills the screen and just can't wait to be interviewed and 'spar' with all and sundry. In contrast, the Eastbourne promoter Jon Cook appears to successfully shirk his televisual duties, and the limelight generally, to the same extent that Ian relishes them.

Luckily for Ian and unluckily for Jon, this is a televised fixture, so the meeting won't proceed at its usual 'natural' pace but, instead, will have to be artificially managed and hurried along to fit in with the demands and privileges of the adverts schedule. In person, Ian is also an imposing character, quite an achievement for someone who in real life isn't the tallest. Then again, you just know he measures seven foot tall in personality terms. Unfortunately for me, I had caught him at a bad time in the few hours countdown before a 'work night' ("even my wife doesn't dare speak to me on the afternoon before a meeting") compounded by the added tension of a forthcoming appearance in front of a national television audience. And need I mention an office also full of riders and the very tall, in person, Kelvin Tatum. I gathered from the conversation that Ian was particularly wary of being "turned over" by some dastardly rival promoters, that he always suspected people and their underlying motives and often correctly saw unexpected Machiavellian plots around many corners, which apparently grieved and irked him in equal measure on an almost daily basis since he is scrupulously honest. "I don't lie, as you know", he tells Kenneth Bjerre before he adds a few minutes later: "I'm an honest man". He is definitely wily and schooled in the ways of the world. From the reaction of others and as I study him at close quarters, it is clear that he has a lot of bluster with everyone he encounters, but projected in an exaggerated almost cartoon-like fashion that belies the genuine and compassionate man he really is.

Ian Thomas definitely doesn't have time for time-wasters, poseurs, wankers, the self-important or pretentious and, I'd imagine (though this is a guess), not much affinity with communists, feminists, ramblers, Eurovision Song Contest winners etc., etc., and a long list of others, unless he'd met them through his work in show business. And, for that matter, he definitely didn't welcome those like myself, inquisitive strangers with southern accents; consequently, our interview isn't as long or as informative as I would have liked. Still, it gave me extra time to look round my surroundings at the imposing grandstand (probably built for the greyhound meetings of the 1960s or 1970s), lurk by the pits, the track itself, and the whole of the perimeter that surrounds it. I even get to watch the always professional Belle Vue trackshop franchise owner, John Jones, lovingly give a few of his Aces regular customers a tongue bath of heroic proportions in a manner that is instructive to witness but, in my experience, ultimately misleading about his innate character, outlook and personality. And so I have additional time to deeply ponder the lessons I'd just learnt with Ian.

The most important of these was that very little had changed at speedway since his early days' involvement in the sport. Particularly unaltered since time immemorial was the number of riders (4), the laps raced (4), the equipment (mostly the same but with new fancy bits that were mostly for show) and the number of brakes (0). This news has probably excited you as much as it did me, and I'm relieved

the tablets originally brought down from the mountain won't have to be redone just yet.

Ian's notes in the programme shed some more light on his current thinking, the expectations for the fixture and his speedway life in general. We learn that "all the boys responded in magnificent style" against Coventry and, though it arguably does do so, "without wishing to tempt fate, I can honestly say that we can count ourselves well satisfied with our efforts to date". He also takes pleasure in the number of away victories the club has already recorded (eight) which Ian views as a comparatively good omen since last year's champions Poole won only six in their winning campaign. I decide that I will also keep my eyes peeled for the cornucopia of retired riders he mentions that delight Ian with their presence and who naturally migrate to the Kirky Lane pits area, bar or terraces every Monday night.

If Ian tempted fate with his programme notes, then the friendly Colin Meredith – one of the country's leading trackmen, the Belle Vue track curator, and SCB official track inspector - did likewise when he explained to me the philosophy, planning and hard work that went into preparing the ideal surface for speedway racing combined with the need for sensible drainage. His basic approach was one based on "dedication and pride" that involved working with the riders and 'asking what they want'. Simple enough, but often overlooked at many tracks you can visit around the country: "the less able just stand there" whereas the "good trackmen can sort it out".

An immutable law of the black arts of trackcraft is that "if they score a lot of points they're good; if they don't score lots of points, it's your fault!" After many years of brickbats and, allegedly, actual bricks poking through the surface of the Kirky Lane track (courtesy of the stock cars with whom they share the stadium facilities), many riders had throughout the 2005 season queued up to offer praise and supplication towards Colin as he perched on his tractor or by the impressively large mounds of shale in his digger. Tonight, sadly, that definitely wasn't to be the case. The level of criticism, moaning, whinging – all the types of things that would get short shrift from Ian if they had the temerity to happen in his office – and the general all-round blaming of the track surface for everything from the lack of overtaking to global warming by riders and Sky pundits alike, quickly reaches an almost deafening crescendo. Eventually after show-trial-by-television, Colin is forced to issue a *mea culpa* with some additional abasement and prostration "for watering too late" to a whole load of armchair viewers who prefer to spend their money with a satellite TV company and haven't paid to attend the event. It's hardly the kind of crime that will excite Amnesty International to complain about Colin's treatment, and luckily enough it's not yet an offence for which he can be imprisoned. But it didn't sound that far off that night. Speedway has rich tradition of rider and ex-rider imprisonment, often for crimes that are mundane in a similar manner that riding a speedway bike is not, but mostly they are put away for activities that fall outside the Nelson Mandela category of matters of principle and political belief. Afterwards, the vehemence of the reactions on the various Internet forums, invariably from those not actually present, mystifies Colin "you'd have thought that I'd murdered someone or something!"

Bizarrely, since I'm in prime position behind the scenes, I actually see much less of what goes on behind those scenes that night than any viewer prepared to pay the outrageous and increasingly exorbitant Sky satellite subscription fees does, even though the events and people they film are often only within a couple of yards of me. I do get to watch 'famous' television speedway people of the ilk of Jonathan Green, Nigel Pearson and Sophie Blake, along with hordes of technical staff, warm up in their own way for the arduous couple of hours broadcasting live that they face, which requires that they be constantly on their toes. They all appear perfectly normal, approachable and easygoing people.

The Eagles team looks unlikely to spring a shock result with rider replacement for the always combative Adam Shields – who still has yet to intuitively grasp, unlike some of his better schooled team mates, that most often he is likely to be 'beaten' on the Kirky Lane track. Floppy is in the line up, as is Nicki who we hope will be keen to best Jason Crump every time they meet, and it's no surprise that Steen has been overlooked in favour of Oliver Allen who gets the chance to strut his stuff and impress the management and fans alike when we need it most. Floppy suffers an engine failure in the first heat and consequently we concede a 5-1 that ensures the letters written on the wall suddenly appear much larger. A welcome triple of consecutively drawn heats stabilises the Eagles efforts only for a couple of further 5-1s to leave the Aces running away with things at Roadrunner speed (Meep! Meep!), despite the moans about the track rising from a gentle susurration to storm force among the home riders when each of them are interviewed after a race win.

Even more worrying for the few Eagles fans that have "made the long trip north" is a cursory analysis of the heat results. Not only had the Aces taken to the track without Joe Screen for whom they operated rider replacement, but in a sure sign of confidence they had also used their No.8, the young and gifted James Wright, as early as heat 3. Nicki's first outing had him comprehensively defeat Jason, something that in the normal course of things would have been the signal for much celebration (especially as he was last in an almost Jensen like supremely ineffective manner), but for the fact that Andy' Smudger' Smith won the damn thing. Floppy took until his third ride in heat 11 to register a point, while Nicki ran a third before he rallied with a win on his tactical ride in the proverbial black-and-white helmet in heat 9, though this only narrowed the score to 36–21. The few Aces fans that there were on the terraces included the infamous sombrero wearers who kept their beer in their glasses, but let their emotions spill triumphantly all over the place with each and every heat victory. Always a fixture on the Kirky Lane terraces, the self-styled acerbic wit with the amplifier, predictably serenaded all the usual suspects – Nicki, Deano, Floppy – from the Eagles line up with judicious 'funny' comments as they drew towards the tapes or as they warmed down from another futile chase. I would have liked to ask them to "keep your thoughts to yourself until you saved up for a funny one", but bizarrely they still managed to look drunkenly menacing in Mexican headgear and, contrary to received wisdom, were often actually quite witty. It enlivened a fairly dour evening's racing, where we were rarely offered any real competition and, to paraphrase Dave Peet, the riders "looked like washing strung out on a line all night".

The announcer did try to thrill us – on the assumption we were Man City supporters admittedly – with the news that "Nicky Weaver is here". I'm sure this isn't the sort of thing that any responsible person can say in polite company unless they've ensured a good supply of defibrillators have been laid on beforehand specially. The scoreline probably would have been a lot worse but for an expensive evening endured by Russell Harrison who blew two 'Rusty' engines and then had an engine failure in heat 12 that restricted his score to four points, the same as Floppy but in one less ride. Seven would have been the highest score for any Eagles rider but for Nicki's double your money effort which inflated his total to a still remarkably disappointing for a rider of his calibre, ten points. Ian Thomas was so confident of victory that he was again happy to track James Wright against Deano when he was on a tactical ride in heat 12, a degree of confidence that was well founded when the youngster held off Deano to grab second place behind Mooro, who overall was, arguably the star of the night, when he overcame his migraine to gain one of only three race wins for the Eagles on the night. He attributed this success to the ministrations of club physio Jayne Wooller: "I felt really bad before the meeting and the woman who helps David whisked me away to the changing rooms and gave me a good massage. I felt really good after that". Though these efforts were sterling they weren't enough to ensure that he had sufficiently recovered to remember her name when interviewed, though her husband Ashley is actually Mooro's mechanic!

22nd August Belle Vue v. Eastbourne (ELB) 59–35

Another different chapter appears about this fixture in my book *Showered in Shale*.

Pimp My Ride

25th August

Nigel 'Waggy' Wagstaff is a man who inspires strong feelings and emotions in many people connected with the world of speedway as well as the many loyal Oxford fans who have in recent years ridden a Silver Machine, rather than shimmy about the place in their previous incarnation as the sleekly predatory Cheetahs. In fact, the team name change was arguably the most visible impact of the reign of Waggy at Sandy Lane. If this were a corporation rather than a speedway club in Oxford, you could probably lay the blame at the door of an army of expensively hired consultants with newly minted MBAs for the dunder-headed decision to throw away years of tradition and, what I believe in management consultancy jargon is known as "brand equity", for a name inspired in circumstances unknown. It's a decision that has Waggy's hallmark all over it – taken in true entrepreneurial fashion without consultation and on the hoof – and, far from the modernity that this name intended, his choice has a rootless retro feel to it. Maybe it came from a Eureka! moment in the middle of one night *chez* Waggy. It certainly defies the fundamental tenets of "Marketing", but then if you run and create businesses you invariably don't have time to read theories about them.[1] Then again, Waggy already "had previous" when it came to spontaneously ignoring tradition to change a club's name, as he had previously altered King's Lynn's name from the Stars to the much-resented Knights. His time there had more of the Dark Ages about it than the Crusades.

The Oxford Silver Machine (OSM) are a club built to Waggy's own specifications and, almost literally, in his image if the large photograph of him prominently displayed on the cover of the match programme is anything to judge things by. If you judge a person by their actions then Waggy, like Trotsky, would appear to be an advocate of "permanent revolution"; the perpetual and profound team changes under his management constitute Exhibit #1. Some changes are thrust upon any speedway team by injury, bad luck and loss of form, but Waggy has taken it to a whole new dimension over these past few years, but especially in 2005. Hardly a week has gone by without news of another arrival or exit from the team. Even if the results on the track aren't always that great, then the Oxford fans have the ongoing soap opera of all the rider changes thrust upon the club by Waggy to keep them interested or confused, if not exactly amused. You can imagine that they no longer have permanent nameplates over each individual rider's regular place within the home side of the pits at Sandy Lane but blackboards, so that these are always correct, or at least soon will be.

I am fortunate to have an audience with Waggy before the meeting and he is far from the bombastic self-opinionated man that his pronouncements in the *Speedway Star* or live on Sky Sports television would have confidently led me to expect. Once he has found his measure he is, in fact, enthusiastic and knowledgeable about speedway, the club, and is rather good company during the short time we spend together. Admittedly he is a voluble companion, plus I had no expectations other than a conversation. Also my relationship with him isn't mediated by the status of his credit, which has apparently coloured some other people's opinions of him. When our interview finishes, Waggy kindly grants me the 'Freedom of Sandy Lane' for the duration of the evening. This is kind of a poor man's speedway version of the 'Freedom of the City' often bestowed on notables in the past, who are then free to ride their horses about the place, drink in town for free, and have their pick of the wenches. The concept has slipped a bit in practice over time, though; so sadly there were no drinks or wenches for me in Sandy Lane.

It's a short uphill walk to the trackside underneath a peculiar kind of underpass, almost unique to Oxford speedway, traversed by wooden

---

[1] The decision by the new owners BSI under the leadership of John Postlethwaite to change the traditional nickname at Reading Speedway from the Racers to the Bulldogs for the 2006 season is equally brave or inept, depending on your point of view, as a "fresh" marketing initiative and innovation. Perhaps there is something in the Thames Valley air that leads reputedly savvy and successful businessmen to commit to these "brave" decisions without any real thought to the consequences upon the delicate equilibrium that is your dyed-in-the-wool speedway fan. Fine, fiddle with the logo but, even if your stated ambition is "to attract new audiences" and ignoring that you may pride yourself "on not being afraid to take difficult decisions" against (clarion) voices of opposition, it seems short-sighted to bin years of tradition on little more than a whim. Market research might not even be amiss, though this is apparently something that both Oxford and Reading didn't commission beforehand. If they did they should never work with these people again. Still, as it says in *Catcher in the Rye*, "people are never too old to find new ways of being stupid".

boards. These are used by the bikes to gain access over the tarpaulin-covered dog track, weighed down by apparently randomly abandoned large tyres, onto the speedway circuit itself. The Eagles have nearly completed their obligatory track walk and are dressed in their civilian clothes, which in itself provides a *melange* of style statements though there is a smattering of items resplendent with the distinctive Eagles logo. Once this formality has been completed, all the riders hurry back down to the pits for something hugely pressing. All with the exception of Floppy, who not only goes out of his way to pose for photographs but to sign as many autographs as required for a small gaggle of young people with whom he clearly has a quick natural affinity and rapport. He is easy, unaffected and relaxed in their company and they respond to him warmly, though with some predictable cheek and casual testing of the boundaries. There appears to be genuine mutual respect and bonhomie as well as some joshing. This is the 'soft' and affectionate side of Floppy that he keeps comparatively hidden from the general speedway public, often during the 'open access' granted to the *hoi polloi* on race night in the Arlington pits. It is no mistake to think that Floppy sometimes highly values his privacy in the most public of places but, perhaps, this is the convenient disguise or calculated 'game face' that allows him to find the necessary space to concentrate and excel in what is, after all, the rather 'hard' and competitive world of speedway. I admire the skill and bravery of anyone who is prepared to sit astride a speedway bike to earn a crust, develop a career and to entertain the public. It takes a special person to do so. But then I also admire sportsmen who remain accessible, approachable and genuine with the fans; this is true of many speedway riders and is a quality Floppy often has in abundance, no matter how hard he tries to throw us off the scent with his sharp witty comments and his occasional aloofness and demeanour. While I watch Floppy and his admirers, they all laugh *together* in a shared way rather than laugh *at* someone or something. It's a quality I've heard people say that Floppy has but I've not witnessed until now and is one that you can't fake.

Unlike the rest of the team, Jon Cook has not retreated back to the pits and makes a mobile phone call some distance away, as he stands on the well-covered dog track. While he does so, he studies Colin Meredith who zealously reworks the track surface. Colin is everywhere it seems that a track has to be attended to or inspected by the SCB. He works in Oxford because he has a short-term contract to help out at the Sandy Lane track, a job that works out well for him as it dovetails with his similar and mostly highly regarded duties and responsibilities at another Lane of the Kirkmanshulme variety in Manchester. After his call I chat with Jon for a few minutes, as he leans nonchalantly against the safety fence, while all the while he continues to intently watch the progress of the red tractor as it drags the grader behind it. His face wears the expression of a teacher just told that he's been unexpectedly put in charge of the sixth form school winter trip to Bulgaria. "What's he freaking cutting it up for now, just after our track walk?" He pauses before he then wryly answers his own question: "Maybe he's creating the usual Oxford track as they're well used to riding rough tracks".

A notable absentee from the track walk had been club captain Deano, who chooses this moment as the track switches from surprisingly smooth and well prepared back to its traditional very rough, to saunter by to let Jon know he's now finally arrived. Given that he rode at Oxford for a while, Deano's explanation that he mistakenly took the M4 to try to get to Sandy Lane isn't the most believable explanation ever. Better late than never appears to be Deano's attitude:

Off to inspect the track © Jeff Scott

The bikes await © Jeff Scott

The mandatory ambulance-in-attendance arrives © Jeff Scott

Floppy takes his time to charm the youngsters. © Jeff Scott

JC contemplates the track grade. © Jeff Scott

Mooro lost in mid warm up. © Jeff Scott

"The main freaking thing is I'm here" he reassures Jon before he goes off to use the 40 minutes that remain before the tapes go up to good effect.

The whole team must be on their toes this evening since this is precisely the sort of fixture that Jon and Trevor will have previously identified as 'one to win' when they mapped out where they expected to gain the final few points needed to assure qualification for the Elite League play-offs. A win here at Sandy Lane tonight or when the Eagles visit again in a few weeks is certainly a more likely option than victories at Peterborough or Coventry. The Eagles cause isn't aided by the absence tonight of Nicki P who they have bizarrely replaced with Steve Boxall who – no offence intended – isn't exactly what you view as a like-with-like replacement! Eastbourne have been forced to track Steve, as they will already use the rider replacement facility for the injured Adam Shields.

Back down in the pits the team prepare as normal. This basically means that Mooro warms up his bike in trancelike fashion with his ear defenders on, Floppy conducts a punishing regime of arm whirling exercises and gurning gymnastic poses, while Davey Watt earnestly fusses with a few vital last-minute adjustments to his bike. Deano's long-time mechanic, Glenn, remains confident of a positive result. It's an opinion mostly based on the combination of his expectation that Oxford's poor form this season will continue and that a good performance from Deano as the key rider will make that vital difference between the two sides ("Deano is the key to tonight's result") though he immediately and rather sensibly adds the caveat that, "if we stop Hamill, and he's flying, we should be okay". The danger posed by Deano is something that the programme alludes to in its comments on the Eastbourne team and they darkly note in true conspiratorial fashion that Deano had only just been along the week before as the mechanic for Edward Kennett, whom they suspected of "maybe doing a bit of homework on the track". I couldn't possibly comment but somehow doubt it, though I would say that the track often has the reputation that it's often a bit on the rough side.

A brief glance at the race card inside the match programme doesn't leave me quite so confident as Glenn. Our side has been weakened by the Boxall–Pedersen switch inevitably brought on by the giant fly in the ointment for British speedway that is the perpetually disruptive impact of the BSI-run GP Series. In this instance, there is a similar happening with regards to Greg Hancock, who has been replaced tonight with Chris Mills. That still leaves a triumvirate of Iversen, McGowan and Hamill, all of whom more than know their way around Sandy Lane on their day, of which they've started to have a few more of recently. An imponderable factor is how exactly their reserve Pavel Staszek will ride, something that is difficult to estimate, especially since he's the latest addition to the squad that Waggy has again plucked from obscurity and heaven knows where. Staszek has only been around since July 27th and it's impossible to gauge whether his assessed average of 4.50 is hopelessly inflated or, as Waggy claims on practically every occasion, whether asked or not, a real steal compared to his potential. One rider who has improved is the other reserve rider Tobias Kroner who has been around slightly longer this season and is therefore well on the way to what, by recent OSM standards, is a long service medal! On a like-with-like basis, the Eagles reserves of Oliver Allen and Mooro should prospectively more than match their scores.

This was resoundingly proven to be the case in heat 2, when the Eagles stormed to a 1–5 race result that was to allow us to take our first lead of the evening. The McGowan–Iversen partnership immediately replied with a 5–1 in return that saw them relegate our Sandy Lane "track specialist" Deano to third place with Davey trailed off in fourth. This didn't exactly look promising for the Eagles against such a 'weak' side who most impartial observers would expect you to beat, particularly given the recent run of form that had seen the OSM lose 11 of the last 12 meetings and draw the other. Still, Waggy has spoken so often of the fabled green shoots of recovery that they surely have to arrive some time soon!

While many of the Eagles get a race win (Barker, Norris and Watt) and Olly Allen impresses many fans with a couple of wins, the reality is that the OSM side look fired up and are carried along to victory by the apparently unstoppable force that is the combination of Iversen, Hamill and McGowan. Between them they score the same number of points (41) as the entire Eagles team. Equally serendipitously, or cunningly, depending on your point of view, the OSM only ever pull ahead by a margin of eight points and thereby eliminate the possibility that the Eagles could make a fight of it through the introduction of a rider with the black-and-white helmet cover. Though we spend much of the meeting trailing at the point where an Eagles rider could be introduced for double points off a 15-metre handicap, this would be a fruitless tactic given our often poor gating and the difficulty of passing that is a feature of this contest for most of the night. After heat 9, I bump into Glenn who no longer holds out any optimism for an Eagles victory and he acerbically remarks, "it's shit, isn't it?"

However, it does turn out that this is one of those meetings where in years to come you can say, "I was there when Travis pimped Floppy's ride...". In this case, the "when" is the supremely bizarre incident on the back straight on the first lap of the last heat of the match when Floppy and Travis McGowan somehow transpire to get their bikes closely and immovably locked together when they race for the advantage over each other. Afterwards, the usually unflappable Travis McGowan was counting his lucky stars that he didn't lose a leg or get seriously injured by the weird entanglement of these bikes, "I've never seen that happen before and never will – I was lucky to pull my leg out – I was so happy I wanted to hug Floppy and its not often I want to cuddle another man". Their "creation" was later slowly dragged off the track towards the pits where the bikes would be separated rather than displayed as if they were the main feature of a contemporary work of art made of brightly polished metal. As is required, the referee excluded Travis as "the prime cause of the stoppage", though Waggy and Cooky immediately appealed in unison – a touching show of mutual sportsmanship that typifies the attitude that most people involved approach the sport with – to get the referee Dale Entwhistle to rescind his decision and reinstate Travis. So, the fixture concluded with the double collector's item of the introduction of the "Contemporary Movement School of Sculptural Design" and the rare happening of a referee who is actually prepared to admit that they are wrong and change their mind! They are events that almost make up for the loss of some more vital points in the Eagles campaign for Elite League glory.

25th August Oxford v. Eastbourne (ELA) 50–41

27th August

A Bank Holiday weekend fixture against Arena Essex without the talismanic presence of Nicki Pedersen who was again away on his traditional Saturday night GP duty would test the enthusiasm of the Eagles faithful, who are apparently drawn from a wide area that includes Kent, Surrey, West Sussex ('the other side') and South London. In the choice of Peter Karlsson as a guest, who rode to a maximum, the fans had no reason for complaint and Floppy also found his old form. As widely expected, early in the contest they had effectively battered their rivals into submission with only Mark Loram and Paul Hurry showing any signs of fight.

Oliver Allen roared away to great effect from reserve after an initial blip and appears to be a possible solution to the ongoing but seemingly intractable 'reserve problem'. Never short of a few words and while he wears the expression of someone who has been awakened early in the morning by his student neighbours playing hip-hop music, Big Ronnie this week believed that the missing Arena fans desire to regularly see "big wins". This would never happen away at Arlington, though in extenuation Ronnie pointed to a naughty "new Jawa motor" for Mark Loram. In the manner of John Betjeman who used to say to people who didn't know him, "I went to Harrow – except in fact", Ronnie bizarrely claims, "we were in it for a long time as we were only two points down". Though in reality, this was only the case until heat 5! In his mind's eye the Hammers have now even been reduced from their previous metaphorical wagon status; indeed, there was no joy for Ronnie as he watched "the wheels fall off the barrow".

Jon Cook praised a "straightforward win", but had other fish to fry as he tried to secure the club's rightful and long-held ambitions to reach the Elite League play-offs. Nonetheless he sensibly flourished the almost lawyerly caveat, "any more performances like Oxford and Belle Vue this week and we can forget the play-offs".

27th August Eastbourne v. Arena Essex (ELB) 56–37

September

DAVID NORRIS

"Adam Shields makes the Incredible Hulk look like Mister Wimpy really"

Double Header at the EoES

1st September

The meetings between the Panthers and the Eagles have been postponed so many times because of inclement weather in the form of rain that there is general amazement among the riders and fans alike at the clear skies that have appeared over the East of England Showground. Not that the Eagles ever relish a visit to the wide open spaces of the large Peterborough track but the delays in staging these fixtures have arguably done them less favours than the Panthers, who have been on a run of form that has seen them surge up the league into the Elite League play-off slots. The resurgence of the Panthers has been such that they are still vying with Coventry for the second spot, behind the Belle Vue Aces, that would guarantee them an important home draw in the sudden-death semi-final. Given that few teams relish their trip to the Elite League's biggest track, they have additional incentive to perform well against the Eagles.

Rather like a double maths lesson, both the 'A' and the 'B' fixtures will be staged one after the other. Consequently the track has been prepared with the idea that it will not only have to withstand 30 heats of racing, consequently it's missing the piled high with shale effect that so caught Deano's eye on the Eagles last visit here. Pragmatism along with use is another explanation for the state of tonight's track since, unsurprisingly, there is an outside forecast of rain showers and thick mounds of shale become much more quickly impassable and unrectifiable than a smooth surface should there actually be a downpour. Not that this smoother surface seems to have spread that much happiness to the Eastbourne side of the pits where preparations carry on apace very professionally but predominantly with slightly fixed, mostly unsmiling expressions. Then again, not many people (unless they're very lucky) go to work with a smile on their face like a synchronised swimmer, but there is definitely an air of a trip to the dentist about them. It is also late in a long season. Not that Deano is here tonight to see the track in its full glory, then neither is Nicki Pedersen, though the "today he's here – tomorrow he's not" pattern that has characterised Floppy's season while he attempts to recuperate from his early season injury at Swindon actually has him in the pits and warming his bike up in preparation for the parade and practice lap. His presence doesn't quite dispel the make-do-and-mend appearance that the Eagles squad has about it tonight.

Not that Jon Cook hasn't gone to extreme lengths to try to get the ideal replacement guests to ride tonight for the Eagles but he has been frustrated on the one hand by the dreaded "8-day rule" and on the other by the (unofficial) unwillingness of potential play-off rivals to make their riders available for this double-header fixture. It is only human nature and eminently understandable that any rival club wouldn't wish to disadvantage their own campaign for Elite League championship success, but it has been a process that has left JC frustrated and slightly lacking his often sunny but always wry natural disposition. Not only has it been "a bloody nightmare getting someone" but also it is just another instance in a season of mishaps and bad luck that has sapped the tenacity of the Eagles trophy ambitions: "you could write a book about our season and no one would believe you".

As of midday JC has had the chance to choose any suitable rider from the Oxford and Wolverhampton squads (as their fixture tonight is now cancelled) but before that a rider chosen from the Belle Vue team had been the only available option. Jon has plumped for Russell 'Rusty' Harrison as a guest from Belle Vue and although he could now change his mind at the last minute, JC prefers to do as he would be done to and will loyally stick by his man and his own word. Arguably, this exemplifies his own promotional philosophy at Arlington because, despite the clarion voices calling for radical change to the team every winter, JC has chosen loyalty, faith and stability in his squad over either change for change's sake or grandiose gestures often favoured by rival clubs. On the whole, this has been a strength for the Eagles over the years though this season's injuries have derailed the plans and intentions that Trevor Geer and JC would have set out with at the start of this campaign.

Though there are 30 heats to be run this evening, the 'A' fixture represents the best chance that the Eagles have to enjoy success since they won way back in April by a margin of 11 points. In contrast, they were only able to gain an advantage of six points during the 'B' fixture in July. Given the notorious difficulty that they experience with this large track, never mind the recent resurgence of the Panthers, neither lead looks sufficient to take the bonus point from these encounters. As expected the Panthers ease into the lead after the first race but the Eagles then temporarily stun the home crowd with a 1–5 when Mooro and Troy Batchelor (from Premier League King's Lynn) combine together. The win for Batchelor, a few days after his 18th birthday, is in the third fastest time of the night. It is a time only bested by the excellent Peter Karlsson and ex-World Champion Sam Ermolenko. Unfortunately this will turn out to be the only heat win achieved by any Eagles rider and from that point on the Eagles experience a comprehensive drubbing and mostly find themselves in the wake of the tyre tracks of the home team who ride as though something really massively important rests on this actual result. Between heats 3 to 10, the Panthers notch up six 5–1 heat wins and only a second place on a tactical ride for Steve Johnston – riding as a guest for the Eagles from Wolverhampton – in the seventh race provides a brief respite from the onslaught.

In a season characterised by difficulty, aborted comebacks and bad luck, the 'A' fixture represents something of a nadir even for Floppy. After the early promise of a second place behind the exceptionally quick PK in heat 1, Floppy is passed by a recently rejuvenated 'Sudden Sam' – a manoeuvre that has the announcer Edwin Overland salivating, "all I can say is WOW!" – before he then retires from the race. They say that anticipation is often the most satisfying part of any event that you really look forward to and, if that is the case, anyone excited by the idea of David Norris flying away from the start when the tapes rise will have had a truly orgasmic heat 9. First of all Floppy is penalised 15 metres for a tapes offence and then proceeds to get excluded for failing to make the two-minute warning in the re-run. Fortunately, with the scores poised at 32–18 and the bonus point most likely already gone the way of all flesh, in the spirit of competition and mutual understanding Trevor Swales and JC agree to his reinstatement. Not that Floppy exactly hurries to comply with the next two-minute time allowance and only narrowly makes it back to the tapes in time, all the while serenaded by the chorus of "I'm tired of waiting for you" by The Kinks which drifts wittily over the tannoy system. It is then all to no avail since Floppy trails in last. He looks far from happy back in the pits and proceeds to lash out at his machinery while letting off some steam with some agonised shouting.

This appears to do the motivational trick as Floppy finishes second in heat 11 while Adam Shields, on a tactical ride, finishes third to secure the Eagles third and last heat advantage of the night to keep the score at 45–24. When the two-minute warning for heat 13 sounds, Floppy remains rooted in his seat in the pits like a prize fighter who has thrown in the towel and refuses to rise to endure any more punishment. He sits stock still with his back turned towards any prying eyes while the clock runs down and he is excluded under the time allowance. This concludes his involvement in proceedings and is his last away meeting of the 2005 season. Looking over towards the scene being played out in the pits, Clerk of the Course, Dick Swales, watches in 'I told you so' mode. "He's doing his usual trick of just sitting there," Dick notes before he recalls that last season (2004) was the only one where Floppy has really demonstrated an ease and relish for the East of England Showground. "If you've got a dodgy head you'll really notice it on a large track, so you shouldn't freaking ride – plus he's a danger to himself and everyone else". Dick tuts and shakes his head at the madness of it all.

Ye Olde Pits Tea Shoppe. © Jeff Scott

Floppy readies himself. © Jeff Scott

JC and Floppy consider their options. © Jeff Scott

The person in charge of the music rolls out the well-used repertoire of musical congratulations with "That's the way I like it" a particular favourite. The Panthers riders celebrate on their victory laps with displays of greater and greater gymnastic ability that they execute with some flair, élan and exuberance. If the ultimate destination of the Elite League title was decided on the innovation and artistic merit of these victory celebrations, they would have won the trophy some while back. Even the promoter Colin Horton has been infected by the over excitement at what is in reality an entirely predictable, expected and easy victory. He greets the returning riders with a broad smile, thumbs-up signs and generally shoots energetically about the pits area with barely restrained delight. With nothing to race for, Davey Watt races Sam Ermolenko with a determination and relish in heat 14 that belies the certainty of the result and provides a great exhibition of hard, no-quarter-given but fair wheel-to-wheel racing that is a pleasure to watch. It's one of the few pleasures that can be taken from a comprehensive 62–31 in which only Eagles guest Steve Johnston really troubles the scorer with anything like a decent tally (nine points from five riders, one of them a tactical ride!). Apart from Adam Shields on six, every other Eagles rider only musters four points each.

This doesn't bode well for prospects in the return fixture to be raced after a brief interval for the riders to recharge themselves as well as adjust and maintain their equipment. The expected news of Floppy's withdrawal doesn't heighten these prospects at all, though it does provoke some reshuffling of the line up. Johnston now replaces Norris instead of Barker who is instead replaced by Rusty Harrison in this 'B' fixture. The rest and recuperation provided by the interval cuppa only appears to invigorate the Panthers who continue where they left off with a series of untroubled heat victories after a stumble in heat 1 when the Aussie pairing of Johnston and Shieldsy secure a one heat only lead for the Eagles.

Strangely given that they now have an even more depleted team, the Eagles put up much more of a fight. That is how I would like to see it rather than the view that the Panthers might have taken their collective hand slightly off the throttle. They still celebrate with some passion and are lauded throughout by the packed but partisan grandstand terrace crowd. Davey Watt is mostly responsible for the improved combativeness the Eagles now show. He combines with Harrison for a win on a tactical ride in heat 7 before he races to another two heats later with Batchelor. In an evening of exciting, closely fought but competitive racing, this heat stands out as the real race of the night that has all four riders always in contention, always thrusting for advantage and providing superlative entertainment. Though Ermolenko finishes third and Jesper B. Jensen fourth, they could just have easily have won as only a couple of bike lengths separate all four riders at the finish.

By the time Shieldsy has also taken advantage of his tactical ride and ridden to victory, the match score has narrowed to 38–34 and the aggregate score has the Eagles still in charge of the bonus point. The possibility of an away win, never mind a bonus point suddenly looks on the cards.

It immediately goes back off the cards and stayed off with the events of heat 12. It is the second sign of madness to quote yourself but, I believe, that I sum up this incident quite well in my book *Showered in Shale*:

"The spirit of fair, safe and competitive racing appears to be thrown to the wind by Jesper B. Jensen, which results in a very painful-looking crash, for the vastly improved and competitive Troy Batchelor, who hurtles into the bend 2 air fence and results in a broken arm for the young rider. Viewed from my position on the centre green directly by the incident, it appears as though Batchelor – who has consistently pressured Jensen and has frequently attempted to manoeuvre past him round the outside – misjudges the space available to pass Jensen. Though it is a misjudgement that the wilier and more experienced Jensen could, in my opinion, have mitigated if he had chosen to ride a slightly different racing line and thereby not narrowed the gap as quickly as happened, that then caused Batchelor to hit the air fence at speed.

Perspectives on incidents like these in the immediate aftermath usually divide down party lines. Just as one person's terrorist is another person's freedom fighter, so it is with the conundrum of when is it 'dirty riding' and when is it just 'hard riding'? In this specific case, the incident is viewed by some people as "just showing him his back wheel" and by others as "deliberately sticking him in the fence". It all depends on your point of view and, given the high speeds the riders reach, it all takes place in a fraction of a split second. A short while later, Panthers co-promoter Neil Watson defends Jensen when he observes, "Troy said they're riding too hard but these youngsters should learn to shut off; it's time some of these young lads learnt that that they can close the throttle as well as open it, before complaining". Eastbourne's Jon Cook avoids the relative merits of a throttle control debate and prefers instead to sarcastically advise upon the need for an urgent eye test for Jensen. Jon also pointedly draws a comparison between the "racing room" left by the experienced Sam Ermolenko a few heats earlier in an aggressive, excitingly competitive but "fair race" and what he sees as in marked contrast to the "lack of space Jensen had left Troy" to safely race in. Without the benefit of an adjudicator for these diametrically opposed perspectives, we can all agree that the net result is a premature end to Troy Batchelor's season; to the great disappointment of the rider, Eastbourne on the night but, most of all, his parent club King's Lynn."

If the ambitions of the Eagles had inflated like a balloon, then Jensen provides the prick that deflates it. In the re-run of the race 'Rusty' Harrison then comes to grief which in turn forces a second re-run that has Jesper B. Jensen and Henning Bager glide to an unopposed 5–0 and the difference in the scores moves to a nine-point gap that will ensure that the bonus point remains beyond the grasp of Eastbourne. Though the message of impending defeat clearly hasn't communicated itself to Steve Johnson who continues to ride in inspired fashion and thereby beats the strong Panthers pairing of PK and Ales Dryml by a tyre length on the line after they have vainly chased him for four laps without finding a way past. There is still time for one last hurrah in heat 14 when Mooro wins and Watty takes third. This tees things up nicely for a last heat decider where a 2–4 or 1–5 heat win for the Eagles will ensure that the bonus point sneaks back to Arlington. After a re-run forced onto the referee by Ermolenko crashing into the tapes, PK rides to an untroubled win ahead of the rejuvenated Johnson to ensure that the victory and the bonus point end up where everyone expected it to beforehand – in the Panthers' paws. At the interval you would have got long odds on the Eagles managing to get so much of their talons into this contest and, literally looking on the bright side, it didn't rain though a dark cloud still hangs over the Eagles' chances of qualification for the play-offs.

1st September Peterborough v. Eastbourne (ELA) 62–31
1st September Peterborough v. Eastbourne (ELB) 52–43

Another different chapter appears about this fixture in my book *Showered in Shale*.

Nearly Naked

3rd September

The last home league meeting of the season finds a resurgent Coventry visiting once again; they had already won easily at Arlington earlier in the season. Since that fixture, the Bees have gone from strength to strength, a run of form so good that it looks likely that they might even overhaul the favourites for the title, Belle Vue, in the play-off finals. It's particularly impressive given the Bees appalling start to the season, which saw them lose six of their first seven league fixtures. It's safe to say that the expectations of the home crowd were at best cautiously optimistic and were not improved, as I entered the stadium, by KC's announcement "I have some good news and some bad news". Ever droll and after a pause for comic effect, KC continues, "the good news for Coventry is there's no Nicki Pedersen and the bad news for Eastbourne is there's no Nicki Pedersen". You almost expect him to say, "boom boom" as Basil Brush would if he had told such a joke. It's the sort of joke that aspires to have the punch line "but apart from that, how was the play, Mrs Lincoln?" The large crowd around my position near the starting gate groans, mostly at the news, but also at KC's smirking presentation. It's definitely not at all good news for Eastbourne.

Still, given the avalanche of fixtures that every team must endure during the period immediately before the cut-off date for qualification for the play-offs, it's practically impossible to predict the final standings. Well, except for Belle Vue who will definitely finish at the top of the league and thereby enjoy home advantage in the semi-finals, but this, by no means, guarantees success in the final sudden-death rounds. Even Jon Cook doesn't know what the future holds and he's the manager of the Eastbourne team! When he writes the notes for his column in the programme, JC decides to err on the side of certainty and predicts both possible outcomes. He notes, "we could be heading for the heartbreak of finishing fifth or the triumph of second spot" before he gnomically observes, "love them or hate them the play-offs are here to stay". The play-offs have only been in existence for a few contentious seasons, solely it appears for television and club revenue reasons, but already they've achieved the status of the poor, since by now they will always be with us.

Without Nicki, every Eastbourne rider must perform to their best against Coventry and hot on the heels of learning we will ride without our important Dane, we learn we'll again see our slightly less consistent Danish national, Steen Jensen, line up at the tapes for the Eagles. Just like the poor and the play-offs, it also appears Steen is always with us. JC goes out of his way to ignore the evidence of his and everyone else's eyes to ludicrously exaggerate the possible impact Steen will have upon the team and its fortunes in his programme notes. JC stresses the "rich vein of form" Steen has supposedly recently exhibited for his main team in the Premier League – the Isle of Wight – though those always unreliable Internet forum postings about the Islanders somewhat contradict this rosy perspective. JC is more than happy to ponder the future likelihood of success for Steen, "I think now is the perfect time for him to have another shot at Elite racing as he should be full of confidence". He also utters, well writes, what would in many other sports render the final kiss of death: the dreaded full vote of confidence delivered when JC claims Steen "has our full support". You can only assume the "our" mentioned here is Trevor Geer and Jon Cook, but it could even be the shadowy phantom that is the present incumbent and serial speedway franchise owner Terry Russell. I'm sure that few would object if Steen were to try to further his career at Terry's other much loved speedway club Swindon or even the club run by his ebullient brother Ronnie in Thurrock. In the meantime, the chatter on the terraces remains sceptical.

Almost parallel with the start line I'm surrounded by many passionate female supporters of the Eastbourne Eagles. During each meeting I enjoy listening to their loud exhortations to individual team members to try to improve themselves or, between the races, their down-to-earth observations on a variety of matters. The ladies in question are Margaret Rice, a committed Elvis fan who always attends along with her husband Dave after journeying from their Elvis shrine – 'Tupelo' – in Dorking; Judy Hazelden, from Horam, who always attends with husband John, their daughter Karen, their knowledgeable son 'Mark the Bark', partner Billy and motorcycle mad son Jordan; plus Jane Rogers, who always leaves hubby Wayne and her children at home in Uckfield. You couldn't ask for a more committed or partisan group of fans, all of whom prefer to stand in our so-called 'usual' spot by board number 51 to watch the beloved Eagles race on a Saturday night. Judy claims only to have come along tonight for the same reason the rest of the crowd apparently has, namely, "everyone's here for the last meeting of the season to hear Jon Cook's excuses!" Opinions differ sharply about the likely outcome of the meeting, season, play-offs or indeed the team line up for next season, which Mark has, on good authority, will still include everyone we "should have got rid of years ago". His list of sacrificial victims in the end of season cull he hopes for varies slightly throughout the season, but is created by a perspective that definitely feels you (well JC) can actually have too much loyalty to under-performing riders. No one suggests an automatic team spot for Steen for 2006, but Mark gleefully thinks the unthinkable and suggests riders that he believes "could do a job, a real job for us!" To save any unnecessary embarrassment or misapprehensions I'll not name the 'guilty' parties from the present squad, or, indeed for that matter, list the full range of his fanciful suggestions, which I think everyone politely listening knows has absolutely no chance of becoming a reality at Arlington in 2006.

Tonight's fixture begins under perfect racing conditions – dark but surprisingly warm. Before the tapes fly up for the first time, KC puts in his tuppenceworth with a putative forecast for how the season will pan out, "it's fourth where Eastbourne have a realistic chance of finishing I would suggest, it is so close, it's so soooo close, it's hard to say!" Things start well; with a heat win for Floppy in the first race and with Adam Shields third, it's a 4-2 heat advantage to the Eagles. Heat 2 witnesses a textbook display of passion from Jayne who, when not lost in deep prayer, likes to live each race on the edge of her emotions, so much so that she often screams advice or suggestions to the always oblivious riders. The initial object of her attention tonight is Mooro to whom she repeatedly screams, "Go on Andrew! Go on Andrew!" as if it's a type of incantation or religious mantra that will bestow luck on all who are named. As it happens, three laps of aggressive shouting appears to work as Mooro glides past the combative Martin Smolinski at the start of the last lap. Despite JC's hopes of renewed confidence and vigour in Steen Jensen's riding, he cuts a forlorn figure as he lags at a considerable distance behind the other riders as though involved in his own private race. JC's faith in already naming Steen for Wednesday's encounter away at Arena Essex already looks like extremely misplaced optimism, despite his so-called credentials as an "our Arena track specialist". A few topsy-turvey and entertaining races follow, all of them drawn, where the standard of the racing is top class, but to predict the race result proves exceptionally difficult. Luckily we're not able to place bets and so manage to save money and watch all at the same time. The Barker-Watt combination come out twice in three heats with Watt looking in sublime form, whereas in contrast Deano looks comparatively out of sorts and he gains only a solitary point. But just to look at this meagre total would miss the extent of his contribution. Jayne shrieks, "go on Barker!" throughout both races before she sagely notes, after heat 5, in the manner of a Zen philosopher, "a point's a point and it's more than he got last time out". Truly it is a single point, albeit a hard-earned point in an enthralling race for third place with Sebastian Ulamek, a race so hard fought and without any quarter given that you'd have thought the destiny of the individual world championship title or the honour of a woman was at stake.

An absorbing evening's racing continues when heat 6 sees a long awaited head-to-head encounter between David Norris and Scotty Nicholls, but ends with a disappointing Floppy well off the pace in last place and with Nicholls surprisingly well beaten by Adam Shields. The next race gets off for a bad start with a case of mistaken identity for Jane: "Bloody hell it's Barker, oh God, no, it's Steen Jensen". To invoke the Almighty is a rarity, but Jane is apparently devout, since before many important races she appears to pray or to lose herself in deep contemplation with her eyes closed with her palms held together. After she calls on higher powers for help and guidance for the Eastbourne cause, she often urges our riders on with a selection of advice with language peppered with words that would surely be out of place in a church. This race almost has a bad but comical end for Billy Janniro who afterwards, in the midst of his celebratory wheelie (unusually joined by Davey Watt who finished a close second) nearly hits the tractor driven by Bob Dugard. KC winces aloud, "Whoa, here comes the tractor". With the meeting even again, the Bees maintain parity in the next race when Harris nips (bombs?) past Mooro on the finish line. It's poor reward for four laps of effort by Mooro who has tried pretty well everything to get past the often wild but always combative Smolinski. KC marvels at the injustice of it all, "how can you race like that and get no points, what an unfair sport it is!" Eastbourne go into the interval with a slender two-point lead after Shieldsy beats Janniro and an out-of-sorts Floppy manages to hang on and beat Smolinski for third.

During the interval I accidentally bump into Jon Cook, as he scuttles along behind the home-straight grandstand on his way to the referee's box. Despite the lead he's not confident of success tonight, "we're looking weak in heat 15, so we're up against it and Davey's dropped a few points while Andrew dropped one through inexperience". Once again I marvel at how readily JC is prepared to chat, albeit briefly, at such an important juncture. I can't imagine the (then) manager of my football team, Sunderland's Mick McCarthy, as ever being so available that you could actually bump into him. And if you did, you'd undoubtedly get only platitudes or, most likely, told where to go in choice industrial language. As I return to my place I overhear two girls talking. The eldest says to her younger sister "Dean Barker's riding rubbish tonight". After they spot me chatting to JC, the fans I regularly stand with by board number 51 take the mickey and then bravely ask, in the full knowledge that they're completely out of earshot, "Did you tell him that we need a change of promotion and management?"

Immediately after the resumption, heat 11 establishes itself as an early contender for the likely lifetime award winner for the 'You Just Couldn't Make It Up' category of race. Well, at least a comedy of errors section inspired by the 'Carry On' films. It features Floppy, riding rider replacement for Nicki and Mooro, who replaces the hapless Jensen, versus the Coventry duo of Harris and Ulamek. Norris makes his first effective start of the night before he is caught in a four-rider crash cum melee on the third corner that results in Ulamek's exclusion as the primary cause of the stoppage. So far, so normal. Then the real fun and games commence as a consequence of Floppy, who suddenly doesn't feel well enough or sufficiently chipper to take part in the re-run. KC tries to clarify the situation from the pits when he informs the crowd that "he's not 100%, but he's okay to go again, I just been told he's withdrawn as he's just not 100%". There's then a short delay during which Judy vents her frustrations, "he shouldn't have bloody well come then, should he? I don't care what they say this is pathetic!" KC then announces that Floppy has been replaced by Steen Jensen, before less than a minute later he reclarifies his clarification, "Steen has already been replaced by Andrew Moore so he can't be reinstated for Norris". We all just stand there as it remains completely unclear and chatter impatiently as the minutes tick by. No one suggests that Floppy should try the homeopathic cures that Deano apparently relished as a cure for his early season bouts of influenza. I'm interrupted from my reverie by KC, who conjures up a marvelously evocative image for the patient crowd, from the "School of Too Much Information", when we learn, "David Norris has not withdrawn, although he's in the toilet and Jon Cook is in negotiation[1] with him to ride in this race". It's quite an image to contemplate which JC later, with a straight face, describes and simultaneously justifies as, "it looked pretty messy and, I suppose, it was!" KC with considerable joyousness in his voice then announces, "let's just say that he's not very well but he's going to have a go". An unfortunate choice of words but we all reassure ourselves that this "go" will be of the on the track variety. As he returns from his ablutions onto his bike and out to the start line, in the toiletry equivalent of rising from his sick bed, Floppy just goes through the motions, while withholding them, and cruises round for a vital third place point. Although he did not really race during the actual race, he certainly shows a remarkable turn of speed when he shoots from the track with some alacrity back to the pits. The eager post-race chatter leaves no time for our collective minds to boggle at the possible scene that is being played out there.

While the queue for the toilet waits patiently, KC interviews the ever-philosophical and ironic JC, this time in slightly clichéd sick-as-a-parrot mode, "at the end of the day we'll get what we can and see what we can do". Looking for the positives and to try to boost morale JC avers, "it's a change in the boys from the last time Coventry were here as this time we've been absolutely tremendous". With a nod to a season plagued by misfortune and injuries, JC closes with, "I've started thinking we've only got six riders as I've never seen us ride with a full team". A bit of an exaggeration but we know what he means.

The consensus view is that with Floppy on the throne and probably unavailable for the rest of the meeting, our chances of success have been flushed away. Things looked even worse when Janniro leads Deano easily in the first running of heat 12, which then had to begin again after Risager was excluded after falling. It's an immutable law of speedway that if a race is stopped, then the rider who was leading at the time will not perform anything like as well in the restaging. Sadly, Janniro didn't appear to be aware of this canonical law of the speedway universe, though Deano remains extremely close behind throughout in hot pursuit. However, cometh the hour cometh the man, and Deano determinedly answers his youthful but disdainful critics from the interval, as they're still too young to succumb to his reputed off-track charms in the bar later, with a real captain's performance on the track. Deano just wins on the line by a fraction with a last-gasp pass of Janniro to ecstatic cheers from the crowd. KC's delighted enough to immediately relive the tension of the race when he excitedly notes, "Deano was sizing him up, sizing him up but not quite passing" until the end.

It's a win that stretches our lead, just as the next race similarly stretches our credulity when Deano reappears in place of Nicki Pedersen for an unlikely and incongruous partnership with the out-of-sorts Jensen, who rides in place of the indisposed Floppy. The collective groans at the sight of this comparative nightmare riding partnership as they idle on their bikes round to the tapes turns to consternation and disbelief when Deano trails even Ulamek. Jane decides to forsake additional appeals to the Lord for the more direct approach when she screams, "Come on Barker, he's not had a freaking point all night!" Pride and determination then has Deano masterfully pass Ulamek who still gains his first point of the night when he easily defeats the forlorn Steen Jensen, in what was to be the Dane's last race in Eagles team colours for the 2005 season and, most likely, ever! With Nicholls's race win the aggregate lead for the Eagles is reduced to two points at 40-38. This tempts Jane into another bout of ostentatious prayer with her head bowed before heat 14. The power of the Lord moves in yet more mysterious ways. It's a divine purpose that apparently relishes the bizarre! As we watch Janniro withdraws with bike problems, Mooro is lapped but obliviously and for no good reason carries on racing to the finish, apparently unaware of the rules that dictate that he was already excluded for having been passed, while Watty trails home behind the "dirty German" Smolinski. The Eagles fans glumly listen to KC make light of this rare 2-3 heat loss.

[1] Presumably by the toilet door.

So, on to the last race of the night, as the Eagles cling to a slender one-point lead. Jane leads a one-woman call to worship with her head buried in prayer and supplication in her hands for many minutes. Keen to hedge her options, in a range that delightfully runs from spiritual to carnal, she promises us "if we get a 5-1 in this race I will dance naked". A stewards inquiry among the rather pedantic nearby male members of the crowd in front of board 51 remains perplexed why, technically, we can't see her dance naked if we get a 3-3 draw or a 4-2 win since both of these results would ensure an Eagles victory. No matter, the Coventry and England pair of Nicholls and Harris race to an easy 1-5 race win, thereby putting Coventry ahead for the only time in the match. It's a win that cements their play-off credentials as "the form team" – as Sky Sports talking head Jonathan Green has termed it *ad nauseum* every week for the last two months – and makes the return visit to Brandon appear all the more daunting. We stand disconsolately and ponder what might have been. Especially John, Dave, 'Mark the Bark', myself and other innocent passers by, who are oblivious to the fact that the cream of English speedway talent has cruelly deprived us of the spectacle of Jane's nakedness. It's a bitter end to the evening that you just don't like to dwell on, particularly in case we get even more upset about the defeat and the realisation that it has deprived us of the only chance in our lifetimes to see Jane in the buff! Pondering what has eluded us we grumpily file out to the car park.

3rd September Eastbourne v. Coventry (ELB) 43-46

Sandy Lane Memories

5th September

Along with visits from Arena Essex, it had begun to seem like my own version of *Groundhog Day* included Oxford as well. I was again at Sandy Lane for the speedway and another fixture with Eastbourne. It was warm and sunny though with a few clouds, but not enough to threaten any rain later. It's an intense period of late season fixtures for the Silver Machine with 10 league matches to race at home and away before the season's most important date – the cut off for qualification for the play-offs. You can still race your meetings after this date but the points gained will no longer count towards your qualification for the vital end-of-season play-off encounters. Not that Oxford will qualify but it's a situation that the Eagles still want to find themselves in, so this fixture means a lot to them. They're unlikely to win if the most recent performance here by the Eagles, 10 days ago at this stadium, is any sort of forecast for tonight. It will be a particularly difficult task because they are again without the vital and ever-exciting Nicki Pedersen and it will be even harder, since they've once again lost the services of David Norris. The on–off, now he's riding now he's not, fickle and temperamental nature of his injuries has been the theme of the season for the Eagles, and a significant reason why they still haven't already definitely qualified for the play-offs. David's inconsistency, in comparison to his performance last year, throughout these many brief returns to the team has compounded the difficulty of effectively challenging for Elite League glory. Even with the reliable Billy Janniro replacing Pedersen, the most optimistic Eagles fan wouldn't expect an away victory, though – if the speedway gods smile upon you – you just never know!

As I stand in the small queue of fans eager for the gate to open to the Sandy Lane stadium, the man in front of me holds forth to his friends about how this is the "strongest team we've tracked all season". It's a shame that the season is nearly over, even though Oxford have many more of their fixtures to complete than anyone else in the Elite League. The consensus seems to be that it's too little, too late. A strong sense of gallows humour surrounds the repeated and multiple team changes inflicted on the club by promoter Nigel 'Waggy' Wagstaff. Some of these frequent changes were a function of the club's response to injuries, but others verge on the whimsical, the impatient, and the downright strange. No matter what your perspective, whatever the change is to the line up that Waggy makes he always manages to make it sound plausible, as if there's a logical master plan and well thought out rationale that underlies it. The fans in the queue have long since shelved their frustration and impatience and, since results have recently improved, have become much more tolerant of Waggy's changes. Happy to argue the virtue of the situation a la Waggy, they almost sound believable themselves as they trot out the usual careworn reasons. These include: building for the next season/the future/he's an exciting prospect/it's a change forced on us by injury/he's experienced and I'm sure he'll do a good job/he's someone I've looked at for a long time. It's an endless list, but one so practised I often wonder if the BSPA issues all promoters with a handy ready-drafted list that they can quickly refer to when they make public statements.

As we slowly trundle towards the entrance turnstiles, the family credentials of the Oxford Speedway business are confirmed as they've just been unlocked and opened by Mrs Waggy and her daughter. Their presence doesn't cause anyone to moderate their critical comments of Waggy; in fact the older fans appear to delight in deliberately speaking loudly and critically, just as the Wagstaffs similarly affect temporary deafness. The chap by me says, in a penetrating stage whisper, "with Freddie Eriksson we've made it to number 18 in the squad numbers, lets hope to God we can finish the freaking season without getting to number 20!" The other old blokes further in front have an animated discussion about rider wages. Their theory is that they're way too high nowadays, but that Oxford are stingy and thereby don't attract the best talent. They estimate that the club's star rider, Greg Hancock, is cheaper than many of the younger and possibly better "superstar riders".[1] Speculation about what speedway riders earn is a perennial topic, shrouded in mystery and the figures cited range from the extraordinary to the wild to the miserly. Whatever the amount or however you calculate it, we usually resort

---

[1] Whatever the accuracy of this claim or the sums involved, this still didn't stop Greg complaining in the *Speedway Star* during the winter about his understandable disgruntlement at sums outstanding and unpaid to himself after Waggy ceased to be a promoter at Oxford. Though, typically for Greg, he did this in a "nice" way that was all the more brutal and cutting because of its comparative politeness.

to our own list of clichéd and standard responses: it's a short career/the pay reflects the danger/the pay doesn't reflect the danger/if they offer to pay you that you'd be a fool not to accept it/the sponsorship is where they really earn serious money/with all the leagues they say he earns half a million/he deserves it/I just wish they'd show more loyalty/effort/commitment/he's worth more than his points and money as he's an asset in the pits. Whatever the reality may be, we all hope that our riders will excel this evening and be appropriately rewarded for the risks they take.

I bump into Waggy on the open terracing and though he's distracted, he kindly gives me permission to visit the pits to observe the pre-meeting atmosphere. As he stands on the tarpaulin-covered greyhound track, as is traditional at Sandy Lane, Eastbourne manager Jon Cook looks wistfully towards the track and the tractor that slowly grades its surface. He's his usual friendly self and is happy to chat, reasonably unguardedly, about all things Eastbourne. We walk to the pits and sit on the bench where we're ideally placed to watch the riders and mechanics prepare, work on their bikes or warm up the machines. Everyone is absorbed in his own world of preparations and Jon still remains pretty angry about Jesper B. Jensen's aggressive riding the other night at Peterborough. I was at that meeting myself, and saw the incident in question happen right in front of me from my ideally placed vantage point on the centre green. It was abundantly clear that there was a lot of anger on the Eastbourne side of the pits.[2]

I make the mistake to compliment Jon on the witty sarcasm of his subsequently reported comments about Jesper's eyesight, which he initially and slightly sparkily misunderstands, "you thought that was funny, did you?" After I quickly re-establish that rider injuries aren't a topic I find any humour in, we move on to chat about some interesting speculative ideas advanced by Jon in his notes in the last home match programme. In order to stimulate debate and to put the cat among the proverbial pigeons (eaglets?), he proposed the dual heresies of a switch to a regular Friday race night along with a suggested change of the club name to the 'Sussex Eagles'. These aren't the sorts of ideas that will be popular with traditional die-hard fans but they have the force of pragmatism behind them. "It's just a talking point, really" admits Jon, "though we do have a problem getting coverage on the local television news". This is primarily because the local television studios are located in Southampton and Canterbury, "so we're caught in the middle of Kent and Hampshire which, being called Sussex, rather than Eastbourne, might help?"

For tonight's meeting Jon has struggled to find a guest rider willing to ride, "it's almost impossible to get a guest for a Thursday night". This is partly due to the reluctance of the riders asked ("Nicholls and Harris both didn't want to do it"), a suspicion that rival teams might instruct or hint to their riders that it might be best not to come to the aid of a competitor at this vital stage of the season but also because of the restrictions imposed by the "8 Day Rule", which severely limits the number of teams that could even be approached to help. Without a great deal of conviction, Jon matter of factly insists, "we have an obligation to put on a good performance and that's what we'll do tonight". Although the

Loyal and always well turned out Oxford fans Dot and June. © Jeff Scott

Eagles riders on parade. © Jeff Scott

OSM parade. © Jeff Scott

[2] This was reflected afterwards on the official Eagles website where Jon commented: "I felt Jensen left no room whatsoever for young Troy, unlike Sam Ermolenko in the previous heat, and several of the riders were incensed by his move, when I questioned him as to why he did it, he said he simply didn't see Troy which should call into question why we aren't testing his eyes rather than his carb".

possibility of qualifying for the play-offs is still a goal to strive for, the likelihood of victory in the away fixture appears remote, "so we should really see the season as being over and start building for next season". That said Jon is clearly sensitive about the criticism the team's performance received from some quarters during the season, "if people in the Eastbourne crowd are complaining, I think that they have very little grounds for doing so". The team has suffered from injuries in general and the saga of David Norris's recovery has been a major contributory factor. Jon has shown loyalty towards and belief in Floppy, something that he was criticised for but equally something that, if he hadn't shown this level of commitment, it's equally just as likely he would have picked up on by ever-critical fans for his lack of support. It's a situation that whichever way you jump, you're probably wrong. In plain terms, Jon and Floppy were both convinced he would return to the team but, sadly, events proved both wrong. I have to leave Jon as he continues to amend the race card in his programme, motivate the team and fulfil his other team manager duties.

Contrary to general expectations in the crowd and in the pits, a massive shove by Deano on Greg Hancock on the first bend allows the Eagles pair to ride to a convincing 1-5 win. This is followed by a couple of drawn heats before Billy Janniro and Andrew Moore combine to repeat the medicine to take Eastbourne into a shock 8-16 lead. I'm pretty surprised. The two ladies next to me by the start line wall, both smartly dressed and made up in the way that ladies of a certain age have perfected for when they go out, affect to be surprised at the turn of events too! Nothing really astonishes them at speedway any longer, since they've come to watch Oxford race for well over 50 years. "We haven't missed that many, but then in the old days we used to go to Reading, Swindon, Cradley Heath and Rayleigh too!" They've brought some soft drinks and a selection of pick 'n' mix sweets selected at the supermarket with them, which they retrieve after they rummage through the contents of their rather large and sturdy handbags. This is the kind of bag my Nana took great pride in owning when I was a child; it was always filled with something vital and useful, no matter how unexpected the situation. Both June Saxton and Dot Webb started to come to watch Oxford about the age of 12. They didn't come together initially, although both started to attend in 1949, "when I took myself" as Dot puts it. They've experienced it all since then, both at the track and also away from it with their husbands and families. We have quite an in-depth chat between the heats about the recent Golden Wedding photo fiasco in the *Oxford Mail*, where a colour photo was paid for, but a black-and-white one was printed. Luckily with some persistence, a quality that I imagine that they both have in abundance, the photo of beaming Dot and Fred posing happily together ran again in the Monday edition, this time in glorious full colour.

They ask whether I have seen these photos and, because they've learnt that I am a 'writer', feel it would be dead easy for me to get a copy retrospectively. The Golden Wedding celebrations themselves took place at Butlins in Bognor ("the food was beautiful") rather than Paris on account of a seriously ill cousin who has now subsequently recovered. The cousin's recovery is echoed by the performance of the Oxford team tonight who, after their shockingly bad start and some lengthy grading of the track between heats 5 and 6 suddenly miraculously recover their momentum in a huge way. The charge begins with a win for Greg Hancock in heat 6. The ladies bluntly note, "he hasn't rode so well this year". Dot and June have a facility to chat ten to the dozen between races, fill out their programmes and then concentrate intently on the race for 60 seconds before they again seamlessly resume where they left off. They appear to complete each other's sentences or anticipate the next train of thought. They miss the crowds of yesteryear when "it used to be absolutely packed, you just couldn't move as you were squashed". In fact it was so crowded they used to just "have to stand still" on the pits bend "and not even go round looking for boys!" It is now some years since they had to make this sacrifice. They stand on the home straight now, just by the start line with all the room they need and their bags rest on top of the low wall that separates us from the greyhound track.

Let practice begin. © Jeff Scott

They tell me that during the early years, the "riders had to ride for their place and to keep their place; if they had two bad weeks or so they were dropped". We joke that under Waggy it often seems that, in this respect, he's unofficially trying to reinstitute a return to the "good old days" with his frequent personnel changes. They both think something has been lost as "today it's much more of a business, they buy them in or fly them in, and they don't have the same connection to the place". They have a grumble about "the cost of the price to come in, £11! When it's often just follow the leader".[3] They have a rather balanced, but contradictory view of Waggy as a promoter, "if it wasn't for Wagstaff, with his money, we wouldn't have any speedway so you've got to look up to him". June likes to look at things from both sides. Consequently in the next breath she says, "I don't like Wagstaff, he's a lot of the problem here; he's arrogant and not a very nice man to work for by all accounts". On top of that, Waggy "doesn't give people a chance and brings in riders no one's even heard of, who mostly aren't any good, before he gets rid of them again!" They certainly know their speedway do these ladies, and have sympathy for the plight of these newly arrived riders from around the world, who are often so quickly discarded. Some of them are so out-classed that "it's not fair on them, you might as well leave them in the pits".

By this point, the Eagles' early promise has faded considerably and Oxford effectively dictates the rest of the meeting; they lose only one heat of the remaining 11 races. After a poor first ride, Freddie Eriksson looks pretty unbeatable for the rest of the night, a particularly valuable performance in combination with the able support he receives from Billy Hamill and Travis McGowan. The ladies feel that the absence of Nicki Pedersen, tonight and recently, has weighed heavily on Eastbourne's chance of success at Sandy Lane and elsewhere. "We love Nicki Pedersen, we always loved him when he rode here; not everyone sees that though and they can be so unfair about him".

Though the Eagles lose without a fight at the end, these ladies have distracted me so much that the final result almost seems incidental to a great evening's entertainment just talking about the present and times gone by with them. Indeed, June and Dot are happiest when they reminisce. Their favourite modern "rider of the decade" is Hans Nielsen. The rider that they speak most fondly of from all their years at Oxford is Frank Johnson, "he's dead now, but rode way back in the 50s". The consensus between them is that he was a "madman". June says, almost wistfully, "he had something about him, I dunno what he had, he wasn't good looking or nothing, but he would speak to anyone and not ignore anyone". Dot nods and chimes in with the observation that "he was no good as a rider, more on the floor than past the post. When he fell on the floor, which was

[3] That is the reduced rate for pensioners. Adults pay even more to watch "follow the leader" at Sandy Lane.

Magnificent sunset over Sandy Lane. © Jeff Scott

often, June used to climb over the fence and run over to check he was alright!" They laugh and the years fall away from them both, caught in the moment of their memories and youth, before June says "Yeah, and he would go off on a stretcher and then always get off at the pit gate". They laugh some more and I tell them I'll find them next time I come to Oxford. "We'll be here, we're not going anywhere, we've been here all our lives anyway!"

5th September Oxford v. Eastbourne (ELB) 49-41

7th September

It's the night before September 8th – the Elite League's end-of-season cut-off date – but access to the Arena Essex stadium on the A1306 Arterial Road appears to be beyond the capabilities of anyone travelling by car. It's a double-edged sword that the stadium is so close to the M25 motorway. It is a part of the UK road network that suffers, as they note on the radio pretty well every day, a traffic jam and "motoring organisations report slow moving traffic and hold ups due to an earlier accident that has now been cleared". This is definitely the case on this sunny late afternoon in early September as it melts into the evening. As with courtesy on the streets and silence in the library, courtesy has long since disappeared from the roads. The result is an extremely frustrating virtual gridlock on the large roundabout that you have to negotiate when you exit the motorway in order to reach the service station roundabout that has the entrance to the speedway. I spend a very long time inching imperceptively forwards as I try to arrive well ahead of the first race in order to observe and record the atmosphere, impressions, and events.

By the time I've successfully negotiated the labyrinth of lorries, buses and cars of all types and ages, I learn that the start time has been delayed to accommodate the hordes of fans that the Arena promotion sincerely hope are still stuck on the motorway. All the extra contemplation time I've had has been mostly spent considering the immutable law of car ownership that grips the driver of expensive, executive type cars, namely, that when you own a more deluxe and high-powered car you immediately assume that you're exempt from the rules and regulations that necessarily govern other road users behaviour. And after 90 minutes of totally masterful but obscene examples of aggressive, hostile driving to gain the advantage of only one additional car length, I'm ready for the traditional live-and-let-live but friendly atmosphere that you will invariably find among most speedway crowds. The Arena crowd are no different, but because of another poor season's results and the grunky traffic, the open spaces of the concourses and banked dirt terracing appear very much emptier than usual.

However, the track shop is already open and attracts pretty well everyone who enters through the turnstiles to stop off for a chat or purchase. After that they usually find the bar, their favourite spot, or stand on the road that slopes down towards the pits gate. It's a great spot to engineer chance encounters with the riders, officials and mechanics as they either prepare for the meeting in the pits or walk up and down the hill from the riders' portakabin dressing rooms. In charge of the shop, with a word for everyone it appears, is the extremely genial Tom Woolhead and, lurking just inside in his own cubbyhole, Alf Weedon, still supremely active at 85, who sips on an inevitable mug of hot tea as he relaxes before he begins his photographic duties for the evening. They both welcome me and ask about my progress with my book *Showered in Shale*. I regale them with incidents and people from my travels, though only intermittently between the constant stream of purchasers, browsers and well-wishers that the shop attracts. For every person, incident or story that I can recall, they more easily trump it with much more interesting stories against which all mine pale in comparison. With legions of experience in and around speedway between them, they relate all the relevant gossip or information you would want to know – about the present or the past – with an effortless stream of wit and words.

The chaos on the motorway is everyone's initial topic of conversation when they arrive at the track-shop booth, especially as the arrival of this week's *Speedway Star*, hot off the presses and usually sold here a day in advance of even when the subscribers will receive it, is sorely missed by everyone. Sales of the *Speedway Star* provide a regular weekly flow of income for track shops up and down the country and I imagine that the summer circulation figures dwarf that of the subsequent out-of-season months of the winter, when we are all without competitive speedway fixtures at tracks around the country. Tom wittily invites everyone who is disappointed to go and collect their own copy, in speedway's version of 'pick your own' beloved of local farmers in the strawberry season, from the man from the *Star* who's presently within a mile of the stadium but stuck in gridlocked traffic. Most people shrug and then stop to finger some of the many other accessories, gifts and memorabilia displayed on hangers outside the booth or attractively laid out on the glass-topped display that Tom stands behind or nonchalantly leans on.

The latest issue of the bi-monthly retro speedway magazine *Backtrack* hasn't yet arrived, since it's also stuck on the motorway *en route* here. It's less popular than the *Star* and Alf reminds disappointed punters that along with *Backtrack* the latest issue of its sister publication, the *Vintage Speedway* magazine is also held up in traffic. After he finds no takers to the by now well-worn suggestion to actually "go and meet them on the motorway", it at least allows Alf the pleasure to smile weakly and for Tom to guffaw as if he hasn't ever heard this before. As they loudly consider the tragedy of these magazines losing potential buyers while they languish in the back of the knowledgeable Editor Tony McDonald's car (known to him as the "crapmobile"), Alf stirs himself from his chair to totter to the doorway. As he clutches his mug of tea, Alf begins a relatively brief reminiscence about the "young" Tony McDonald. These memories reach back to the time when Alf was editor of the *Speedway Mail* along with his partner Robert Bolle. "One day there was knocking at our door and when I opened it this young lad of 16 was standing there. 'What do you want?' I said, and he told me he wanted 'a job reporting on speedway'. I could see he was keen, must have been to have done that knockin' on the door and asking for work, so I gave him a job. So it was me that started him off, giving him his first job at 16 and now look at him. He's a West Ham fan, you know?"

As this happy memory brightens Alf, I take out my small digital camera, to ask them both if they can identify the distinctive-looking lady in a sash emblazoned 'Miss Arena Essex Speedway' that I took last time I was at Thurrock. Tom immediately identifies her, "that's Sheila, they call her Scary!" while Alf's years of interest in photography causes him to curiously examine the camera and ask a lot of technical questions about its specifications and complex functions. I can answer none of his questions, so he explores its potential by insisting that Tom stand stock still behind the counter. According to Alf, "all models should know that they never move when they pose". Alf takes an age trying to achieve the exact composition he wants before he then struggles with the camera's mechanism.

"If you don't hurry up I'm going to have to charge you overtime as well as my modelling fees," jokes Tom.

"It's you moving all the time that's stopping me, if you shut up for a minute I'd be finished by now," admonishes Alf distractedly.

"I'm not moving at all, it's your hands shaking like leaves movin' it 'cause you're so old now," retorts Tom. All this is said in the familiar, affectionate, but slightly scolding manner of a married couple or those who over the years have become well used to each other's foibles through regular company together.

I'm still interested in Sheila and keen to learn more about her. I ask if she's called that on account of her resemblance to 'Scary Spice', not that they share any features at all obvious to the untrained eye. "Nah, they just call her Scary cos she's Scary!" As if by magic or aware that we were just talking about her, Scary passes by focused entirely on getting somewhere for something important if her distracted and determined walk is anything to go by. She again wears a bright and distinctive sash; one that this time proclaims 'Miss Behave' in very large letters. Alf has by now become temporarily enraptured by my camera which I retrieve from him to show Scary the picture of her that I took on my last visit. Alf retires to his cubbyhole to retrieve his latest acquisition "my first ever digital camera, you'll like it when you see it, I'm not used to it yet as it's new but I think it's a bit better than yours though".

It so happens that Sheila is happy to be known by her soubriquet of "Scary", though her real name is Sheila Le-Sage. "French, I think, but it's said Lee Sar-ge, like Sarge in the army or police," she informs me. Scary closely studies her photo silently for some time, and ignores my questions for a moment, before she launches into a monologue about the sheer variety of the many different things she does or helps with "at Arena". She's followed them for some years now – 17 or 18 – and sort of just fell into her involvement without plan or intention. Among other things she notes, "I do the Lucky Chance, the Membership cards plus I design and print the Dinner Dance tickets though lots of others do the arrangements – it's a team effort like many things here". I think that she might also be the supporter's club secretary but I'm not sure as I lose the thread slightly as I listen to her talk so quickly about some many different activities. "Basically I chase the riders, often catching them and then I let them go again! That's why my sash says 'Miss Behave' as I do – badly!" she laughs, and cackles but unselfconsciously, at her own well-worn joke, though it's at her own expense. After she quickly readjusts her sash, dress and her pop-star sunglasses, she's off to the pits to catch some riders or get on with the million other responsibilities that she has at Arena. Though I imagine she'll struggle to move that quickly in her heels and dress should the chance to chase any riders arise. If everyone else who voluntarily helps the club behind the scenes at Arena Essex has half the energy levels and enthusiasm that Sheila clearly has, then not only is it a truly frightening prospect but the "team work" that "Scary" is so proud of will always get the tasks done in a quarter of the time!

All this while, Alf has been absorbed in fiddling with his superior camera so that he can give me a brief photography tutorial, more like a master class given his years of excellence with a camera. "No matter what camera you use or what you're taking a photo of, you should always fill the frame with your subject. It's the first rule of photography, look at all the space round your one whereas the one I took of Tom fills the frame." Even though I'm the camera klutz, I'm able to help Alf with the storage functions on his more upscale camera "I got just for fun". As Alf returns to the comfort of his chair in the cubbyhole, Tom warms to his chosen topic of the differences between modern speedway and its predecessors. "This is the top league but it's not necessarily the best racing, though everything's changed so you can't really compare properly". Tom believes it all started on a downhill slope after the late 1970s, "the old National and British Leagues were the best, it was more fun then, now it's all money, money, money". The courtesy and consideration of the riders has diminished and the relationship between the promoters and the riders has changed. In speedway as in life, there's a lack of care in the rush to get everywhere and to wring the most you can from everything. "If you look back, Bruce Penhall was a true gentleman of speedway, he'd always ask: 'can I put this there or that there?' He was always considerate". Even then there were those riders and promoters who thought that they were the 'Big I Am'. The ones who always had "the 'don't you know who I am?' attitude, which there's lots more of now – with their entourages, their trailers, mechanics in every country and all the flying here and there!" Overall, though, Tom wouldn't do anything else or not be part of it. Despite all the changes, "it's still a good sport".

Just a few paces away from the track shop on the steep camber of the second bend exit near the pits area, I bump into lovely and always friendly Nicola Filmer, Dan Giffard's rather delightful girlfriend who has dedicatedly done as many miles as any speedway riders – in her case loyally following her man as part of Team Giffard. She provides a marked contrast in personality and attitude to Dan who always appears pre-occupied, sullen and aloof – reluctant to talk to me, at any road. Whereas Nicola has a much more sociable, slightly shy but gentle manner about her and a curiosity about others around her. Whenever I've met her, she politely affects to be interested, that's my impression, even if she has other things to do, is tired or after another long journey ahead. She's a credit to herself and her parents. Tonight, Dan has been called into the Eastbourne side at the last minute as a replacement for the just injured Steen Jensen. Nicola and Dan are excited by the prospect that Dan will actually get to ride within the same Eastbourne team on the same track as the current and defending World Champion, Jason Crump, who has been shrewdly chosen by Jon Cook as a guest to replace the absent Nicki Pedersen. A quick glance through the race card in the programme reveals that they'll actually ride together in both heats 6 and 9. Since she has already looked through all the heats he will ride in, Nicola says Dan is much more concerned that he'll have to race against the wily and very experienced Paul Hurry and Roman Povazhny in the reserves race, heat number 2. "They're both rather good to be in that heat, really, aren't they?" Nicola notes rather politely. As we continue our chat, now that they've fought their way through the gridlocked traffic jams on the M25, Nicola is rather surprised at the comparatively small size of the Arena track and the bare functionality of the stadium. It's her first visit to Thurrock and she can't help but exclaim about the mostly gravel terraces, "it's a bit far away the track, isn't it!" After I go down the steps to the road that leads to the pits gate barrier where the various keen fans congregate I happen to pass Dan in his kevlars as he chats with Eagles photographer, Mick Hinves. All I hear as I pass is Mick enquire, "Are you all ready for tonight?" to which Dan, ever nonchalant and always frighteningly blasé, replies "yeah, you gotta be, don't ya?"

Eastbourne's co-promoter and team manager Jon Cook hovers by the barrier that separates the pits from the great unwashed in the form of the smattering of fans that presently loiter and congregate just here, having just hung up from an earnest-sounding mobile call. Jon has suffered much tonight. He struggled just to get here and then has found himself beset by the many travails and trials that afflict the life and lot of a speedway professional. "I've had an idea: you should call your book The *Trials and Tribulations of being a Speedway Promoter*, you just wouldn't believe what goes on sometimes".

My question "what sort of things?" is parried noncommittally with "it'd take too long, just give us a call when the season's finished and we'll get together". The need for a late replacement was definitely one issue on Jon's plate earlier. He doesn't appear best pleased, "Steen Jensen only just declared himself unfit this afternoon though I'm not sure what exactly he's injured". My sarcastic "what your Arena track specialist?"[1] gets a knowing smile, short shrift and another elliptical answer that can be read both ways, "as it happens it's not too much of a problem".

Though Crump is an excellent choice of guest to replace the absent Pedersen, the Eagles team has a slight make do and mend look about it that's not helped by injuries. I learn from the Eastbourne physio, Jayne Wooller, that "Deano has a trapped nerve and with his riding the muscles swell in the neck and he needs it massaging after every meeting". Deano remains something of a hate figure for some sections of the Arena crowd after he spent last season riding in a chequered and often lacklustre fashion for the club. I'm not exactly clear what happened but there's no question about the strong antipathy that his mere presence generates in this part of Thurrock. It's a negative feeling that appears mutual.

On the roving mike this evening we have Bryn Williams, who informs us that he's a stand in since "we have no Geoff [Cox] here tonight, though he was on BBC Radio Essex on Friday talking about modelling and the making of a model of the leaning tower of Pisa". If his absence was sufficiently exciting to generate a headline in the local paper it might read "Cox out for Arena tonight" or "No Cox at Arena". From quite excitable but always interesting Bryn, we learn a variety of news about the club and the riders as well as the deliberately emphasised fact that there's a sale of speedway goodies in the track shop. Only too happy to fill the silence while a huge queue of fans still try to force their way through the turnstiles, Bryn's thoughts turn to "this Saturday's Lonigo GP", since Scary Sheila will be there. "God help the Italian fans and the country as a whole, as Scary Sheila will be there – I don't know if they know what they're letting themselves in for. Look out for her tonight as she comes round to sell you tickets for the Lucky Chance, you can't miss her – tonight or in Italy!" The crowd has swelled appreciably and I notice that the chair-hire shop, also in the arcade that houses the track shop, ice-cream parlour and the renowned cafe, has actually opened tonight and is doing a roaring trade with chairs at £1 each to hire for the night. I decide not to hire one for my usual position on the back straight; I'll stand there in the hope that I'll get to watch the Eagles race to that vital away win that will ensure that they continue their push to make the top four

---

[1] To echo Jon's recent programme notes description of Mr Jensen before this trip to Thurrock. Made I believe, slightly tongue in cheek, but definitely making the best of a bad lot and remaining a professional promoter who talks up his riders on pretty well all occasions.

places and thereby ensure their place in the Elite League play-offs before tomorrow's cut-off date. To do so, the Eagles will still require the results of other teams to run in their favour and the chance to gain three more vital points looks much more probable tonight at Arena than it does in their final fixture away at the very in-form Coventry Bees.

Prospects of an easy away win for the Eagles look good immediately after Davey Watt and Adam Shields win the first race convincingly. This was the signal for Arena to reply in kind through the exceptionally strong reserve pairing of Paul Hurry and Roman Povazhny. At the start of the next race, Adam Skornicki breaks the tapes though Deano somehow manages to ignore the red flags held out by the marshals and refuses to stop until he's almost reached the fourth bend, probably out of delight to actually lead a race at Arena! The local fans reaction leads me to gather that they think he has both wilfully ignored the flags and is going to perform exceptionally well tonight just to spite and irk them. The inevitable exclusion of Skornicki for the tapes offence has reserve Roman Povazhny arrive at the tapes as a replacement and he rides to an easy win with Barker second. A predictable and easy win for Jason Crump and a retirement for Paul Hurry evens the score at 12 each. The Eagles then edge into a slender lead which they retain until heat 10, when not only are the Arena fans delighted by a maximum 5-1 from Sergei Darkin and Gary Havelock, but Deano finishes last to widespread delight, derision and cat calling.

Ronnie Russell, the Arena promoter, then takes to the microphone to make a lengthy announcement to the crowd, in which he discusses – in honest, almost stream of consciousness, fashion – the many reasons that "cloud my mind" about whether he will manfully endure the aggravation that comes with the territory and continue to promote Arena at Thurrock in the Elite League next year, if at all. It's very much a catalogue of woe and introspection, let alone an unusual way to inspire and motivate your fans through the long winter months of uncertainty that must inevitably surround the club after such a candid public confession. The most bizarre reason behind Ronnie's confessional bout of soul-searching is the horrendous delays experienced by the fans on the M25, the surrounding roads and roundabouts, as well as at the turnstiles before tonight's delayed fixture began. "Things like the traffic tonight put doubts in my mind", says a conflicted Ronnie Russell. Strange really, if you can't expect traffic delays at a sports stadium sited next to the country's most congested motorway – just at the point where it suffers from the notorious bottlenecks and jams caused every day by the tolls at the Dartford Crossing, on one side by the tunnel and on the other by the Queen Elizabeth Bridge – then where on earth can you expect them?

Jason Crump proves to have been an astute choice of guest. In heat 11 he races to an easy victory, escorted by fellow Aussie Adam Shields, for his fourth win of the night that thereby restores the Eagles lead. It's an Eagles partnership that fails to work its magic later in heat 13 when Sergei Darkin becomes the first and only rider to beat Crump tonight. With help from a strangely muted Mark Loram who takes third, the overall scores are brought level for the first time. The next heat is drawn to set up a tension-filled last-heat decider, vital for the Eagles to win if they are to maintain their challenge for an end of season place in the play-offs. Like many of the crowd I've made my way over to the far side of the track to watch the last heat near the exit to the car park, so we can all make a quick

Cuddly Havvy poses with fans and car. © Jeff Scott

Arena back straight slowly fills. © Jeff Scott

escape afterwards. While we wait for the team managers to choose their line ups and for these to be announced, I stop by for another brief word with Tom in the track shop. He's very affable, as ever, although by now slightly sloshed, which seems a sensible response from any Arena fan given the uncertainties over the club's future and all they've had to endure in these last few seasons at the Elite League level. He's got many stories about speedway from his youth and years around the tracks. He fondly recalls "when we used to live in a caravan with mum and dad at Rye House, when Jack [—] owned Rye House, the pub and the grounds. We were woken at 1 a.m. one morning by one of the foreign riders with very poor English, shouting "bandits here!" and Jack running round chasing the thieves with a golf club. You just don't get that sort of thing anymore nowadays." Many other stories flow from him before he is gripped by either clairvoyancy or paranoia and rhetorically asks me, "The Russell brothers owns both teams; so what do you think is going to happen now [in the last heat]?" and before I can answer, Tom continues, "Terry'll say to his brother let's have a close meeting for the fans before we [the Eagles] win 5-1 at the end".

It has been a very close meeting throughout and, to my mind, Arena have performed in a manner that belies their recent track travails this season. Spookily, or maybe just through happenstance and the necessary but inevitable randomness of speedway, the deciding heat is an anti-climax as the Eagles aussie pairing of Jason Crump and Adam Shields emerge from the tapes with ruthless efficiency and speed off to race to an unchallenged 5-1 heat victory. I make a point to pop back to Tom who triumphantly shouts as I pass, "what did I tell you? It's a carve up …"

7th September Arena v. Eastbourne (ELB) 43-47

8th September

Fortunately the Eagles had already secured a play-off berth before this fixture with the resurgent Bees who themselves needed the win to secure the home advantage to be gained by a second-place league finish. The Bees are quite rightly fancied to become the champions since they are presently the form team and injury free. The closest the Eagles ever got was only four points behind their hosts and this was after we lost our first heat 5–1! Prospects weren't helped by the absence of Nicki Pedersen through injuries sustained while riding in the GP series, and Billy Hamill could only ever really be a simply competent replacement.

The win was so predictable that it barely warranted a mention in the context of the club's wider ambitions. Indeed, for Joonas Kylmakorpi it didn't register at all, even though the Eagles are one of his former clubs. Because of recent history, only the win over Peterborough loomed large in his mind: "They treated me like crap when I was there and did some silly things afterwards!"

Jon Cook confirmed, and would have said if this were *'Allo 'Allo!*: "For you, Floppy, ze season is over". The Hailsham-based star and resident club wit now hoped to fully recuperate after his various attempts at a comeback during the season sadly failed.

8th September Coventry v. Eastbourne (ELB) 58–37

Foiled Again

12th September

The Elite League Play-Off Semi-Final will be simultaneously televised on Sky television along with the other semi-final between Coventry and Peterborough. Because of their respective first and second place positions in the Elite League table, both Belle Vue and Coventry will have home track advantage for the sudden death play-offs to determine who will actually meet in the two-legged Final. As usual in speedway, the viewing experience of the spectator who attends an event will be secondary to the perceived needs of the viewer sitting comfortably at home on the couch. As we watch patiently at Kirkmanshulme Lane we will have to regularly endure a wait for what seems eons of time between each race, because these will be run alternately for the edification, pleasure and delectation of what Sky calls the "dedicated stay-at-home fans of the sport". For myself, I am in Gorton once more at a speedway meeting at Kirky Lane with a strong sense of déjà vu. As for the riders, they've been here so often this season (with more trips planned) that they must feel like they're stuck in their very own endlessly repeated speedway version of Scottish football. Though everything changes each time, what's remained the same is the defeat on every single visit. The Premier League in Scotland is often derided as a joke because of the frequency with which each of the teams plays the others throughout the season. If frequency and familiarity breeds contempt in Scotland, we will have to invent another sporting comparison to cover the regularity of the many Aces and Eagles encounters in 2005.

To be strictly factual, this is the third encounter at Kirky Lane and the sixth in less than five months. For once, the fact that the sport causes a high number of absences through injury keeps the whole thing reasonably fresh when it comes to the exact line-ups of the teams. It's also safe to say that as Ian Thomas has complained so vociferously at the iniquity and unfairness of it all, in print, online and on television, that we're all very much aware that Kenneth Bjerre won't ride for Belle Vue in tonight's fixture or the rest of the season. It is an absence that will, as Ian frequently but correctly claims, ultimately prove to be a critical influence upon Belle Vue's effectiveness during the vital closing weeks of the season.

Initially I hadn't intended to travel all the way to Manchester again as the probability of a substantial defeat looked very much on the cards and the fixture was to be televised as well. But, watching speedway live is infinitely preferable to the packaged television version; however, the armchair viewer does get the behind-the-scenes access to the pits and the contemporaneous thoughts of the riders and managers via these broadcasts. It is arguably the best and most enlightening feature of these broadcasts in comparison to the often hyperbole filled and histrionic commentary, along with the usual statements of the obvious and the frequently errant choice of camera angles. Both the questions and the stock responses often limit the insights generated. In life and speedway, there is always a certain fascination observing 'behind the scenes'.

But let me tell you what I really think! The questions asked live on Sky are rarely challenging and inevitably follow along the lines of "You really rode well there, how did it feel?" if the questions are asked by "Sophie in the pits". Or if asked by "Kelvin and Jonathan", these mostly centre around Kelvin – usually after Jonathan has teed things up with a banal summary of the situation as he (often inaccurately) sees it and copious references to "this important fixture" – as he extemporises about the last race incident and then often shoves a microphone (or has the Sky outside broadcast headphones with trendy microphone attached) into the face of the victorious rider to ask "how did it feel to put your troubles behind you? ... [Or] carry on with your winning streak?" The follow-up question usually is "we can show you film of the last race, maybe you'd like to talk us through it from your point of view?" Just before the next race commences we'll then be treated to the further opinions of the commentary team. These often involve a re-statement of the "bleedin' obvious" from the relentlessly enthusiastic Nigel Pearson or Tony Millard in conjunction with whomever they have with them to add colour and perspective.[1] Often this will be Sam Ermolenko using the full range of his cliché American commentary-speak from the 1970s. He always uses the vernacular of imported television sitcoms seasoned with liberal smatterings of "you betcha, golly and wow" leavened throughout with his trademark but random, breathlessly irregular speech patterns and occasional technical details. His voice will rise and rise further to double emphasise the supposed excitement of whatever has just transpired, whether or not it merits this

verbal attention. Another regular in the booth is Steve 'Johno' Johnson who can be relied upon to speak a clichéd Australian. He doesn't actually wear a hat with corks that dangle down on strings although he occasionally gives one the plausible impression that he models his commentary style on a mix Dame Edna Everage and Crocodile Dundee. The strine in his voice at least aurally confirms that Sky Sports is international in its outlook and well travelled in its perspectives on the sport, at least in its selection of the riders it favours to appear in the commentary box. Invariably optimistic Johno consistently mispronounces words and fails to recognise speedway riders' names, but he doesn't have the sheer élan for mispronunciations and malapropisms that Kelvin's unvarying confidence in his own opinions frequently produces. Johno always believes that he should see no evil and therefore he never speaks any evil on television. Consequently, the house style of everyone being a "great bloke" who "really tried hard there", who "gave no quarter even though he's really good mates off the track" or who receives the ultimate accolade of the designation of owning an "amazing talent" that sometimes "just hasn't had the results he deserved or you'd have expected" is never questioned.

Though I'm biased, I do enjoy the slightly yokely dulcet Sussex tones of David 'Floppy' Norris on the telly. He temporarily sets aside his love of profanity and tones down his prickly and sometimes vaguely slightly prima donnish default setting that he sometimes reserves for the great mass of the general public when he represents Eastbourne in the flesh in favour of his adopted, much more bantering on-screen persona. This persona is charming, snappily dressed and, nine times out of ten, very perceptive. He's also often extremely witty, not quite as much as he thinks he is, but still, impressively so. Floppy also presents often overlooked but simple truths with a remarkable conviction and sincerity that renders them much more compelling than they'd sound in the mouths of others. His only real competition for the crown of 'Curmudgeonly but Insightful Experienced Speedway Rider Who's Seen It All Before and Got The T-shirt' is Gary Havelock.

Havvy has a significant advantage since he's actually an ex-World Champion, but Floppy has the advantage of his natural humour and ability to just speak good naturedly like one of the lads. Gary has to try harder to achieve this effect and the effort reveals itself in his often caustic and slightly intransigent comments rather than the witty *bon mots* he believes he's hired to deliver. They're both still laddish but in subtlety different ways – with Floppy you sense that this is an affectation as well as an effective way to mask his shyness, whereas for Havvy it's much more of a lived experience and compliments his slightly wry outlook. Floppy can sometimes appear brittle and hypersensitive, but he still manages to convey the impression that he's the 'speedway rider next door'. While Havvy, on the other hand, comes across as more of the 'speedway rider next door that would steal your car and get your daughter pregnant if you didn't keep a close eye on him' type. You just know that he's always generally on the cusp of possible trouble or sailing perilously close to it. However, that said, along with Chris Louis, Floppy and Havvy are runaway the best value, most insightful, and natural rider-commentators employed by Sky Sports for their television

[1] They say that a really good sports commentator ADDS to the spectacle of what you can already see with your own eyes. Think of the skilful, evocative use of language – painting with words and the skilful use of silences to enhance the effect of the visual spectacle – by gifted sports commentators, true exponents of their art, like Peter Alliss, Richie Benaud or John Arlott and the gulf of what we're served up on Sky's speedway coverage is thrown into dramatic relief. Sometimes you feel even Garth Crooks might help things!

coverage. Kelvin is often a parody of himself and manages to affect an on-screen persona that combines bar-room braggart, careworn professional and a Tony Blairesque preachiness that projects an attitude that's undoubtedly sincere but often closely borders on that most modern form of hypocrisy, just saying things for effect or because you feel you should say them even if they're not quite correct. Though it is very touching that Kelvin can confidently say so many things, perspicaciously about technical matters but often completely wrong about the rules.[2]

In the end I decide I will travel to the meeting given the remote possibility that I'll witness a historic Eagles victory. It's more of a hope than a realistic expectation, rather similar to my request to the Belle Vue promoter, Ian Thomas, to kindly consider granting me free access into the stadium while I am still researching my book. He had grudgingly allowed me in the last time in a manner that strongly suggested I was a freeloading ne'er-do-well. They say you know when the magic has gone from a relationship and that you also know when it's never really been there. A few brief words on the phone with Mr Thomas are enough to reconfirm the presently unmagical nature of our relationship. He reacts with his customary but endearing bluntness to my request in a way that suggests that I had just volunteered to return to his house to burgle it for a second time. One quickly learns that when Ian dons his stern, schoolmaster "game face" prior to a meeting, then warmth and humanity aren't qualities that he will exhibit with the natural ease that has at other times. Indeed, his default setting of affected grumpiness and distain is a useful mask that skilfully ensures that interruptions are kept to a minimum on race night when there is much more important business at hand to attend to – like winning speedway meetings!

Mr Thomas quite rightly replied to my cheeky suggestion that he would consider giving me free entrance to his facilities for research purposes as if I was a naughty and greedy schoolboy. "You got in free before, didn't you? So you've had your go, haven't you? And you got a free programme, so I think that's quite enough, don't you? So if you want to come in tonight you'll just have to use the turnstiles like everyone else and, to be fair, usually everyone expects to pay, don't they? And they haven't got in free in the past!" After this retort, I'm desperate enough to clutch at my last straw and mention the talismanic authority of the fax introduction and support sent to every track in the country in May by the Chairman of the BSPA, Peter Toogood, this cuts no ice at all. "I'm not bothered, I haven't seen it, and anyway you've already been." is the concise polite version of this response. Finally, after a slight pause, he relents and kindly agrees that, after I pay my entrance fee, I can watch from the pits "so long as you don't get in the way or bother anyone."

My own inflated sense of entitlement as a budding author was so offended by this treatment that I immediately rang Eastbourne promoter Jon Cook to seek his advice on this situation. As usual he was polite and matter of fact, even when bothered by this complete triviality. "It's his prerogative as the promoter, although others may have done different. You'll just have to chalk it down to experience."[3]

Contrary to the usual view of Manchester as a perpetually rainy town, it was another sunny late September afternoon when I arrived in Gorton by bus from the re-branded Premier Travel Inn on Portland Road in the City Centre. The entrance gates had just opened though the anticipated huge crowd of loyal Belle Vue fans hadn't yet arrived. It was still very early and considerable time remained before the tapes went up for the first race. I lurked for a while in the main grandstand bar by the track shop. There the balding franchise holder John Jones confidently predicted to all and sundry, who arrived to peruse the stock he had laid out on his display tables, a clean sweep of every remaining British speedway trophy for the Belle Vue team. At this point in the season, the trophies still available were the Elite League Championship, the KO Cup and the Craven Shield. John was cockily arrogant and definitely believed, "we'll 'ave 'em all!" He uttered this phrase like a religious mantra over and over again in a loud, slightly whiney voice to anyone who lingered within earshot and warmed to his theme at some length, if anyone cared to ask for more detail on his thoughts, which it seemed everyone did.

John Jones also advised his customers that he was in the process of having commemorative badges made to celebrate Belle Vue's

---

[2] That said, he is often very insightful when genuinely describing things close to his heart and experience – like bike set-ups, the riding lines taken, the meteorological impacts on man, machine and the environment at different tracks as well as on the psychology required to achieve high-level success or overcome injuries. This often well hidden by his blatant need to say what he thinks he should say on behalf of his employer or what he perceives to be their interests. He has also become fatally infected by the "I'm just about to verge on having a particularly loud orgasm" style of commentary that's almost become favoured as the Sky house style. If Kelvin received an electric shock every time he exclaimed "whoa" he would be quickly burnt to a frazzle. He would be even more thoroughly burnt for uttering our fave Kelvinism "Crikey – O'Reilly!", whilst remembering his trademark but always deliberate glance at the camera. In comparison, if Nigel Pearson was similarly wired up to the mains, he would be burnt to a cinder after a few heats if he was penalised for exaggerating the excitement unfolding on the track.

[3] In fact, since my initial encounter with Ian, he has been generous to a fault, always keen to help with my book *Showered in Shale* and he has always gone out of this way to help, whenever he can, as well as offer perceptive and thoughtful advice. Many people have tried to take the piss with Ian and all have got short shrift. I can now number myself among them. Ian Thomas is definitely a person with a strong sense of right and wrong, of what's expected and fair and what's not. Many long-standing and loyal Belle Vue fans wouldn't expect free entry to any meeting, never mind an important semi-final like this fixture, and I shouldn't have had the temerity to do so either. The club's owner, Tony Mole, and loyal fans understandably take great heart in Ian's appointment and the down-to-earth stewardship that he provides for the club.

anticipated victory in the yet uncontested Final of the Elite League, "I'm already planning having badges done with 13 times champions on them!" While it might have been a formality for Belle Vue fans to expect to progress to the Final, widely expected to be against the very much in form Coventry 'Bees', it was definitely jumping the gun and ungracious bad form (if not luck) to prematurely assume victory. When I interrupt to ask, "isn't 13 an unlucky number?" John retorts, "yeah, we thought about that but these are the facts so that's what we'll do!"[4] John immediately bats off my suggestion of an Eastbourne victory tonight with a loud laugh. He retorts, "with B-jair in the side I'd definitely say no! But you don't know," then has a slight pause, followed by a snort-like guffaw, before he continues, "okay I'm just being diplomatic you haven't got a freaking hope in hell!"

Outside on the terracing there's a sparse crowd and a complete lack of sombrero-wearing Belle Vue fans. No doubt they'll all start to arrive shortly. Given, the play-offs are such an important series of meetings in the Sky Sports speedway calendar – one they're often widely held to have instigated as a condition of their extensive coverage – they've practically taken over the pits area with their huge variety of outside broadcast equipment and their distinctive predominantly silver-coloured interview booth that awaits its presenters and the riders is in place. The riders of both teams are already here with their bikes. Most of them have already emerged from the changing rooms in their kevlars. It's such an important meeting that they've all made themselves available extra early to get things right with their bikes or chat to the crowd of fans, reporters and sponsors that slowly gathers here.

The reporters are very much in evidence. There's the BSPA Press Officer, Sky commentator and West Bromwich Albion fan Nigel Pearson, who stands on the centre green gesticulating wildly throughout a lengthy and very animated mobile phone call. Probably yet another booking for this one-man media industry within the British speedway world that extends from online to print and broadcast outlets. When he's finished, he appears to have or needs to have a brief word with absolutely everybody of any importance around the vicinity including Tony Mole, Ian Thomas, Colin Meredith, Jason Crump and, very briefly, me. Nigel mentions that he spends half his time working for the radio station Talk Sport and the rest of his time working in various capacities within speedway. His involvement in both sports requires extensive travel round the country to football matches and speedway meetings, where he usually either reports or does the commentary. Nigel stresses that it's a "great life and beats working for a living!" At certain times of the year, one day he does football and the next speedway. I ask if the daily grind of the travel ever gets him down at all. "It seems like a lot, but it's nothing like the amount of travel that the speedway riders do and it's only in this country, too". Unconsciously Nigel reveals his own bias towards and predilection for the riders in the upper echelons of the sport – the superstar rider

[4] Interestingly, given that assumptions are usually the mother of all subsequent freak ups, Ian Thomas's column in tonight's match programme incorrectly stated "Tonight we offer a warm welcome to Poole, the team who finished fourth in the league table by the cut off date of September 8th". Admittedly this was also the widely expected outcome but, as they say, the table doesn't lie and this wasn't how it eventually turned out, since the Eagles and not the Pirates are present for this meeting. Ian's notes also sensibly include some caveats about the use of rider replacement by the Belle Vue team caused by Kenneth Bjerre's injury, "we are all going to have to dig deep and see just what we can do". Immediately afterwards, in a style reminiscent of a politician who tries to dampen down the expectations his own comments have created, Ian mentions, "when we took over the running of this great club we stated that our target was a place in the play-offs, something that Belle Vue had never achieved before. Well, we achieved that in some style … in the days before play-offs we would have been crowned League Champions". Unfortunately, despite his cavils, these were not the rules on how the Champions would be determined that Ian had already agreed to before the start of the season but he still remains hopeful of having some "silver where (sic)" to adorn the "top table at our Dinner dance".

part of the speedway fraternity with their weekly grind of English, Polish and Swedish League racing mixed in with all the Grand Prix and international events dotted around Europe – rather than the common, grass-roots experience enjoyed by the majority of speedway riders. As Bryan Ferry used to sing "I'm part of the in crowd, I go where the in crowd goes", sadly this isn't the reality for the vast majority of the country's riders who spend most of their time commuting long distances round Britain's congested road networks with, if they're lucky or talented, a few overseas trips thrown into the mix.

I see another person at the glamorous end of the reporting spectrum this evening, Sky's attractive interview lady in the pits, Sophie Blake. Throughout my travels, it's a standard observation among the Elite League riding community that Sophie really is a 'bit of all right'. Sophie had struggled to gain acceptance initially – mostly because she wasn't the original glamour speedway interviewer, the stunning and fragrant Suzi Perry – but also partly due to an initial "jolly hockey sticks" earnestness as well as the universal and negative perception of her complete lack of speedway knowledge and insight. These are non-essential attributes if you are a professional media presenter today and, given the well-documented declining support base of speedway, hardly surprising for a woman in her mid-30s. Contrary to her critics, Sophie never claimed to have the insights, but does have the reporting and presentational abilities that her job requires. She presents herself on television as genuinely hard working and enthusiastic plus she has dramatically improved her knowledge of the sport over the past few seasons. There were also the topless shots of her in *Nuts* magazine, which appeared in the summer around the time of the British Grand Prix in June that further boosted her notoriety and profile. These caused quite a sensation as though everyone couldn't quite believe that someone involved in our sport of speedway, "our Soph", would dare to, and get well paid to, pose with her kit off. In the strange way of these things, this helped to improve her credibility with the speedway community, too.[5] I've watched her at quite a few meetings now and have spoken with her briefly a couple of times. I've found her remarkably friendly, personable and absolutely professional every time. She's also prepared to patiently give the adoring (mostly male) speedway public all the time they need to speak with her, get autographs and photos, or generally stand around ogling her. This they do with a zeal that they usually reserve for the bikes and the riders. She appears not to mind and is remarkably taciturn in the face of all of this extra attention.

I take my place in the queue of adoring admirers and eventually get to quiz Sophie about her work. She has a wide sports reporting background and has covered clipper boats, pool (the Mosconi Cup), some form of boarding sport, the American Transatlantic Wrestling Challenge, and football. This variety positively shouts satellite channels but also signals that she's very much in demand. With football she mainly conducts interviews and surveys the players' lifestyles. It's a genre that's become increasingly popular as the celebrity status of footballers growls along with their rapidly inflating incomes. Sophie instantly becomes quite coy when I turn the subject to the transgressions and *faux pas* of the soccer players she's met. Sophie effectively restricts herself to 'no comment' but she increases the mystery and my curiosity when she stresses, "I wouldn't like to say as some of the footballers are my good friends". Hmm. Sophie is much happier to draw the distinction between her football interviewing experiences and her speedway work, "I'll just say that it's very different, totally different – the guys are so nice with no pretensions, you get what you see. It's a great sport where anything can happen, and does! The riders often refuse to give up and everyone connected with speedway is very passionate. Even when they've just crashed, they'll always talk with you – honestly – and they're always like that whether they've won or lost. It isn't like that in other sports, especially when they've lost."

Sophie always has a lot of time for the speedway fans. I saw this myself when after the meeting she took the time to pose for as long as necessary with a crowd of sombrero-wearing Belle Vue fans. "I don't mind it at all and they're always a good laugh, real fun but respectful with it. There's fans who dress up everywhere, don't forget those Coventry women who travel everywhere in their pink hats!" The wonderfully fragrant Sophie smiles broadly, then excuses herself to continue with preparations for tonight's work.

Over by the gate that separates the main home-straight grandstand terraces from the speedway offices and general pits area, the gatemen are excited about the possibility of Belle Vue winning through to the Play-Off Final. Like many fans in Manchester, they believe that the team's finish at the top of the league after all the regular season fixtures, effectively means that Belle Vue are really the only deserving champions. The Eastbourne fans also felt this in the first year that the play-offs were introduced, though it still didn't stop our subsequent loss in the Play-Off Final to Wolverhampton. The talkative Alan Wilkinson has been a Belle Vue fan since 1965 whereas his

---

[5] In the interests of research I had to buy the end of year edition of *Nuts* magazine that featured "Britain's Top 100 Babes", all posing topless. Sophie was number 84, 85, 86 or thereabouts and I finally got the chance to see the photo that affected everyone, but was recalled so fondly by Trevor Swales of the Peterborough Panthers. Trevor drew my attention to, and was indeed correct about, the prominent mole that had been airbrushed out of the photo, but that is visible when you meet her. The photo features a 'wet look' Sophie and, while we must bear in mind that different looks float different boats, my opinion is that she's way more seductive and feminine in person fully clothed. I have previously noticed too that she is, sadly, a smoker although at Belle Vue I don't spot her snatching a quick fag. To my mind, she appears more attractive in the flesh than on the medium that she works in.

fellow partner on the gate, Patrick Stanford, has been one for 42 years "since the year before Peter Craven was killed". Patrick worries, "they could still flop after winning the league, I really don't agree with the play-off system". Patrick can't remember a time when he wasn't involved in speedway, but he can vividly recall the first time he visited Hyde Road. He'd come to the zoo with his parents and remembers "standing at the tunnel and hearing the roar of the bikes and noticing the smell". After getting hooked on the buzz of "the speed with the riders so close together", it's an addiction he's transmitted to his cameraman son, David, who "rode for a couple of seasons – for Stoke, Manchester juniors, in Denmark – until a bad foot injury put him out of speedway". Patrick knows it's in his blood in way that football has never been. Despite living only 20 minutes from Old Trafford, he's never been there in his life. Alan and Patrick hope I enjoy my evening "but not too much as we want Belle Vue to win!"

Close to the pits, there's a small enclosed and tiered area that the riders and mechanics, those who don't gather by the fencing, can use during the meeting to watch the racing. After the pits area has been cleared of interested members of the general public, I stand there too and keep out of the way as instructed by Ian. I try to say "hello" to Ian as he passes, but he's oblivious to the world and looks frantic but smart in his dress shirt set off by his black jacket, as though he's about to perform some magic on stage, while he rushes about the pits area and concourse with instructions for all the riders, staff and mechanics he encounters. All the tension shows on his face and makes him look suddenly older than his age. He's hot and hassled, compared to how I remember him from my interview in his office last month or from how he appears during his often combative interviews on television. This affectation of calm for the cameras must be down to his professionalism rather than make up artists since Sky Sports doesn't appear to stretch to the luxury of these for an outside speedway broadcast.

It must be infectious, as everyone rushes around and looks hassled although, on the Eastbourne side of the pits, both Jon Cook and Trevor Geer appear studiously calm about their roles as joint team managers. Each person is wrapped up and absorbed in their own activities without the time to stop to chat. Someone who does have the time to talk is Tony Mole's friendly partner, Zanna. She's here in the pits area with her daughter Emily who looks especially cute in her very smart school uniform. Although Zanna's daughter is young, she is very much at home around the roar of the bikes and the hurley-burley of the pits, as I have observed tonight and when I've previously seen her marauding round at Workington and Stoke earlier this summer. Zanna has brought her straight from her school in Walsall to watch tonight's important meeting for Tony's most prestigious speedway club. When I ask her "you must be a very grown up girl to be here – how old are you?" she only has time to say, "I'm four next month, I'm three years and 11 months now" before the lure of a passing speedway bike as it's wheeled out for the rider parade proves too much of a distraction. Zanna smiles, shrugs and wishes me well with my research before she chases after her daughter.

By the edge of the pits it's hard to miss one of Davey Watt's sponsors, Dean Saunders, because he's so tall he's literally head and shoulders above everyone else. It's good to see him again and catch up on some of the inside information that he's gleaned from his regular involvement round the Eastbourne pits as a valued sponsor of one of the riders. The main news, as it has been all season, isn't the intermittent appearances of Nicki Pedersen but rather the on–off saga of David Norris's appearances for the Eagles. "Jon has told David not to ride again this season so he can sort himself out properly. Chris Geer, his mechanic, said 'he can come back to the pits and not know where he is' – that can't be right for him or for the team can it?" Mostly though we talk about Watty, the rider he sponsors. Davey has "lost a bit of confidence recently, if he has a good first ride it goes well, but if not it doesn't". There have been quite a few distractions off the track apart from his mid-season injuries. Davey has lost his major sponsorship from JT Commercials, which meant that he lost the use of the workshop that he had there. Plus, he wants to sell his house and look for a "bigger place with workshop". Watty and his wife have a young child and she works from home in her job as a structural engineer. All of this has "been playing on his mind" and affects his track performances. Dean relates "John at JT says that he's never met a rider like Davey who has kept so much information on tracks and engines". Davey's records include "details of the set ups for every track he's every rode on for every meeting he's ever rode in – listing what worked and what didn't as well as other stuff which he keeps updated all the time". He has an engine for every track and "with Davey everything has to be 110%". Despite all this attention to detail and preparation, Dean believes that, "if he's not riding well it does his head in and what with the distractions, these mind games have got him down. People think that riders are something special, but they're not they're just living their lives like everyone else!"

When I ask Dean about the impact on his own business from the increased visibility of sponsoring Davey, he pronounces himself satisfied. "I wouldn't say that I've picked up any work from it really but I've enjoyed it. I've met one bloke through speedway, I got another lead in Hoddesdon for a car park, just a few little jobs really. I've probably thrown at it £8K or £10K including the clothing but the enjoyment is the thing as it gets you away from it all, from work and the like – so I'm going to repeat it next year".

Sitting on the edge of the wall by the riders and visitors viewing area is Jayne Wooller, the Eastbourne Eagles physiotherapist and close by, enjoying a well-earned cigarette, is her husband Ashley, who is here as Andrew Moore's mechanic. Jayne fully qualified four years ago as a physio, after three years' training, and got involved with Eastbourne by accident after she had helped various riders with their injuries and ailments. It started for her at last year's World Cup "when I made friends with David Norris and he asked if I could do anything with a lump in his shoulder – I've been working ever since". They'll never be a shortage of lumps and bumps since speedway is a sport that has its fair share of spills along with the thrills, though it's a position that she's only recently started doing in earnest "after Jon Cook realised that I had value to the team" when she remedied Andrew Moore's migraines and sorted out various other niggles that had beset other riders in the Eagles team. She's very personable, justifiably proud of the value of her skills and consequently has "made friends with lots of the lads on our team and the others – they're a lovely lot but they've all been through a lot in their own ways. I really want the boys to win and feel fit – though if I've had a meeting where I haven't had to treat anybody I'm really happy!"

Her husband Ashley has been Andrew Moore's mechanic since they met him at last year's end-of-season dinner dance. Ashley is a man of few words and prefers to let his deeds speak for him. He raced sidecars for 20 years and, after he'd finished, he found that every meeting he attended "horrible – just watching and not being involved". His work as a builder just didn't create any exhilaration or thrills. Serendipity stepped in at the dinner dance through the chance meeting with Andrew and they've taken it from there. Andrew is very easy to work with. They share similar interests in more rural pursuits away from speedway such as "driving diggers; mucking about landscaping with diggers or with tractors on the farm, and clay pigeon shooting". Jayne adds, " though Andrew's only 22, he has a very old head on young shoulders". Ashley lives on a farm close by the Eastbourne Stadium and has been going to Arlington "since the 1950s when it had a dirt track on cinders". He got to know Charlie Dugard well after he regularly borrowed the "only rotivator around for miles to level off the track after stock car meetings".

After the riders have been introduced to the large crowd that now fills the grandstand terracing and have scattered themselves round the stadium, the racing begins with Eastbourne fielding Mark Loram in place of the talismanic Nicki. The first heat provides an instant shock when Deano roars from the starting gate like a man possessed, which catches Jason Crump, the World Number 2, completely unawares and so unable to catch the impressive Eagles captain. With Adam Shields heading Simon Stead for third place, Eastbourne find themselves in a shock initial lead. They retain this in the next race when Mooro provides the race win, though his bike packs up immediately after he crosses the line. Ken Wrench, Belle Vue's temporary stand-in presenter for tonight's meeting, notes afterwards with some chagrin, "his bike's just packed up mind, just a bit too late for the Aces". Based on this unexpectedly positive start, it appears that Eastbourne will offer much stiffer competition that they have on recent visits to Kirky Lane. Jon Cook's face betrays little emotion at this turn of events, though he does raise his eyebrows as he rushes past from his position by the fence to the pits. Throughout the evening I notice that JC and Trevor Geer shun, wherever possible, the corrosive oxygen of publicity that Sky's live national television coverage exhales. They're apparently much happier to leave the limelight to their own riders when possible. This contrasts with Ian Thomas who makes himself much more available to Sky to share his thoughts and comments with a wider audience as the events of the evening

unfold painstakingly slowly. With more race victories on the night allied to their impending qualification for the Play-Off Final, Belle Vue would necessarily be more newsworthy for Sky Sports. But a difference in approach and attitude is quite noticeable, since Jon and Trevor remain content to lurk in the shadows while Ian basks in the glare of publicity.

Already the time between heats has begun to drag noticeably with an inordinate gap between each race at Kirky Lane, while we all patiently wait for the completion of the alternate races in Coventry. This level of delay and boredom through the interruption of the traditional pace of a speedway meeting is a high price to pay for the fans who are committed enough to bother to leave their armchairs and offer their team support from the terraces.

As I stand near the pits, I observe that each race follows the same formula among those not riding in that race. Just before the tapes rise practically every rider, manager and mechanic crowds to the edge of the fence of the first bend to look towards the starting gate. The others stand on the steps of the viewing area and watch the action intently. No matter where they watch, just before the conclusion of the race they will all, practically to a man, rush back to the pits. The most experienced pairing for Belle Vue of Jason Lyons and Andy Smith, the club's only ever-present rider throughout the whole of the 2005 season, restore the expected order of things with a comprehensive tapes to flag victory that brings the overall score to 10-8 in Belle Vue's favour. The brief initial advantage enjoyed by Eastbourne is as good as it gets for them all night.

Heat 4 has the first head-to-head confrontation between Jason Crump and guest Mark Loram. Recently Nicki hasn't exactly set the world alight during his performances in Manchester. Mark Loram honours that tradition when he suffers the first of his four defeats of the night at the hands (or is it the wheels?) of Jason Crump. All head-to-head encounters between them result in defeat every time for Loram and arguably are the defining encounters of this fixture. JC is a passionate advocate use as a guest Mark Loram wherever and whenever possible as a replacement for absent or injured Eastbourne riders ("he always does a good job for me"). They feel very comfortable with each other and have the necessary mutual respect that, in speedway as in business or life, is 99% of the battle. It's a decision that, apart from Crump, is justified by the fact that Loram defeats every other Belle Vue rider he races against during the evening. With the absent roundabouts balancing out the absent swings, the overall strength of the home team, in comparison to that of the visitors, is ultimately the deciding factor. Initially this is not apparent, since every heat from 4 to 8 is drawn 3-3, which thereby keeps the overall aggregate scores equal.

The prolonged gaps between races cause torpor for riders and fans alike. Heat 4 wakes us slightly when Andy Smith rides in his usual forthright and indomitable style. That's what you'd definitely call it if you were a Belle Vue fan. If you were to judge his typical race tactics from the point of view of a supporter of his opponent's team, you'd quickly form the impression that he rides against them with a consistently savage level of aggression. If everyone rode like this there would be a regular furore about how the sport has degenerated into an unduly dangerous and physical battle. But, it is a "man's sport" and, most commonly, the officials repeatedly view the aggression and determination exhibited by Smith on the track as just part of the rich tapestry of the sport. It is completely within the rules and regulations of speedway that, after all, it is for the referee to enforce. In tonight's instance, Andy Smith's attempt to intimidate his opponents during the first bend of the race with a wild broadside of his machine under them as they enter the second corner, results in his own debacle after his dramatic lunge only unseats himself. In the typical never-say-die fashion that you want to see from all your riders, but don't always get, Smith remounts to forlornly trail in comprehensively last. This is playing the percentages professionally, since a subsequent mistake by his opponents, or an unfortunate engine failure, would then leave him well placed and back in the points.

Stood in the same area as myself I meet James Wright's mum Lynn, who's here with her friend, long-time Belle Vue fan and Buxton co-promoter, Jayne Moss. They're here to watch the meeting, but also to savour the fact that James has progressed so far in the sport in such a short period that he's now been named as the Number 8 for Belle Vue tonight. He looks relaxed and stands dressed in his Aces kevlars, while he watches the racing with a mug of tea in his hand. Jayne is a passionate advocate and fan of James Wright and has religiously followed his progress at every Under-21 World Championship meeting she possibly can throughout Europe. She remains confident that his natural ability will enable him to win a championship before he's too old to take part in the competition any longer. Even if he doesn't triumph in this year's final in Austria, Jayne is at pains to point out "he's still learning, he's only 19 and has another two more years after this to win it!" Now I've met his grandfather, mother, brother and James himself, I'm already a convinced fan myself and look out for his results everywhere he rides so I need no additional persuasion in regard to the merits of his precocious talents. He's also extremely determined, charmingly polite to speak with, and a credit to himself, his family and speedway. It would be great if he eventually went all the way and became a British World Champion. Sadly, we don't get the opportunity to see him in action this evening.

Also there to watch the racing, plus chat animatedly to fellow riders and friends, is Manchester born and based rider Carl 'Stoney' Stonehewer. He goes back a long way with Tony Mole and Ian Thomas at Workington. Stoney has his little son Beau with him and holds him tightly all evening. Many of the riders stop to have a word with the currently injured Stoney and affectionately tousle his son's hair. Joe Screen stops and talks for ages with his close friend. They both started to ride in Manchester at roughly the same time, so have grown up on and off the track together. Though Joe has a less than svelte shape more suited to rugby than speedway allied to a slightly ungainly gait on terra firma, on his bike he is grace personified when he invariably displays an effortless skill and control, allied to an acuity of mind, that is a delight to watch. Tonight, he performs brilliantly and determinedly throughout.

The last Eastbourne rider to taste victory during the evening is Adam Shields who easily wins heat 8, after he evades a predictably aggressive scything manoeuvre from Andy 'Smudger' Smith on the second corner of the second lap. These attempts to baulk other riders work superbly when Smudger upsets the trajectory of his opponents but backfire miserably when the trick fails like it repeatedly does this evening. While he misses the chance to unseat or disorientate Shields, Smudger does well to recover his lost yardage to finish second, though Shieldsy is never in danger of being caught after he outwits this increasingly one-trick pony. Throughout the meeting and especially during the long gaps between races, the extremely taciturn Jason Lyons smokes up a storm. He smokes with the arm action of a purposeful smoker, using quick stabbing gestures to the mouth and nonchalantly deep inhalations. Luckily for him, this is Manchester and not Sweden so he doesn't have to choose between a smoke in the pits and earning his living like he did earlier in the season in Sweden, when it apparently cost him his team place there.

From heat 9 onwards the home side assert themselves on their own track and gradually pull away from an Eagles team that fails to post any further heat advantages in reply. Not that this path to victory passes easily and it visibly generates tension among both the Belle Vue riders and, more revealingly, the Belle Vue management. Though Tony Mole's daughter Emily sleeps through it all oblivious in his arms. By this stage of the contest, Shields appears to be the only Eastbourne rider who might win another race. He goes so far as to lead the world number 2, Jason Crump, for nearly two laps before Jason carefully lines him up for an overtake on the last bend of the second lap. With his home track knowledge, superior equipment, track craft and confidence it was always likely that Shields's resistance would prove futile. The announcer definitely thinks so afterwards, "once Jason got close that was it – routine!" The usually calmly quiet Tony Mole obviously doesn't view it that way, since he shouts at a passing Ian Thomas, "Ian, get him to get a grip!" just as the Belle Vue promoter stomps past towards the pits with his jacket flapping open. Ian barks back equally irritably, "I know! I'm going to!" Actually, though neither of them are spring chickens and have vast experience of such meetings, the level of passion and commitment that they both exhibit, during a contest that they're expected to win easily, impresses me. It's a fundamental determination to win everything and leave nothing to chance, even though most impartial observers would see no danger to Belle Vue of an unexpected last-minute defeat by the Eagles. Whatever words Ian delivers have an immediate and salutary effect in the next race; especially on Smudger who, for once, decides to masterfully overtakes Deano and Olly Allen in one fell swoop rather than distract them by riding cavalierly amongst them.

The massed ranks of fans on the grandstand terraces chant with a gusto that indicates that they totally expect the inevitable Belle Vue victory. Quite a large number of the Manchester Mexicans wear sombreros or wave inflatable palm trees and cacti in the air. The mischievous man with the sharp wit and the amplified microphone/loud-hailer is, as ever, there. Consequently, we're treated to many of his more partisan but often funny chants during the many *longueurs* of the fixture. His critical comments about the Eagles waft over in disembodied fashion. We learn that the absent "Pedersen is a turd", and that they suspect Deano of a closet enthusiasm for raiding the pantry, "Deano ate all the pies". With the apparently predictable effect on his girth of these raids they go on to claim, "Deano is a fat bastard". Hardly the height of wit and though they betray their football ground provenance, these chants consistently show verve. For the last few races with the home victory not in doubt, this voice repeatedly chants in singsong fashion the refrain, "that's the way the Cooky crumbles, that's the way the Cooky grumbles". These chants are distinctly audible by the pits where all the riders and mechanics stand but remain unheard or studiously ignored by Jon Cook, if judged by the expressionless look on his face. JC doesn't complain at all, nor has he reason to since the Eagles have given a surprisingly good account of themselves compared to some of their recent performances in Manchester. They've been much closer to an upset than the final score suggests and have competed with Belle Vue much harder than anyone predicted. Still they have sadly fallen at the second-to-last hurdle in their campaign for the Elite League title. With the ifs, ands, buts and maybes that speedway is justifiably famed for, I can imagine Cooky saying 'who knows what would have happened if we'd had a full strength side here tonight?'

12th September Belle Vue v. Eastbourne EL Play-Off Semi-Final) 53-40

21st September

After one of the longest breaks ever between the first leg of the KO Cup at Arlington, the second leg is finally held in Thurrock. It's not the ideal way to fill the stadium with crowds of eager fans but, like many things this season, events have undoubtedly conspired against the Arena Essex Speedway Club. Still they say that anticipation is often better than the event itself and, on this basis, the wait since the first leg on July 23rd should certainly have got the juices pumping. Something else that's also pumping is promoter Ronnie Russell as he actively considers his future in the very public forum that is his report section in the match programme.

The basic problem is that Arena Essex speedway doesn't attract enough regular and consistent support through the turnstiles to make it financially comfortable for anyone to bear the higher costs incurred in the Elite League. This decision, like many in life made in haste, can often be repented at leisure. Particularly in this case, since the choice to advance the club to race at this Elite League level and, maybe more importantly, to change the longstanding race night was made by Ronnie without, as was his prerogative, any real consultation with the fans. He did this for a variety of reasons that probably includes maximising sponsorship revenues, a desire for advancement and keeping up with the Joneses in terms of his brother and fellow promoter Terry. Ronnie in his notes acknowledges the reality of many modern sports, namely that the paying spectators who turn up (or don't turn up any longer in Arena's case) no longer provide the majority of the revenues a club earns as they once historically did. The most important reality of contemporary sport is the huge importance of sponsorship income. This is an area that Ronnie devotes a huge amount of his time, attention and effort to ensure that all goes successfully in 2006. Helpfully, but also rather ominously, Ronnie notes, "my wife and family fully support me at all times in my wish to promote speedway here at Arena Essex, but I do have to take into account their feelings". It must be a great solace and consolation to have their continued support during these difficult times.[1]

Ronnie makes a point though, after the usual caveats about "best intentions", to criticise the fans who use the public medium of the Internet to disparage the strategic direction of the club and the competence of it's officers. The ability to air your comments to a wider audience is a function of the medium. It's one that Ronnie distrusts and he has publicly stated that he regards it as a possible contributory factor to the decline in attendances. His real concerns though are the negative and critical postings of the "very small minority of people on the forum of the club's excellent official web site" that "take every opportunity of trying to bring this Club down". The virulence and ubiquity of the complaints and "personal attacks" upsets those more sensitive members of Ronnie's family who read them and also potentially discourages sponsors since it colours their view. It's an unusual situation, and one that you can't imagine as a possibility in other sports, for the fans to be able to use the "official" site to explore their grievances. Usually this is done with great gusto on the "unofficial" forums. You have to have some sympathy with Ronnie as he energetically strives and sometimes occasionally flails around to improve the future prospects of the club. But, if the comments didn't appear on the "official" web site they wouldn't go away completely, only move to a different web site forum, as Ronnie rather endearingly still hopes that they would!

The match itself, arguably, represents the last decent chance for both teams to potentially guarantee themselves some form of silverware for the trophy cabinet; if they have such a piece of furniture, they'd relish the chance to clear away the dust that's gathered there over the past few years. The dust has been accumulating since 2002 in the case of the Eagles and since 1991 in the case of the Hammers. Injuries plague the line-ups of each team. Floppy is still absent for the Eagles and Sergei Darkin fights for his life in intensive care in his native Russia. On a lighter note, the Eagles will miss their ostensible "track specialist" Steen Jensen, while Jon Cook has publicly stated

---

[1] In fact, the atmosphere on the terraces was bubbling, due in no small part to Ronnie's decision to invite free of charge many local businesses to get an experience of the heady experience that is speedway. He even produced a special A4 programme that listed the names of all the companies that he had invited. Consequently, the first bend hospitality area was buzzing and this initiative not only added to the vibrancy of the 'cup tie atmosphere' but might even have resulted in the Doggo 7 sponsorship received in 2006 from a coalition of small business sponsors. Ronnie is to be applauded for his ambition, looking to the future and zeal in rootling out prospective new sponsors during a season of poor fortunes on the track.

Always a warm welcome on the Arena Gate. © Jeff Scott

Trackshop at Arena Essex Raceway. © Jeff Scott

Attractive display of merchandise © Jeff Scott

"if we can't defend a 15 point lead we might as well give up". This is a task that's definitely helped by Nicki Pedersen's return to the team for this fixture.

Over at the track shop, there's the usual stream of punters who want to purchase the latest hot-off-the-press edition of the *Speedway Star*. Tom Woolhead and Alf Weedon are both there, one behind the counter and the other clutching a mug of tea in the cubbyhole genially supervising operations. They inevitably have a kind word, cheery greetings, or brief gossip with the passing fans. It's late enough in the season for a "sale" of selected items of Arena-branded merchandise in the shop. Alf very slowly writes a sign to advertise those items that will be available tonight at bargain prices. Alf's hand like his handwriting is shaky. The effort involved frustrates him and he is distressed at the battle he's having with age[1]. "I'm going freaking senile, I keep thinking one plus one is freaking four!" he exclaims irritatedly. Tom looks on sympathetically and compassionately observes, "the problem with senility is that you don't know that you're senile". The ravages of time haven't yet completely affected Alf's business sense and insight. He dismisses talk of closure, "of course Ronnie will be the promoter here next year, there's all the Sky money and all the money from the GP including the backhanders". Tom is keen to accentuate the positive about this season's performances by Arena, "let's not forget that we are the only team to beat Belle Vue at their place this season so far and we didn't even have Rickardsson then!" It's unarguably a great achievement and a highlight of the season for Arena but long forgotten by the loyal fans who have suffered at Thurrock and all locations round the country since then. For some of these fans, regularly moaning on the Internet and grumbling on the terraces, this one swallow still doesn't make anything like a summer.

Alf has finally finished writing the list of items on sale. He suggests that I run over to the referee's cum announcer's box and give it to the announcer and say "Alf says can you read these out a few times during the evening". The box itself is near the start line and looks like a 1960s era metal shed. It somehow perches in the air and overlooks the natural bowl that the track itself compactly occupies. To gain access you must climb some steep metal stairs, which will then bring you into a rather cramped area, which will later be rather cosily shared by the referee and the man in charge of the musical interludes and sound, as well as the announcer. Everyone is there already except for tonight's referee Ronnie Allen. They appear used to receiving instructions from Alf and promise to promote the track-shop sale in a series of breathless announcements during the evening. The outlook from the box gives you an uninterrupted and panoramic view of the track and stadium. You'd be able to see the rolling countryside beyond the stadium, if there was any to savour but the general area has the desolate look of an abandoned airfield, undulating and unsuitable for landing planes. But well suited as a lorry park or a site for car boot sales and also somewhere which to transport the wrecked and burnt-out hulks of vehicles that have crashed and met their unexpected end on the congested lanes of the nearby M25 motorway.

Back at the track shop Alf has forged ahead with yet another handwritten sign about the sale. He's concentrating magnificently, although his individual letters appear somewhat random in their sizes and the words slope dramatically across the page. A crowd of teenage girls quizzes Tom who's doing his best to

[1] Though he is a very spritely 85.

understand what they'd actually like to try to buy. They definitely want to buy something, but something that's either new or unique: "what's just come in?" Tom's list of the few recent new arrivals in the shop leaves them completely cold and they definitely want nothing that's on sale that Alf then, ever the salesman, helpfully suggests. They eventually decide among themselves that they want the latest baseball cap and then ask, "do you have one with that blond rider's name on it, you know, what's 'is name?" Tom and I simultaneously guess that they mean Adam Skornicki, the pony-tailed rider who's recently joined the club. It's a late season, stopgap measure for both the club and the rider that signals both parties' comparative lack of ambition. Tom disappoints the teenagers though they look at him sceptically as he patiently explains that he doesn't stock caps emblazoned with the name of unexpected late-season replacements. They give an impression that suggests "what sort of shop owner is it that makes a virtue of deliberately not stocking what customers will obviously want to purchase"? They look even more derisively at me when I suggest that the Skornicki caps should really come with a false ponytail that dangles at the back for authenticity's sake.

I follow the girls as they decide to move to the fence that overlooks the pits area to "look at the talent". From the fence there's not many riders to see at this early stage of the evening with about an hour before the tapes will go up. Though, they are very impressed to see the dashing Lewis Bridger who, sets the pulses going and provokes a racy discussion among themselves as he stands and talks earnestly to Jon Cook, the Eastbourne promoter and co-team manager. Lewis wears an impressive quantity of industrial strength hair gel in his blond streaked hair. Given the slight chill in the air and how cold it will be later, the T-shirt and jeans he sports don't seem appropriate for the weather but they add to the girls' loud appreciation of his figure and form. I imagine that they're similar in age to Lewis, who is 15, but nonetheless they still talk graphically of what they'd like to do with him, should they ever manage to be alone with him. Oblivious that he's an object of teenage desire for the girls pressed against the nearby fence, Lewis nods a lot and waves his arms expansively.

I detour back on myself and descend the stairs to the road that slopes in one direction to the rather austere riders' dressing rooms in some converted portakabins housed behind some more fencing. In the other direction it slopes down towards the car park for the riders' vans and the entrance to the pits area itself. The girls will be disappointed because Lewis appears not to have brought his van tonight so they won't be able to rampantly shag him later in it as planned – which, anyway, his Granddad drives as he's presently too young to legally drive himself to meetings. Lewis is only at the meeting as an interested spectator to continue his speedway education and, possibly it is rumoured as a future Eagles rider. Entry to the pits is impossible for ordinary members of the public as someone in a florescent bib efficiently guards access to it and the road is blocked with brightly coloured solid barriers of the type used by the police to deter possible terrorist attacks by car bombers at party political conferences. The fans keen enough to watch the comings and goings of riders, mechanics and other assorted speedway staff congregate in small groups or individually close to this road furniture. As the riders run the gauntlet of fans spread out along the length of the hill from the pits to the changing rooms, the congregated admirers of varying ages and passion frequently stop them for autographs and photographs.

If you only stand around for a few minutes, you'd imagine that all the riders are here to film a commercial for Red Bull drinks. It is the riders' drink of choice prior to the meeting. There's also quite an outbreak of large holdalls cum sports bags with the riders' initials prominently displayed on the side. The culture of sponsors' adverts on riders' vans, clothes, and bikes has infected the riders so much that they have started to monogram other possessions as well! If only we could get access to the changing rooms, we'd probably also find that there's a culture of sewing name tags into their ordinary clothes. In homage to both trends, when Mark Loram and Deano slowly walk together up the hill to get changed, they both carry monogrammed bags while Loram thirstily drinks Red Bull. Deano sports some piebald bleached jeans that probably must be very presently fashionable on the nightclub scene in Bexhill, Hastings and other small Sussex towns. They're followed shortly afterwards by another Red Bull drinker, the very decidedly ex-World Champion, Gary Havelock, who also enthusiastically slurps from his can. Now I think about it, none of the younger riders who drank the stuff, since they were no doubt saving themselves for some brightly coloured alcopops later. Perhaps as Red Bull is claimed to give a real jolt to the system, the drink is actually the liquid equivalent of Viagra for the ageing speedway star?

After I watch all the comings and goings with all the other fans, I pass Alf when I walk back to the gravel-banked terraces. He's now ready for his photographic duties. He carries his camera and wears a bright blue anorak for this purpose. When the racing starts, Deano once again tries the manoeuvre that recently has become his very own party piece. Namely, he wrestles with his bike rodeo style as though it's a wild bucking bronco. No sooner is Deano out of the gate than he immediately indulges in an intense bout of hand-to-machine wrestling on the first bend. He eventually regains control of his steed and then remounts to resume his chase of the other riders who by now have already shot far away ahead. Not to be outdone on the bizarre things to do with your bike, Deano's Eagles teammate Shieldsy waits until the third lap to fall on the first bend. So far as per usual except that he then appears to be completely pinned to the track as though told by a hypnotist that his equipment suddenly weighed a ton. He's trapped for so long that the referee has no choice

but to stop the race to prevent the other riders from colliding with him on their next circuit of the track. Arena are then awarded a 5-1 race result, an unexpected start that's continued in the next race with a 4-2 score. Andrew Moore finishes last in that race and throughout the evening is infected with the absent spirit of Steen Jensen and so rides to a magnificent zero in four outings. In fact, apart from Nicki Pedersen who manages to ride five times and win five times, the Eagles collectively make very little progress towards the final of the competition. Throughout most of the night, it appears that Jon Cook's words that he'd be very disappointed not to be able to defend a 15-point first leg lead definitely look like they will come back to haunt him. Though, to be strictly accurate, Nicki does get some support from Shieldsy who scores well after the blip of his initial first race fall. But apart from some token resistance from Deano that his final score doesn't properly reflect, the rest of the Eagles team conspire to ride frequently and steadfastly into the minor or irrelevant placings. It's something they accomplish with some panache while they make the Arena riders look like world-beaters for most of the fixture.

There are some racing highlights to report; notably Mark Loram bosses his way past Davey Watt in heat 7 and causes the Australian to trail off into an eventual last place finish. It's a race that's enjoyed by the man on the jingles who immediately seizes the rare chance to play the song "Greased Lightning" from the film *Grease* in loud celebration. To the delighted cheers of the crowd, Nicki is unceremoniously thrown from his bike in heat 11 when Paul Hurry clips him from behind. Despite the obvious fact that the Dane is the victim, the Arena fans loudly boo the referee's decision not to exclude Nicki and put all four riders back into the re-run of the race. This is the most significant decision and race of the night, since Pedersen's subsequent win counts for six points because it's a tactical ride, while Shieldsy's second place ensures a welcome 1-8 result for the Eagles. This result dramatically narrows the substantial lead that Arena had threatened to start to consolidate and increase to possibly gain an unexpectedly large home victory.

Since he rode at the Arena Essex raceway last season and did not enjoy the greatest success, Deano has a difficult relationship with the home fans. After just one season in their race colours, he has easily managed to achieve the status of "the man they love to hate". Consequently in response, Deano rides with considerable zeal and determination throughout the evening, which is typified by heat 12. After a very obvious rolling start by the Arena pairing of Skornicki and Povazhny that the referee doesn't notice, Deano uses all his experience and track craft to gradually wheedle his way from last to first place. Once at the front, he pulls away to lead easily into the last bend where he then suffers an unfortunate engine failure. Temporarily unable to access their keyboards to log onto the official web site forum to slag off their own speedway club, instead the Arena crowd loudly delight in Deano's misfortune. The long walk back that Deano has from the far side of the track to the pits area, gives the fans on the back straight full value and the opportunity to vent their frustrations with colourful language and obscene gestures. Not one to shrink from his more vocal critics, Deano lingers enough on his trudge back to clearly communicate that he doesn't hold these people who barrack him in the highest mutual respect. He restrains himself from replying to obscenities with obscenities in favour of suggesting that "they're all mouth and no action" via a series of expressive and interpretive gestures. By the time we arrive at the last heat, there is still a possibility that Arena could still force a run off if they score maximum points in the last race. It's not a probable outcome despite Arena's improved form tonight and, as a result, Jon Cook doesn't even bother to nominate the Eagles outstanding performer, Nicki Pedersen, to even ride in the race. It's a confidence that combined with an insulting acknowledgement of the lack of firepower and prowess of the home side that proves well founded when Shields finishes second to ensure that the Eagles qualify on aggregate for the Knockout Cup Final with Belle Vue.

21st September Arena Essex v. Eastbourne (KO Cup) 52-41

Revolution or More of the Same?

24th September

It was a lovely clear evening for a revolution though it all appeared frighteningly normal as I drove from Brighton to Arlington. As usual a couple of limos magisterially headed in the opposite direction, and I notice that the limo fleet now includes white ones as well as the traditional black. The country lanes in the surrounding area had some adverts for a foodfair in Upper Dicker on the Sunday that they were pretty excited about.

As a keen student of Marshall McLuhan and politics, as long ago as the sixties Gil Scott-Heron had already announced, "the revolution will not be televised". This was definitely the case tonight with the Sky Sports cameras noticeably absent for the friendly encounter between Eastbourne and Poole, as they competed for the meaningless but recently cast 'South Coast Trophy' though they were to trial a brand new method of scoring at a speedway fixture. It was an attempt to inspire greater competition among the riders and excitement in the crowd. The riders and promoters of both teams had pronounced themselves "excited" to be at the forefront of this dramatic break with tradition and they had quickly allied themselves with the necessary forces of innovation, unafraid to boldly embrace all that is new and radical. The fans who mooched about on the sparsely filled terraces were either markedly less keen to embrace the 'permanent revolution' Trotsky advocated or just plain apathetic. JC appeared hopeful about the likely success of the "new format" in his programme notes, so we're all poised with our pens at the ready to make an absolute mess of our race cards in the name of innovation. The club has kindly included an explanatory section in the programme that outlines the "supplementary rules for tonight's challenge" though, after a casual glance, I can see that these are as clear as mud, but much too arcane to be outlined in detail here. So we'll all have to indulge in that most British of activities – making do and mending while learning through doing.

It's safe to say that the average die-hard speedway fan doesn't welcome most forms of change, whether gradual or cataclysmic. However, they still have to suffer regular and dramatic changes to the rules, formats, and league structures that are frequently foisted on them in the name of progress. This happens after every close season when the promoters closet themselves in meeting rooms and bars in faraway locations to supposedly try to guarantee the "best interests of the sport". The definition of these "best interests" is never specifically or satisfactorily identified but invariably evolves with incredible frequency. Said "best interests" also appear to operate as a convenient shorthand for whatever pragmatic changes the promoters and the UK governing body, the BSPA, wish to foist without consultation onto the paying punters. These often contradict – or "refine" as the speedway parlance of the authorities has it – previous seasons' decisions. At least, in a sport with a very complex SCB rulebook, they're never afraid to consider even greater complexity. Often these changes are suspected to be at the behest of Sky Sports television or made with their business interests in mind, even if they haven't explicitly requested it. This situation is compounded since some key people within the sport who have a close conjunction of

---

[1] For example, the relationship between British speedway and Sky Sports leaves the impression that the tail wags the dog. Though, then again, relationships have sometimes become so complicated in the triangle of the BSI, BSPA and Sky Sports that it's difficult to establish the dog and the tail apart.

business connections that link the various bodies in charge of the governance of British speedway with their own commercial organisations, which are often customers/business partners of speedway.[1] And so it is that the rules of the sport of speedway in general, and its dwindling fan base in particular, often find themselves manipulated at the behest of the business needs of outside commercial interests. Sadly, the medium and the message have become inextricably bound together in a decision-making process that imposes and communicates often arbitrary but radical changes in a manner that many modern business organisations would consider inappropriate when dealing with their "customers".

All these changes and the complicated close ties off the track, adds up to sustained nonchalance, but underlying cynicism, on the terraces from the fans who, in the last few years, have seen too many dramatic changes and too many vested interests. Some of these changes have included alterations to the rules that govern the league format; team constituency and qualification; helmet colours; point scoring; guest riders; tactical substitutes; tactical rides and so on. My list is illustrative but not exhaustive! Tonight the riders and fans are faced with another innovation, in this instance a revolutionary new scoring system. Consequently, if afterwards the sport decides to alter the scoring to a new format that removes the traditional, unique and distinctive characteristics of the current scoring system in order to replace it with soccer-style scoring, then we must, as usual, be very British and shrug our shoulders.

While I purchase one of the remaining few tickets for the Dinner Dance from Kath in the Speedway Office, I overhear Alan Rolfe, the very experienced Eagles Start Marshal discuss the revolutionary new system. "It won't catch on or, if it does, we won't use this system in the League – they've tried many things in the past that just haven't caught on". Among the older hands on the terraces, news that only ten tickets remain for the Dinner Dance provokes trips down memory lane to the good old days, "it used to be £10 and a right piss up with lots of drinking and punch ups". The venue for this scene of Bacchanalian revelry used to be the Sovereign Centre Leisure Centre and Swimming Pool in Eastbourne. Grown men become all wistful and sentimental as they recall "Barker and Norris scrapping" or Jon Cook getting "punched on the nose". I make a silent wish that these recollections are either embellished versions of what was idle horseplay when everyone lets their hair down or completely out of step with the current philosophy of the forthcoming Dinner Dance at the Langney Sports Club.

Talk then turns excitedly to news of the latest young Polish rider to get a try out trial around Arlington. Excitement puts it too strongly; careworn cynicism would be a better description. Near by to me, loyal but occasionally long suffering John Hazelden remarks, "it's another one of Cooky's sensations that we'll probably not be seeing again!" To be fair, promising Polish nationals with the youth, ability and developmental potential to successfully ride speedway in Britain are a hugely sought after and precious commodity, particularly among Elite League promoters. Over the years there have been truly gifted Polish riders who've become wonderfully successful here. Poland already is a country that has League racing of considerable skill, excitement, and renown, as well as legendarily fanatical crowds of supporters; it's very understandable that most promoters would like their gifted performers to ride over here. Consequently, the arrival of another trialist with great potential should be the source of great anticipation amongst the Eagles faithful. Though this is immediately tempered by the thought that we all know the majority of Polish racetracks are huge amphitheatres dedicated to the sport, where ability at very high speed is a prerequisite for success. Well, in fact, all of them are huge in comparison to most British tracks. As a total contrast, Eastbourne has one of the mingiest racetracks in the country where throttle control on the tight corners and the short, narrow straights of the circuit is a prerequisite skill. Most Polish riders therefore are often congenitally unable to come to terms with the Arlington track. This is confirmed by bitter experience and encapsulated succinctly by 'Mark the Bark', "most Poles we see here are through the fence on the first bend or, if they make the second bend, they're going through the air towards the bar". Consequently, no one holds their breath about Lukas Romanek. Though, since assumptions are often the mother of all mess-ups, it would be better if instead we watch closely and speak as we find!

The excitement of a potential star in the making has badly affected KC. As if we're not going to constantly scribble corrections in our programmes tonight, he gives two differing spellings of Romanek's name in the space of five minutes, just long enough for you to have completely filled out the race card before he sows the seeds of doubt about which actual spelling is the correct version. This confusion is nothing compared to the varying schools of thought that even just the few people around me indulge in when it comes to how to complete the programme. Maybe all this debate, concentration and scribbling is the additional excitement intended by these rule and format changes?

The new scoring method, in new money, means that you have to conceptualise the meeting as three sections comprising of five heats. Our conceptual powers are tested further by the appearance of Ricky Ashworth's bike in heat 2. It's a stunning combination of bright primary colours that have some glitter effect added to the glass fibre body. John captures the visual impact succinctly, "it looks like he's built his bike from scrap". The next heat is re-run when, after an inordinate delay by Dave Watters the match official, who finally lets them go only to struggle to locate the red light button to stop the race to exclude Watty, after he has fallen but lingered on the track. With their rider stricken on the track, the crowd beneath the referee's box had loudly suggested this course of action in the common language of men before Watters roused himself sufficiently to act. KC is irked enough to signal his disapproval in a passive aggressive manner when he notes with considerable emphasis, "Heat 3 being stopped *eventually*". Before the crowd knows it, and definitely before the expected excitement can build to the first of the three officially scheduled crescendos, the score is 0-1 to Poole.

KC takes the opportunity to interview Deano during the brief interval before the second third of the meeting begins. Deano refuses to get drawn into a profession of excitement for the new scoring system with a standard but cursory "we'll see how it goes" response. He strongly gives the impression that the intricacies of any scoring system wouldn't be of sufficient interest to ever be a concern to him, except when it came to calculating his actual points money. This is the practised insouciance and flippancy derived from a natural and unaffected equanimity that we've come to expect from him. It either makes the crowd love Deano as a rider and captain or completely tear their hair out at his "relaxed" attitude and roundly excoriate him for every real or perceived lapse. However, Deano is always an engaging interviewee, and often comes across with more natural wit than the often slightly more mannered Floppy. A case in point is when he looks forward to more fixtures with Belle Vue in the KO Cup Final, "we've been to Belle Vue so often this season that we're thinking of getting a season ticket!"

Heat 6, in old money, or heat 1 in the second set of races in the new way, sees another ride for the Polish debutant Romanek. He struggles to get used to the tight circuit and he finishes comprehensively last again but KC, ever the club's man, has seen enough to be impressed with things, "looking smooth is Lukas Romanek". KC's approval cuts no ice with the crowd as Judy remarks, "what's he looking at, he was at the back throughout!" Lukas demonstrates yet more smooth looking but ineffective grace when he again rides to a comprehensive last place in heat 10. Nonetheless, despite two unpunished and outrageous rolling starts by Antonio Lindback, the Eagles have rallied to win the second series of races 1-0 and thereby take the overall score to an exciting draw of 1-1. It's a score that Dave Rice, resolutely not with the regime after all these years doing things the traditional way, insists on calling "1-1 or 31-29".

KC interviews the always laid back Mark Loram, guest rider tonight and for ever a special friend of Eastbourne Speedway. "I appreciate Jon ringing me every time there's a bit of a vacancy – it's nice to be able to have a bit of a relaxed meeting tonight and just enjoy ourselves". KC then moves on to interview Jon Cook with a wide-ranging set of easy questions. JC is keen to highlight the potential excitement of competing in the KO Cup Final, "we're up for it". While he stresses that though the Eagles might potentially be the bridesmaid to the Belle Vue bride, "we're close to being a successful team". JC then comes up with a Tatumesque remark, when he notes, "with speedway there's always a problem round the corner", though it's not up to the exacting standards set by Kelvin Tatum when he works live on Sky Sports. It has a certain accidental truth and *je ne sais quoi*. JC reveals himself not as fully on board with the play-off system that determines the Elite League, when he says he declares Belle Vue as, "the true champions as they won the league". When it comes to his forecast of the play-off final result, JC lists Joe Screen, Jason Lyons, and Jason Crump as "very good speedway friends" before he notes, "my heart says Belle Vue but my head says Coventry".

Afterwards we all thrill as Eastbourne wins the final set of races 1-0 to record an overall 2-1 result or 52-40 thumping in old money over Poole. The new format, if it were a forest fire, would have hardly singed a twig and we would still have a lot of firewood for the winter. Still, we have all gossiped about possible Eagles team line-ups for next season. John Hazelden has passed on top secret "inside information" from a self-styled "Mister Eastbourne" who's really "on the inside and in the know, or claims to be". If Watergate had a 'Deep Throat' figure on the inside of the political establishment, then at Eastbourne we have our own 'slight frog in the throat and irritating cough' informant who, in hushed tones, reveals incredible, improbable but consistently wildly inaccurate changes. "Norris is retiring, Pedersen is going back to Wolves and Peter Karlsson is coming to Eastbourne though we'll be known as the Sussex Eagles next season". It's all too astonishing to believe so, taking full account of "Mister Eastbourne's" previously very chequered history of predictions, nobody does! It is a fantasy – though one with a slight greater chance of becoming reality than the revolutionary scoring system has to become the exciting new wave of the future that has the crowds flocking back to watch speedway once more.[1]

24th September Eastbourne v. Poole (South Coast Trophy Challenge) 2-1

[1] If you spend the evening stood next to the Hazelden family, you can quickly learn that passionate Eagles fan John is a particularly rich source of comment, stories and gossip, which is usually funny, entertaining and, I sincerely believe, mostly accurate. Except, of course, when he repeats hot gossip gleaned from "Mr Eastbourne", who is invariably completely wide of the mark. So much so that I've begun to suspect that he's either brilliantly ironic or the mysterious people who pass on this rubbish to him – 'those in the know' – must deliberately tell him complete nonsense in the full knowledge he'll pass it on and look a complete berk. Invariably at some point during any meeting, an incident on the track will prompt a recollection from the past, which has now assumed the lustre of a more golden era for the club. Given their importance to the club, many stories concern the Dugard family, particularly Bob. I gather that he is a man not be trifled with (I haven't, phew, and think he's truly gifted at his work with the track) and has apparently mellowed with age. "In the old national league days, if anything happened Bob would be out in a flash, he didn't care who he hit!" Not only has he mellowed, but also he's reputedly become less hypersensitive to actual or imagined criticism, plus Martin no longer rides so the family honour isn't as imperiled as it could have been on a weekly basis in days of yore every Saturday night during the season.

"What a brave interviewer our Soph is. Ulamek says he can't speak English and she interviews him anyway"

More Silverware on Offer

1st October

The first leg of the *Speedway Star* sponsored Knockout Cup Final sees the Eagles compete for one of their few remaining chances of silverware this season. In fact as you arrive through the turnstiles, the cup itself gleams at you from a table. Start Marshal Alan Rolfe, skilfully mixes black humour and pragmatism, so sensibly advises, "take a good look at it as it's the only time you're going to see it!" The Eagles ride so often against Belle Vue that it's beginning to seem like we're all caught in some kind of speedway version of a weird parallel universe, as Eastbourne repeatedly crash to aggregate defeat again and again. The sight of the cup coupled with the changing weather is one of many indications that it's actually not a re-run of previous encounters. It's a cold Arlington evening and a light mist hangs in the country lanes that lead to the stadium. A beautiful sunset sky colours the thick formations of high cloud overhead. Despite the repetitiousness and recent history of these encounters, the stadium is already very full of the hopes that invariably spring eternal from the Eastbourne faithful.

The talk of the terraces is, strangely, about the forthcoming end-of-season Dinner Dance. Like most conversations in speedway, it's another instance of the "things were better in the old days" syndrome, not that it sounds that great actually, as the legendary end-of-season fight cum contretemps between Deano and Floppy is again recalled in glorious but exaggerated detail. The exact recollection of the date differs. It's generally agreed that it occurred sometime around 1990 when Eastbourne were in the National League, but this is an unimportant detail compared to a blow-by-blow account of the incident itself that sounds like an encounter of Ali v. Frazier or Foreman proportions. As often happens, even people who weren't there can recall the fight in copious detail. Jon Cook features in many accounts as an erstwhile referee of the fight, with various degrees of success or intent in each of the many but slightly different recollections. In extenuation, everyone agrees that Deano and Floppy were "young and childish then!" (Apparently after this contretemps, Floppy subsequently left on loan for Ipswich vowing "never to return to ride for the club again"). The next cherished speedway folk memory is about a Dinner Dance when "Andersen and Danno were pissed out of their brains and sprayed us with beer". This sounds much more like the spirited rambunctiousness and high jinks you'd naturally associate with any works Christmas party and the stress of compulsorily relaxing with people who are in reality your work colleagues. Though, having listened to these tales as they morph into urban myths, I make a mental note to adopt a dress code where it doesn't matter that much if my clothes are splattered with beer or blood. Worryingly, having already got a ticket to this in-demand but now sold-out premium event, the Langney Sports Centre venue figures as the actual location in question for many of the stories though, hopefully, not as a catalyst for them.

After the theme of 'Great Eastbourne Dinner Dances I Have Known' has been thoroughly exhausted, the terrace talk begins to anticipate tonight's encounter. At least Eastbourne have Nicki back in the team after he missed the revolution that was last week's experimental meeting with Poole – well, with regards to the scoring system rather than the actual races. In his programme notes, it's hardly a surprise that JC, of course, views this as "the biggest and most important meeting of the year here at Arlington", though he does sensibly note that the Eagles quite rightly start out as "underdogs". In a densely worded piece, Jon rehearses the contributions during the season of each of the riders. He notes, "we have discovered an unlikely Captain in Dean Barker" who skilfully uses "humour" to motivate the team and defuse potentially excitable situations. Nicki Pedersen has also meshed into the team fantastically as he "inspires from the front but doesn't count himself as being too big to join in with and on occasion be the butt of the boys' jokes". Oh how we laughed and it appears Nicki did too, which is lucky, since the combination of relentless ribbing and the puerile nature of our British humour, on the one hand, and the traditionally dour reputation that Danes often have towards life, on the other, doesn't bode well. Something that has been no laughing matter has been the ongoing season-long challenge to fill the notoriously difficult Reserve position alongside Andrew Moore. Steen Jensen, though, is notable by the absence of any mention of him in the programme. He has now finally achieved the *persona non-grata* status that the quality of his riding for the Eagles often deserved.

This is such an important meeting that considerable additional verbal fanfare is made about the introductory lap of honour by the riders

by, to use one of his favourite phrases of introduction, "Arlington's very own" Master of Ceremonies, the inimitable Kevin 'KC' Coombes. It's such a special occasion that the riders, for once, don't ride round and wave to the fans on their own bikes, but instead parade on a variety of sparklingly shiny and impressive motorcycling beasts clearly owned by the riders' proudly beaming chauffeurs. Sadly, Nicki doesn't quite make the entrance he'd like when the vehicle he parades upon runs out of petrol. Hopefully, it's not an omen for or symbolic of what's about to happen to the Eagles' season. As he introduces the riders with his customary flair, panache and barely suppressed elation at the mere mention of each rider's name, KC then introduces the match official "and tonight's referee is Chris Dunno, that's spelt D-U-N-N-O". I initially imagine that it's a brilliant jest, by perpetual funster KC, at Chris Durno's expense and that of referees generally as he subtly implies that they're a bit amateurish or vague on the actual rules of the sport. Not that Chris is, of course (it must be another of his colleagues) as he's one of the country's rising and dedicated referees. When he repeats the incorrect spelling again, it transpires KC either loves his own wit or isn't joking but is only being his usual detailed albeit, in this instance, slightly mistaken informative self.

Just before the first race I finally find Jules Martin, Lewis Bridger's number one fan and photographer par excellence. She's travelled over from Weymouth to watch tonight's meeting at Arlington en route to another one at Mildenhall tomorrow afternoon that features Lewis. It's a chilly evening and it's always really cold at Arlington towards the end of the season, so Jules in her jacket, T-shirt, beaded necklace and combat trousers will likely suffer as the evening progresses. As opposed to the Conference League fare she traditionally watches, Jules professes to be excited to get the chance to see this clash between these two senior Elite League teams, but it's really just an incidental bonus to the main purpose of her visit, which is to watch Lewis warm up for tomorrow's prestigious individual 'Bronze Helmet' with a few second-half rides. Jules is so obsessively committed and enthusiastic about Lewis that she's become a welcome and co-opted participant in his unique first season of speedway. Her website focuses on her photographic work and her coverage of speedway majors on all things Weymouth 'Wildcats' Speedway which thereby allows her to give full exposure to many beautifully captured images of Lewis gained throughout his exceptional 2005 season, mostly on the track but also off.

Jules has also just organised a spoof auction of Lewis's discarded but stinking race socks. Indeed, she has billed the event as a unique once-in-a-lifetime opportunity to purchase some speedway memorabilia from the "Future World Speedway Champion". The auction was surprisingly popular but unfortunately misconstrued by the apparently humourless 'Berthoven', a frequent poster on the British speedway forum. The feverish world of the Internet forums, often unfairly, excites strong negative opinions among the more hypersensitive and thin-skinned promoters. 'Berthoven' is, perhaps, typical of this breed of earnest regular posters, long on opinion and, in this case, often low on humour. But like all earnest posters, he comments because of his enduring love of the sport. He's quickly managed to test the tolerance and equanimity of Jules with his criticism of her auction and her apparently inflated opinion of Lewis that, thereby, misses its tongue-in-cheek approach.

Whatever point of view you choose, Jules appears as a sincere, very engaged and huge LB fan. She benefits in comparison to others by being what, in the USA, they call an 'early adopter' as well as being warmly accepted by Lewis's family. She's close to Lewis, obviously, but is also warmly welcomed by his guide, mentor and mechanic Alan Thompson (aka "Granddad") and his wife Jackie. Alan and Jackie have raised Lewis from infancy. By all accounts, he's loved to ride bikes since he was old enough to balance on one and has always demonstrated a real gift and ability. Granddad and Jackie have always supported and nurtured this interest and now Lewis is, potentially, on the cusp of great things within the sport, however early it may be in his career. Jules will stay over in Bexhill tonight with the family before she has the privilege to travel up in the van with them to Mildenhall.

For Lewis, these second-half rides are the meaningless preliminary to the most significant individual meeting of his young career to date, the Bronze Helmet. Given his potential at such a young age, it's not unrealistic to think that he might ultimately compete in the biggest individual championship of them all, the World Championship. Though, for practically everyone else inside the Arlington Stadium, they only have eyes for the latest Eagles fixture against the Aces. As expected Crump wins the first race before heat 2 results in a heat advantage for the visitors after the experienced and combative Andy 'Smudger' Smith wins impressively. This race has some Weymouth interest for Jules since Dan Giffard races in place of reserve Steen Jensen. At the Conference League level, Dan is one of the bright heat leader stars for the Wildcats, but he's stepped up two levels in quality in terms of the riders he will race against tonight. This evening will be altogether a different proposition for him. To be fair to Dan, he tries hard and then scores exactly the same total as Steen probably would have scored when he finishes comprehensively last. Jules is quick to rush to his defence as she notes the Arlington track "is much bigger than we have at Weymouth and he didn't do too bad, as I bet these have had a lot more practice round here". The second point isn't quite accurate since Dan is an Eastbourne asset, so he actually initially learnt his riding technique and practised his skills around both the Arlington practice and Arlington professional racetracks. Jules also notes the appreciable difference in control and skill levels between the riders in the Conference League and those in the Elite League. It's only the second time she's watched a top-level meeting, "they look a lot smoother here, there's much less of the wobbling you see at Conference level". The difference in the noise made by these Elite League machines also surprises her though, as "these all sound really throaty and powerful whereas at Weymouth they sound much rougher".

What's rough, from an Eagles perspective, is the way the Aces begin to run away with the meeting almost immediately. By the end of heat 4 the Aces lead 9-15 and Crump appears in dominant form since he's already easily beaten our best rider, Nicki Pedersen, on his home track. Things would have been much worse but Simon Stead, frequently lauded as a potential English star of the future, falls when another Aces heat advantage looked the more likely outcome. At least on the terraces we can amuse ourselves as we debate the vexed question of why England (no one uses the British word) no longer produces World Champions or even why we have produced so few. The debate is sparked by the fact that you rarely see races at the Elite league level that feature four British riders, whereas at the Conference level for a single foreign rider from outside the Commonwealth to compete at all is the exception and not at all the rule. Dave Rice near by surmises it's all down to "us being too nice sometimes, we just seem to lack that killer instinct that you see in riders like Crump, Rickardsson and Pedersen". As if to prove his point Jason Crump wins his third race easily in heat 6 before Nicki does the same in the next race. A run of five drawn heats allows the Aces to maintain their six-point advantage and Dave frets, "our riders are already mentally at the end-of-season Dinner Dance!" By then Crump has won all four of the races he's been in though, happily, just before the interval the deficit is cut when Nicki combines with teammate Shieldsy to narrow the score to 29-31.

Since I know Chris Durno in the referee's box, I ask his permission if Jules and I can briefly join him and watch his work during the last five heats of this leg of the Cup Final. He's as welcoming and enthusiastic about his speedway as ever and happily answers Jules's many questions. I'm a bit distracted from their conversation, as I'm all a bit overcome and gobsmacked to have finally made it into the booth that I've stood below for so many years. It's always appeared to me to be a referee's and commentator's booth transplanted to the Sussex countryside from a 1970s Formula One finish line. It's white, windowed, overlooks the circuit from a considerable height and hints of glamour from a bygone era. From below you can always see the referee and the mysterious line of other people that always appear at the windows. I'm also delighted that tonight I'm going to finally get the chance to closely observe KC since the cold has driven him inside to commentate this evening. Actually, it's an ideal night to watch him since KC is missing his regular help tonight, so not only will he have to practise the black arts of the Master of Ceremonies but he must also multi-task to undertake many other essential duties. Besides being the announcer and interviewer, KC will also be the timekeeper, incident recorder, soundman in charge of the music and jingles, as well as the one who controls the electronic scoreboard via a laptop on the far side of the booth. KC has to leave straight after the KO Cup Final has ended to go to a local wedding reception, so there'll be no rest for the wicked as he'll be the disc jockey there until 2 a.m. So it's quite a busy night for him, but he takes it in his stride and you can't doubt his sincerity when he says in a flippant manner but clearly in all seriousness says, "I love Saturdays!" This part of the booth has a long bench-like desk against the large windows. KC uses one

end of it, while the control panels and phones that are the match official's responsibility to operate occupy the other end of the cramped bench.

Even during the interval it quickly becomes apparent that there's real skill required to announce in a professional, interesting and enthusiastic style, as KC does, despite the many distractions and other competing tasks that would throw a lesser man off his stride. The ability to concentrate while others talk right next to you, while you make your announcements is a skill that takes practice to master, especially since a lack of skill would lead to chronic and embarrassing on-air snafus if you allowed your mind to understandably but momentarily wander.

KC easily ignores the chatter of the animated Durno–Martin discussion on the mysterious absence of female match officials in speedway. Jules questions the lack of "women refs" and Chris ties himself into PC knots before he bluntly admits, "not many apply". There's a lack of female participation in many areas of sport, never mind speedway and photography is a prime example. Jules herself is one of the rare female photographers within speedway, and besides another lady who works at Wolves and Stoke, I can't recall seeing any others. But, sports photography in general is still primarily a male preserve if Jules's experience of covering football and rugby in her local South West area is a reliable measure. Weymouth is her team and a club Chris likes to officiate at, mainly due to the positioning of the referee's box, and he closely quizzes Jules about her perspective on the events and characters at her local club. She is unequivocal about her own personal view: "Lewis has been the highlight of my year". It's an opinion that stirs and briefly engages KC who temporarily has a moment to spare, and nods in agreement before he adds, "it's easy to be enthusiastic with young talents like Lewis coming through!" Luckily for Chris, who had already earlier won a 'Political Correctness Lifetime Achievement Award' for his earlier glorious attempt to even try to be PC during a speedway meeting – a very rare flower indeed around any matters of the shale – the discussion then doesn't move onto the lack of similarly talented female speedway riders. We're saved by the bell, well the buzzer, when the interval ends and everyone returns to match duties as Chris sounds the two-minute warning to summon the riders back to the line.

Once the meeting is back underway, I notice that KC and Chris work in tandem very capably and smoothly together in the cosy box. Heat 11 is a very significant race for everyone connected with Eastbourne as it's dedicated "In Memory of Steve Heath". His contribution over many years to the development of young riders is a testament to his dedication as well as his skill as a mentor, but the fact that he's still sorely missed, due to his tragic, premature death earlier in the summer, is further testimony to his qualities as a man. Fittingly enough, an Eastbourne rider, Nicki Pedersen, wins this memorial race and serendipitously it also features Dan Giffard, a graduate of the club's training schools that Steve famously dedicated himself to.

What's most fascinating, as I watch the races from the box, is the manner in which KC and Chris operate so seamlessly and efficiently but both still manage to remain so thoroughly absorbed by the racing in front of them. They behave as the true fans of the sport that they are, albeit ones that occupy positions of responsibility, as they live each lap of the race. They both unconsciously signal their absorption through a series of involuntary jerks, twitches, imprecations and loud exclamations. They compliment each other professionally in their work; Chris calls out the finishing rider order, which KC confirms before he shouts out the official time that Chris in turn reconfirms, before they both independently write down these details. Then KC announces this over the tannoy to the fans. This tableaux happens every race but it's their complete absorption and personal integration into each and every race that fascinates me as I stand silently behind them throughout. After KC informs the crowd of the official result, which he does while he simultaneously also operates the laptop that controls the scoreboard and effortlessly cues up the next music, never one to ever miss an anniversary, KC moves on to congratulate the lone Sussex-based Conference League rider at Arlington, "it's a working birthday for Dan Giffard – Happy Birthday Dan!"

As the music plays, Chris sounds the two-minute warning and they both agree with Jules that Giffard "isn't looking disgraced at this level". The officials then banter on between themselves as Chris, with genuine bonhomie, compliments the standard of the Eastbourne facilities "this box is one of the better ones [slight pause] though the windows could do with a clean". This elicits a sharp but smiling "watch it!" from KC before he resumes his work and smoothly transitions into confirming the line up for the next race to the crowd.

The next heat is a disaster from an Eastbourne point of view. The Belle Vue pairing wins easily and thereby extends their overall lead to 33-39. KC the fan – rather than KC the Eastbourne employee or KC the SCB Official – spends the race imploring Deano to alter his race tactics, "the dirt! The dirt! Get out in the dirt, Dean Barker! You're not going to win it on the inside!" Nicki finally beats Jason in the next heat and when Smith falls the gap slightly narrows. Between multi-tasking on his many duties, KC isn't optimistic about Eastbourne's chances of success in the KO Cup: "if this was a boxing match we'd have thrown in the white towel by now". But as he reflects on the season, he immediately reminds himself that there have been many more highs than there have been lows. The most enjoyable aspect of the season for KC has been "the crowd getting behind the boys" which is helped by the "design of the place as everyone can get close and it really builds the atmosphere". If he had had his usual help with the music and the scoreboard, KC would have been out among the crowd, chortling on the centre green or chuntering on in the pits with his sensible questions, "as, no offence to Chris, I'm an outside kind of a guy!" Not that this is a confession about any proclivity towards dogging but, as so often with KC, a bald statement of fact. Most of all, as if it needed any further confirmation, KC "loves Eastbourne winning, as a successful team makes the job a lot easier".

During the next race, as the riders compete for position, KC enters his own private fan world, as he commentates to himself for all four laps in a manner that would gain peculiar glances in the High Street, but in the cloistered world of the box isn't remarkable. In heat 14 Andrew Moore, unusually, blasts off from the gate with some panache and great alacrity to make such an amazing gate, without a hint of movement from the referee's vantage point perched high above the start line, that he easily wins the race that he leads from start to finish. Davey Watt's subsequent overtake of both Aces riders to join with Mooro makes KC gasp before he chants "one-two, one–two" as though it were a Buddhist incantation. Since he truly savoured the race so much, KC's excited announcement to the crowd of "it's a brilliant win for Andy Moore" comes across with an authentic sincerity (and, once and for all, punctures my long-held cynicism about the practised professional efficacy all these types of remarks previously uttered by KC on many other nights at Arlington). With the scores tied, KC and Chris are both delighted that there haven't been any accidents tonight because that involves both potential injuries and its concomitant twin evil copious form filling, "touch wood we haven't had the need for any paperwork". The tentacles of Health and Safety legislation, the regulations of the BSPA, as well as the restrictions of the club's insurers mean that the referee's boxes all round the country are nowadays flooded with paperwork. KC has a smart square executive briefcase of the type your mother would buy you for your first office job in the mistaken belief that it would make you look a suave businessman. Into this go sheaves of papers and paperwork, half completed between tasks by KC as the night progresses. Though in pride of place, casually hung from one of the many pockets on the internal divider of the briefcase, right next to an impressive array of pens that wouldn't disgrace a science-minded schoolboy, is a badge that identifies KC as an authorised 'Speedway Control Board Official' for the 2005 season. It's an authority KC carries lightly but nonetheless, very professionally. Even before the last race is at the tapes he's already begun to pack his things away to make a quick exit into the night for his disco duties.

As the riders make their way round to the start line, Chris observes, "if Ian Thomas has any sense he'll have a 5-1 here [to Eastbourne] otherwise, if they win, it's a couple of hundred off his gate on Monday night". Looked at in coldly commercial terms, the overall result and the destination of the Cup is not really in doubt, barring a miracle. Although the dedicated fan probably wouldn't mind watching a foregone conclusion in a final, they might soon mind if they had to do so every week. They will always overlook it at the prospect for some glory. However, the sporadic attending or 'floating' fan is a different beast, by very definition and as the history of the last couple of decades at speedway would indicate, one who only attends on a discretionary basis. Let's assume that each adult fan spends around £20 on entry, a programme and a drink. If you lose 200 discretionary fans that costs £4000; or the loss of 500 costs £10,000. These are

significant amounts of money in a sport with notoriously precarious, wafer thin or disastrous (but always secretive) finances. Even at a reportedly major club like the Aces, despite the presence of an enthusiastic investor Tony Mole, Ian Thomas's mission and *raison d'être* has been to, where possible, track an attractive side that offers entertainment and competitive racing to regularly attract back the legion of 'lost' Aces fans. There's no doubt that he's been successful as he's staunched and, arguably, reversed the recent inexorable decline of Belle Vue under the much-maligned John Perrin in one short season. A great accomplishment, but then Ian is also a seasoned promoter well aware of the exact value of his and Tony Mole's money. As it happens, the Eagles win the last heat 4-2 as Nicki P beats Jason C for the second time. The overall score of 46-44 is unlikely to trouble the Aces too much on their home track. The result delights the Eagles fans and the riders indulge in a celebratory lap of honour that, once more, illustrates the close bond that exists between the sport's participants and its spectators. The riders high five or touch the outstretched hands of the celebrating fans as they ride past, helmetless and mostly smiling, on their bikes.

KC and Chris now add the finishing touches to the copious quantities of paperwork that they must compulsorily complete. KC closes down the laptop because, even if he stayed, the junior riders results don't have the honour of their results appearing on the electronic scoreboard. KC takes off the headphones that give him the slight hint of the 'air traffic controller look', and then flamboyantly snaps shut his leather-effect executive briefcase. Ken Burnett will handle KC's duties in the second half. Ken is well known in Eagles circles and hails from the speedway video production company T2TV ("Relive those magic moments") who, along with his friendly wife Jackie, usually film every single Eastbourne meeting. They film at many other clubs too, so Ken is very well versed in speedway matters and has trained to become a referee, though sadly he failed to make the exacting grade they have for this exalted position. Nonetheless, despite being lost to the ranks of the SCB referee's, Ken is definitely a well informed and capable replacement, although he doesn't have KC's infectious Tigger-like enthusiasm or his verbal presentational élan, since he prefers a less-is-more, studiously muted public address approach. With a few hearty goodbyes, KC disappears down the box's steep stairs and speeds off to deejay the night away elsewhere.[1]

Ken and Chris know each other very well. They became pen pals when they were 12 and used to exchange programmes. They also work capably together but without the same intensity or bonhomie. But then the junior racing doesn't have the same urgency or hold of the tense atmosphere of senior riders who compete in a Cup Final. Also Ken, unlike KC, doesn't gyrate on the spot in the box living every twist and turn of each race, shouting comments or uttering suggestions to the riders throughout. Nonetheless, as usual, it's a very entertaining and strongly contested – if often an individual personal battle between rider and recalcitrant but dangerous machine rather than rider against rider – second half of racing. Tonight is again packed with the falls, incidents and general mayhem that you'd expect from young men as they learn the sport as they develop and acquire the

---

[1] SCB referee Chris Gay explained to me that many announcers/presenters in the country often only give the listening fans the bare minimum of information and don't explain the intricacies of what has happened on the track or the reasons behind the referee's decisions. He often has to prompt some announcers to provide this information. This is not the case with KC who leaves none of these informational stones unturned. Chris commented, "he's one of the best, if not the best there is, he really cares about what he does and really explains everything to the crowd in an easy way so everyone knows what is happening".

necessary skills to properly master a powerful 500 cc speedway bike. As a night to digitally capture Lewis Bridger while he hurtles around Arlington, it's definitely a disappointment for Jules. Not only is the racing cut short from six to four races only, as a result of time restrictions, but Lewis also endures an unfortunate evening.

In many respects it's a typical evening of junior racing that keeps all the officials consistently on their toes. Though there are only three riders in each heat, only two of the races are actually completed. The first heat has Brendan Johnson win easily; he is another rider that Jules wants to photograph, since she knows both father, Dave, and son well. He easily beats my local favourite Niall (pronounced 'Neil') Strudwick.

Interestingly, in a sport that loves statistics, in the box I had noticed earlier that the club has another sheet that records each rider's fastest race time and average speed during the 2005 season. This list includes the juniors and it's notable that Lewis's best time is almost identical to that of Steen Jensen's. I did also notice that some poor other lad (who I won't name) had an exceptionally slow time that would lead you to think it was a cycle speedway time recorded on a sundial.

In the next race Lewis has an engine failure, Adam Filmer falls and gets excluded, and so the rider in last position, Gordon Walker, is awarded the race. The race after actually has a full complement of four riders competing, but this swiftly diminishes as they keep falling and so are gradually excluded. After a re-run, the referee again awards the result. Lewis wants to make amends in the next race, but he falls and then retires. Jules would have to have been extremely quick to capture any exciting action shots of Lewis on his bike. Adam Filmer falls again, but retires before he can be excluded. Once more, this leaves Gordon Walker to power to his second win of the evening with a race time of 71.1 seconds.

They say that one of the many joys of speedway is the chance to be able to casually mix with the riders in the bar afterwards. I can't say that it's something that I've ever made a habit of but, for once, I do venture to the Arlington bar by the pits area to meet with Jules. The place heaves with florid and flushed Eagles fans with their families, friends or better halves, as they drink in celebration of tonight's outcome. In the annex room of the bar, which houses the pool table, there's also quite a crowd. This includes Deano in a bobble hat without a bobble, who chats animatedly with Floppy, who's there with his wife and one of his sons. Though Floppy hasn't ridden tonight, it is a given that he would be here in the stadium throughout, if not the bar. I imagine that it's a comparative rarity to find him for any real length of time in the bar, since last year he famously quit the demon drink in order to fully concentrate on his chosen sport and career. It was a level of commitment and professionalism that paid dividends when Floppy had his best-ever professional season in the sport in 2004, when he performed at an exceptionally high level. This season, though, he's had the kind of luck with injuries and come-backs that would lead anyone to drink heavily.

Jules sits with friends from Weymouth, in fact there's a huge number of people from that Dorset seaside town, who have invaded Arlington this evening. They sit in a group and wait for Lewis to arrive in the bar and for Granddad to finish dismantling his bike, so that they can depart for Bexhill. The people with Jules are all mad-keen speedway fans having been brought up that way by their mother Debbie. Her daughters, Sarah (13) and Sam (16), are both start line girls at Weymouth speedway, but since they're dressed in civilian clothes away from the starting gate I don't recognise them as such. They've enjoyed the meeting at Arlington and now actively scan the bar for their favoured quarry – any speedway riders that may lurk nearby. Slightly mischievously with all the intense talk of hunky speedway riders, as she has her back to him and I know how much Jules 'admires' Dave Norris, I wonder aloud who that is over by the bar. Just as Jules spins round to glance at the happily married Mr Norris, who is now attired in a smart casual shirt set off with designer-looking jeans, he starts to walk over towards us. It's all a bit of an unexpected surprise for Jules, who in the same instant breathes very deeply, exclaims "Phwoaw!" in a low moan, and blushes profoundly. She also momentarily loses track of her multi-tasking skills and conversational abilities as, at that instant, Mr Norris wanders even closer and then slowly passes by her and out of the door with his son. After she regains her composure Jules confides to Debbie, "I hope he's called 'Floppy' because of his hair!" Lewis arrives, clutching a pint of orange juice chock-a-block with ice cubes, looking incredibly fresh faced, young and slightly miffed at how the evening has turned out. When he doesn't loudly bemoan how slow Granddad is at packing up the bikes, he noisily rattles the ice cubes round his mouth or chews them impatiently. He's a whirlwind but is clearly very comfortable with Jules who commiserates with him. "When was I crap then?" demands Lewis. To which Jules laughs, "I tell you you're good even when you're crap".

Chris Geer ("he's 19 and can legally do everything" Lewis notes in a hushed but envious tone) comes over at that moment to cries of "Geernob!" as Lewis immediately stands up to do some sort an exaggerated mime of greeting that involves a jerky, humping motion with his pelvis. They shake hands in a twisting, convoluted manner more suited to the Bronx than Bexhill, though with all the mentions of

"cushti" there's more than a hint of 'Del Boy' from *Only Fools and Horses* about their adopted vocabulary. They're not discussing mechanical issues although some form or concept of riding and performance does tangentially enter the equation as they animatedly discuss the latest gossip about off-track conquests among the riders and mechanics. While exotic stories and frank tales tumble out, Jules matter of factly notes "Weymouth is like a giant knocking shop, in the backs of the vans and everywhere though I imagine it's like that at all the tracks". The boys' talk tonight is mainly about a Wildcats rider that favours hairstyles even looked on as outlandish among the younger element of the speedway community, who has boastfully tested the springs of the back of his van with the young daughter of an influential figure in the sport. Though no doubt hypocritically, Geernob and Lewis definitely don't hold her personal moral reputation in very high esteem.

Ever protective, Jules maternally but loudly mentions, "I've often tried telling Lewis about the birds and the bees". He'll soon receive a lot more female attention, partly as a result of the perceived 'glamour' of his calling but also, according to Jules, because of his youthful good looks and for possessing the "loveliest eyelashes". Fortunately Granddad arrives at this point to summon Jules and Lewis to the van, which cuts short the graphic discussion of the smell of his socks ("hair gel mostly") on auction on eBay. Lewis goads Jules with "Everyone feels sorry for you 'cause Granddad really fancies you", apparently deaf to this, Jules asks, "Am I sleeping with the dog?" The bar is still packed with happy punters and, for all I know, the riders' vans might already be rocking away in the car park, but I doubt it - but I have no desire to investigate.

On my journey home, the mysterious disappearance of the limos during the autumn is solved when I spot a queue of them as they wait to fill up at the BP petrol station on the A27. It would be just my luck to find myself behind a queue of these limos if I'd nearly run out of fuel. Each vehicle appears to fill the forecourt and heaven knows how long they take to fill up, never mind the vast quantities of petrol they need in comparison to even a van. I'm sure that they're much more comfortable for shagging in the back though!

1st October Eastbourne v. Belle Vue (KO Cup Final, 1st Leg) 46-44

3rd October

This was a much closer match than the scores suggested. It wasn't until heat 10 that the Aces pulled away for the victory that the Eagles' recent form at Kirky Lane would have led only the most optimistic of die-hard fans to expect. With rider replacement for Floppy and Deano absent but covered for by Travis McGowan, things always looked likely to turn out to be a drastic mismatch.

Afterwards, like the speaking clock, Jason Crump gave all the usual platitudes a quick run round the track: "This team deserved to win something this season and now we have". Thanks were the order of the day for all and sundry, especially Messrs Mole and Thomas, but Jase was content to help "the kids" in the Aces team and he "just did my best in a big team effort".

Jon Cook was also keen to give everyone their just deserts. "I have to say that this has been one of the best teams to be around over the time I have been at Eastbourne and there have been very few occasions when heads have dropped.

We have discovered an unlikely captain in Dean Barker who manages to bring humour to most situations of stress and a supreme points scorer in Nicki Pedersen who doesn't count himself too big to join in with and, on occasion, be the butt of the boys' jokes". Davey Watt had been "a revelation", Shieldsy had "an incredible end of season finish," and the future burns bright for Mooro who "has established himself as a fully fledged Elite League rider, one who I certainly want in the team next season".

Unacknowledged, MIA and apparently not on the 2006 team list was the always entertaining and our very own Admiral-at-the-Rear, Steen Jensen, whose role sadly didn't get mentioned in these dispatches. Floppy's injury didn't cause the team to slip into a slough of despond, but despite strength in adversity, his absence had proved costly as David was "a ten point rider" and couldn't recapture this form during "his subsequent comebacks".

3rd October Belle Vue v. Eastbourne (KO Cup Final, 2nd Leg) 53–37

8th October

The six rider format of this tournament could be the structural benefit that enables the Eagles to travel some distance in this competition since it immediately eliminates the season-long problem of how to adequately fill the No. 7 reserve slot. The Eastbourne management have signalled how seriously they take their chance for one last hurrah to gain some much-needed silverware for the recently resolutely empty trophy cabinet, since they have been able to draft the always reliable and often spectacular Mark Loram in place of the injured Floppy.

This late in the season the weather is always a peril and so it proved, when the meeting was abandoned with three heats still to go. This premature end thereby deprived the home side from the possibility of building an even greater lead than the ten points they gained over Oxford. Ever the diplomat and always reluctant to pour oil on troubled waters, Ian Thomas viewed the lost heats as a sign of incompetence by the Eagles: "I couldn't understand why they had a ten-minute interval when there was rain forecast. We could have finished the meeting otherwise". The Eagles were helped in no small part by a very lacklustre display from Jason Crump and, though Jason Lyons sparkled, Joe Screen was also unable to celebrate his full transfer from Eastbourne to Belle Vue with a large 'freak you' score. He's undoubtedly too nice to think like this anyway, although it would only be human nature to demonstrate to your ex-employer what they are now missing. A resurgent Oxford team, who have finally found a decent run of form, provided sterner opposition. Albeit in this team of a thousand changes, they were still without a settled side as the 'hired hands' of Lee Richardson and David Howe compensated for the absence of the evergreen Yankee combination of Hancock–Hamill that still slips off the tongue with the resonance and ease of a catch phrase.

Back home in Yorkshire, Ian Thomas, with the pained look of a man who has just had his prize pet parrot casually assassinated by the kids next door with their air pistol, smells a rat in the Eagles' lair. He accuses the Eastbourne management of a sneaky change of heart to "move the goalposts" at the last minute: "the clubs agreed to use a reserve rather than bring in guest riders because we all had riders injured. But then Eastbourne said they were going to use Mark Loram as a guest for the injured David Norris". A man of firm convictions, Ian stuck to his principles – despite requests by the Aces fans to do otherwise – to honour his booking of Rusty Harrison ("I wasn't prepared to drop him and cost him three pay nights at the end of the season") rather than seek a guest replacement for Kenneth Bjerre. This would be within the rules, but Ian takes the moral high ground, though it will almost certainly result in Belle Vue's elimination. "Even Mark Loram agreed with me and he'd got the bookings to ride for Eastbourne. He told me he couldn't understand why he had been given the bookings instead of them using their number seven like we had done". Clearly Ian hadn't studied Steen's form or that of his replacements at reserve closely, never mind their injuries, in a jinxed team position for the Eagles.

8th October Eastbourne v. Belle Vue v. Oxford (Craven Shield Semi-final, 1st leg) 37–26–27

13th October

The Eagles narrowly retained their aggregate lead after an evening where they frequently gained the minor places at Sandy Lane. They were unlucky not to have a greater lead to take to the decisive leg at Kirky Lane, particularly when Adam Shields crashed while in the lead, and so gifted the Oxford Silver machine an unexpected bonus of a 5–1.

Belle Vue's chances of advancement were severely dampened when Andy 'Smudger' Smith withdrew with flu. This led to a busy night for Rusty Harrison and even a race where they only had a solitary rider. The only consolation that Ian Thomas could take from the night was a reconfirmation of the moral high ground he'd established earlier, in that he'd "stuck to our pledge not to use guests in the Craven Shield and give the extra meetings to Rusty Harrison". Indeed, Belle Vue are the only club not to have used any guest riders in 2005.

Keeping his post-match comments comparatively brief for a change, Nigel 'Waggy' Wagstaff was content to just briefly state the obvious: "I'm very pleased". Before he went to blather on about Kirky Lane as a difficult place to go to etc. etc., as though you had to trek over mountains with elephants and sherpas, before he gave the usual canards about a "recent run of form" and having their destiny in their own hands a quick canter round the press conference.

13th October Oxford v. Eastbourne v. Belle Vue (Craven Shield Semi-final, 2nd leg) 42–34–32

17th October
This night produced the kind of result that would have led you to believe that this cup fixture had been very effectively tampered with for incredible financial gain by a shadowy Far Eastern betting syndicate. Despite his magical talents, Ian Thomas had nothing up his sleeve for the Aces nor was he able to pull anything out of his hat. At least, the Aces have retained their unbroken record of never having qualified for a Craven Shield Final. Ian Thomas preferred to accentuate the positive and was magnanimous in defeat: "I've enjoyed the Craven Shield format, if not the results. I'm not pleased to have gone out, but this is not the time of season to start shouting at people. It's been an absolute pleasure to work with these people!"

The choice of Mark Loram as a guest was believed by many people to be the decisive factor that enabled the Eagles to draw on aggregate with Oxford at 107 points and thereby manage to progress to the final. In fact, at one stage the Eagles led on aggregate by eight points. But a fight back from the Oxfordshire-based Silver Machine shouldn't distract from an all-round Eagles team performance that was sufficient for us to advance and saw Nicki P achieve top score and receive the best support from Loramski and Deano. A delighted and still tanned Jon Cook remarked, "We set our stall out to try and win something this year. We have worked long and hard to do that. We made the play-offs and we made the cup final". A real cause of celebration was the chance to hit the motorways back from Manchester in an upbeat mood, "it is nice to be driving away from Belle Vue with something".

Before he rushed off to have more blonde highlights put in his hair, Waggy was also ecstatic: "The last few weeks we've seen an upturn and on current form we're probably up there with the top teams". After he swiftly brushes off rumours about his own future involvement with the club, Waggy is adamant that the club is in "good shape" and that "all the boys are up for it". Never one to shy away from the occasionally tenuous speculation, he partly attributes the qualification for the final as deriving from the confidence engendered by the victorious campaign by "the youngsters" in the Conference League, "that's got people talking and feeling good about the club again".

17th October Belle Vue v. Eastbourne v. Oxford (Craven Shield Semi-final, 3rd leg) 34–36–38 (aggregate 92–107–107)

An Attempt to Square the Triangle

22nd October

Beautiful red autumnal clouds hover over the Arlington car park and stadium as I queue to watch the first leg of the three-team format that will decide this season's Craven Shield Final. For all these teams this competition remains the last chance to gain some silverware and glory this season. They say all good things must end and it's been a good season for the Eagles, even though sadly the trophy cupboard remains bare.

Let's take a cursory glance at Jon Cook's end-of-season programme notes in his 'Promoters Piece' section to gauge his reaction to this eventful and nearly season. There are so many people to mention and thank that the typeface has to be specially reduced to flyspeck size in order for all the words to fit into the usual allotted space. Like listening to your team's manager after a particularly poor performance in a football match, these comments from promoters often appear based on experiences in a parallel universe that only bears some vague passing relationship to what you've witnessed yourself from your vantage point on the terraces. However, Jon's column is typical of the man that I've begun to know – hugely committed to his club (the team, the staff and his own work) as well as straightforwardly honest, loyal, down to earth and, if you listen carefully, someone who leaves a great deal implied or left unsaid.

Anyway, back to Cooky's comments, which he weighed carefully with the consummate skill of the professional politician albeit, unusually, a sincere one. JC readily admits that he was initially one of the harshest critics of the three-team format that we'll watch tonight, but, rather like a reformed smoker or born-again Christian, he's happy to acknowledge the error of his ways as he embraces the bright new future – especially when it might, at the last gasp, result in some precious silverware for the Eagles. From a practical point of view, you can also run extra fixtures, charge the fans a premium in addition to the usual admission charges on the basis that they'll see more teams and races than usual, although presentationally you obviously don't mention that many of these will often feature four riders who aren't from your team but happen to ride at your track. Jon notes, "I am certainly a fan of a competition that sees so many top class riders on track at once, four World Champions today for example". Technically, only two EX-World Champions ever appear on track together but you have to big these things up whenever you can as a promoter.

Whatever happens, JC is anxious to hail in print a "successful season" and to thank absolutely everyone who contributed. For diplomacy, courtesy and accuracy reasons even Steen Jensen gets a mention but isn't expected to attend the end-of-season Dinner Dance. But significantly, if you're looking for nuances, out of the list of the riders who have ridden at reserve for Eastbourne during the season, only Olly Allen and Trevor Harding are identified as riders Jon would be "keen to see more of in 2006". For some reason, all this talk of Steen reminds me of the old sign in an office that I used to work in that read "it's difficult to soar like an eagle when you work with turkeys". It has nuances galore since Nicki is praised for being "superb all year, a true inspiration where it counts most on track". This is all you can really ask as a fan and, when he has been available, he has, indeed, been "superb", although by implication, Jon's praise appears to indicate a doubt about Nicki's contribution to the team once the engine has stopped. Still who cares, when we have Deano "a great captain whose team riding harks back to days of old". There's no doubt that team riding is a dying art in modern speedway and a concept that many of the sport's current great individual riders haven't yet been introduced to properly. In Deano's case, this aptitude makes a virtue of a necessity as he has now lost some of the speed that he used to have when he had a nine-point average. It is something we all welcome on the terraces.

The dying art of this old-fashioned skill is applied immediately in the first heat of the night when Deano and Shieldsy combine brilliantly as a unit to ensure that they take second and third place behind another Pedersen (in this case, Poole's Bjarne). It would have been a more notable achievement if they'd been able to force the other Poole rider back into fourth, but as he'd already been excluded in the first running of the race, this exhibition of team riding was left looking more than a little bit silly. Stood next to me John Hazelden hails the pointlessness of this rare exhibition of such skill, "I love it when they team ride, well except when they're doing it at the back like they are now!" Luckily for Eastbourne Adam Shields demonstrates some tremendous end of season form now that he's put his injuries behind him, though Jon playfully notes in the programme that he's "the man who rides faster injured than fit".

In the next heat we enjoy what we've all paid extra for tonight, the chance to watch the drama and spectacle of Poole ride against Oxford in a drawn heat. In the next race, Davey Watt, lauded as "the provider of some of the most memorable passing moves in recent years", spends the entire race stuck at the rear. It's a continuation of his recent weeks' poor form when he's ridden without any verve and in a manner that suggests the season should have finished for him a few weeks ago. His lacklustre form throughout the evening contributes significantly to Eastbourne's failure to take the full use of their home advantage in this final meeting of the season at Arlington. Luckily throughout the preceding months we could rely on Andrew Moore, who has exhibited the resilience and tenacity that leads JC to characterise him as the "most unlikely find in our recent history who just gets better and better". Tonight, however, he doesn't really get going at all and, if speedway bikes had gears, he would spend most of his races in a very low one.

It's my first experience with this format and of the stop–start nature of a structure that has two races that feature members of your team interspersed with one that doesn't. The scorecard itself takes some time to (re)learn how to completely master and fill out correctly too. No matter which way you look at it though, the Eagles don't head towards the expected high score at home that the three-legged aggregate nature of the competition dictates that you must have for any real chance to win the damn thing! Perhaps it's not that Eastbourne ride poorly but they're not quite on their top note while Oxford ride like a team possessed. Also, each side is only made up of six riders instead of the usual seven which, given the Eagles continued problems at reserve throughout the season, you'd have thought might have favoured them. The situation isn't helped by the arrival of a Poole team that has a shockingly poor evening overall and, apart from the combative Bjarne Pedersen and their guest Joonas Kylmakorpi, you get a strong sense that their team are just going through the motions and mentally are already propped up by the bar for the winter.

Poole have also suffered from appalling luck tonight when their guest, Jason Lyons, had to withdraw from the meeting with a freak injury sustained in the pits. KC earnestly, if slightly unbelievably, describes the unlucky scenario as, "a bizarre injury in the pit lane – he reached to hold a wire to stabilise himself and it went through a finger". Jason Lyons is a very experienced rider – at the "veteran" stage of his career, which apparently means that he's at the point where he's capable of randomly riding well one night and really terrible the next, especially the case when he raced away from Belle Vue this season. He rode in Sweden earlier in the season, but was sacked in strange circumstances by his side for his refusal not to smoke in the pits. Which is kind of admirable for its belligerence in the face of a weird set of values that allow you risk life and limb on a bike with no brakes but draws the line at nicotine inhalation. Nonetheless, I hope he didn't sustain this injury to his smoking hand. Whatever the cause, Poole's performance tonight suggests that it will be a difficult struggle for them to acquit themselves honourably, never mind win this competition.

Another factor that the Eagles must battle with at Arlington is the fair and superbly prepared nature of the racing surface, which, while comparatively small and tricky to negotiate, is always fantastically well looked after. Without any hyperbole or need to inflate their achievements, Jon Cook's praise of all involved throughout the season in its loving care and preparation is well deserved. JC sensibly and graciously also acknowledges every sponsor of the club as well as everyone else involved behind the scenes who thereby help ensure that the spectacle of watching the Eagles happens every week. After he thanks the "great team, excellent sponsors and superb backroom staff", he then thanks "our terrific supporters". Apparently attendance has risen and "familiar faces" have returned to the fold along with those most desired and elusive of beasts, "new fans". Those that have come tonight have seen the Eagles win by the peculiar-looking score of 41-27-40, which sound like the sort of numbers that would probably look hideous as vital personal statistics. The star of the evening has been Nicki, ably supported by guest Mark Loram and regular Eagle Shieldsy, though the overall strength in depth for the Oxford squad means that they should really get the plaudits tonight. Deano has ridden his last two home races of the season with skill and panache to gain two (paid) second places behind his winning partner. It's all too much for Dave next to me, one of many fans that doubt the application of Deano on a regular basis throughout the season, yet who grudgingly praises the man with, "Barker rode well there – for once!"

Tonight's referee, Chris Gay, has managed to avoid any unnecessary controversy though, as is his wont, he's often held the starting tapes inordinately long throughout the evening[1]. In Heat 7 Chris contributes his own portion to human fallibility when he puts on the red and

[1] I must emphasise that Chris is one of our experienced and most capable officials whose scrupulous application of the rules – he particularly tries to ensure that no rider gains advantage over others by moving at the start – is rigorously adhered to. This can create the impression that he is the exception to the rule as a referee in this regard, since the tapes appear to have "been held", whereas in fact Chris is merely ensuring fair play all round. He should be applauded for this and not sniped at from the terraces by people like me, though recently this has become less noticeable.

the green lights simultaneously, perhaps to confuse the riders or to see if they're still attentive and awake. As the season draws to a close, John Hazelden is in reflective mood as well, "it's been a really great season, I've enjoyed my speedway but the team's been shit". His son Mark 'The Bark' Hazelden concurs with, for him, the rather measured "I've got to admit that I've seen better teams for us". This mood of bonhomie and reflection hasn't mellowed John who, when I say hello to a passing fan, says afterwards "do you know him? He's a freaking arsehole – he's always pushing in and manoeuvring others out of their place".

Whether they're new or careworn, the majority of fans stay after on this cold night to hear the end-of-season speeches from the riders and Jon Cook. As ever they'll be conducted with some aplomb and charm by the man with the roving mike and the perennial "just a quick question" enquiry, our very own Kevin 'KC' Coombes. Earlier he's made a point to thank his partner in crime for the last 12 years or, to put it in true KC speak, "his oppo for 12 seasons together". I think that this person's name is Barry Geer, but I can't be exactly sure, he's definitely someone unafraid to play cheesy music on a regular basis. First up for a brief speech with a strong 'end of term' feel and some facilitating questions from KC, during the meeting itself, is JC who tells us more of the same that was included in the programme. But we do learn that, "it's an open secret that we have a new team coming up [to join the Elite League], so the team will be cut back, but we'll retain the backbone of the team to kick on for a championship-winning team". Hope does spring eternal and though there's "important decisions to be made", it's good to see that JC already anticipates success next year, a hope that's greeted sceptically by the crowd around me. The importance of your superstar rider to the team and the promoter is emphasised by JC's very public but undoubtedly sincere flattery of Nicki Pedersen. His comments acknowledge that speedway at Eastbourne has readily embraced some aspects of modern digital life when JC notes, "Nicki has said some very nice things about us on his website". I have to note that this is the first time that I've ever heard anyone say such a thing, never mind hear a speedway promoter speak positively of comments on the Internet, even though this might only be because it's a rider's not a fan's website and thereby it counts as almost semi-official comment.

Critical comments that really gall and irk on the ether is the bane of speedway modernity as well as a familiar theme and complaint that captain Deano immediately returns to, sarcastically, when as the next interviewee he stresses that, "I come into some criticism on the Internet from the super fans who come here every week". Like a character from the *Catherine Tate Show*, Deano's not "bovvered" as he has his reasons, allied to a self-confidence that manifests itself as publicly unshakable belief in his own abilities and a logical perspective, "I've had some problems with my bike but I'm here to do a job – which I've done!" When interviewed Davey Watt doesn't achieve his sunniest disposition ever, though he admits that earlier in the season, "I had a great time when it was going well". We quickly gather that this was some time ago mentally and chronologically, because "now I'm so tired and worn out, I don't want to ride any more". He soon might get his wish; at least as far as the Eagles are concerned, next season. The main reason for Davey's slightly sour outlook can be put down to his early return from injury when he was "eager to ride", even though he still continues to have "treatment every week".

Though he's injured and not riding, KC manages to interview Hailsham's favourite son, the Eagles very own Floppy who's in a combative mood, which in the comfortable environs of the Arlington Stadium is always recognised as high spirits and jocular repartee. As ever, Floppy frequently delights in his own levity and the subversion of interview protocols:

[KC] "The season ended for you at Swindon?"
[DN] "The season's been a bit rubbish."
[KC] "What do you say to the fans?"
[DN] "They can remember me and I can remember them."
[KC] "There's light at the end of the tunnel, then?"
[DN] "All I want to do is ride a speedway bike!"
[KC] "It'll be a tough winter?"
[DN] "Nah, I'll be like Cinderella – asleep for months."
[KC, trying to enter into the spirit of things] "Are you available for panto?"
[DN] "No I'm not 'cause I'm asleep, you twat! Don't you listen? You're a handsome chap so you can wake me with a kiss."
[KC] "You'll be an attractive proposition next year."
[DN] "I am now though they gave me away to Reading before when I was injured, so if you're telling me it's happening again – just come out with it and say it to me."
[KC] "No, no."
[DN] "I can take it, I can, just say it, go on. I'm gonna be the hungriest rider in 2006 and hope to God I'm back here at Eastbourne".

After he maxes out with his interview with this most charismatic of the Eagles riders, KC balances things up when he then interviews Andrew Moore, Adam Shields and Nicki Pedersen in quick succession. The season has gone very quickly for Mooro who notes, "It helps not breaking my leg" and enjoys his summer riding, as "I can't stay at home, can I?" Andrew also reveals the precarious nature of most riders' financial positions, since speedway riding is a livelihood that for most riders doesn't provide sufficient funds to last them over the non-riding winter months. "I'll probably get a job, which I really hate, but I have no choice".

KC establishes that Shieldsy will spend some of the winter in the sunshine down under with his girlfriend Karen. He wants to return to ride at Arlington next season, particularly after the trials of this season when both he and the team suffered from injuries. Understatedly he mentions, "I am kind of ambitious and I feel that I under-performed this year" though injuries contributed to this "confusing time". Shieldsy now realises "I love it here!" He enjoys the entire environment at Eastbourne and even, or especially, because the "fans are great, well, they're here listening in the cold to what we're saying".

It's a message of praise and satisfaction echoed by Nicki though, like all many who have become World Champions, it's not a modest message but one that he's pretty keen to pass on to motivate and acknowledge himself. "I've been the best League rider worldwide – in England, Poland and Sweden. I'm learning, I'm really enjoying myself, it really suits me here and I like the people around me". Though he thinks highly of himself and doesn't suffer from false modesty, Nicki doesn't shrink from identifying his weaknesses and working on them ("I've been practising every day I can in Denmark on slick tracks"). Nicki wants to offer both value and commitment to all his clubs. With his own unique but idiosyncratic use of our idiom he notes, "I always give it a show and do my best on the day, that's what I say! I'm trying to focus on each meeting, each night". KC establishes that his ambitions for the winter are "to train physically", "going to Mexico for two weeks with my missus and, of course, I want to come back – if the club want me back". KC asks the inevitable, "is it the crowd?" Even in his third language of English, Nicki answers with practised elegance, "they're fantastic, of course they are – every Saturday when I fly here, I really want to come down, the track they do here is fantastic, I want to come back". Job application over, all that's left is the formality of the last second-half races of the season.

The crowd expects the usual end-of-season finale that involves the always popular and widely anticipated 'Mechanics Race'. Instead we learn from KC that a "mystery rider" will be "on trial". Everyone suspects that in reality that this will be Jon Cook. Sure enough, JC appears in blue leathers as he rides Deano's bike, in his guise as the "mystery rider" for an exhibition of measured riding that has an official time of 68.6. Quite a contrast to 15-year-old Lewis Bridger's season best of 57.6. Like for much of the season, KC gives full reign to his easy, often natural, wit, "a winning time there of around three minutes". A subsequent second turn for the "mystery rider", this time without the distraction of the starting tapes, again delights KC who can't help himself from commenting throughout this ride. "Notice how he's looking down at the bike as if there's something wrong with it!" Next to me John Hazelden notes, "he's riding better now than he used to as a junior". It's a thought that's crossed KC's mind too, who the very next minute notes, "he rode here as a junior in the mid-80s – everyone used to hold their breath when he rode as, shall we say, he looked a little awkward!"

The crowd slowly ebbs away, though some stay to enjoy the never-say-die sight of Lewis Bridger, who easily dominates the second-half racing. He really is an exciting prospect that everyone wants to see appear in Eastbourne's colours next season. Even Mark 'The Bark' is happy to acknowledge the undoubted talent and ability in one so young, but then worries "when he comes off he's gonna come off big time". This simple caveat illustrates the vagaries of opinion that typifies the Eastbourne terraces and every other throughout the country, when optimism and pessimism effortlessly combine simultaneously in almost the same sentence. Perhaps, just as Frazer used to note in *Dad's Army* "we're doomed!" and is a perspective that, at some point in each season, comes naturally to long-suffering speedway fans at most clubs around the country. Nonetheless, it's fun to hear on the terraces in the heat of the moment at the meeting, but it's understandably irksome for the riders or the promoters when it appears on the Internet forums afterwards.

22nd October Eastbourne v. Poole v. Oxford (Craven Shield Final 1st Leg) 41-27-40

26th October

The spunk for a fight from the Pirates team had already deserted them before a wheel had even been turned at Wimborne Road. The continuing human anatomy and physiology lesson that is the lot of any averagely observant speedway fan, led the charismatic Antonio Lindback to withdraw 24 hours beforehand, when muscle problems in his neck apparently caused an aggravation to his back injury. Matej Ferjan did not ride as he was "tired".

With the fixture effectively reduced to a practice session for the Pirates round their own home track – or, for Ricky Ashworth, the late doors chance to test out a new engine in the second leg of this supposedly prestigious competition – the question was whether it would be the Eagles or the Silver Machine that made the most of the night? Amongst the Eagles faithful, the suspicion remained that there would be a natural inclination for the Dorset competition to try just that little bit harder against the Eagles. However, only Bjarne Pedersen had read this script and offered a one-man opposition on the night. This saw him scorch to the fastest lap of the season by any rider in the skull-and-crossbones race bib, only 0.61 of a second outside Ryan Sullivan's track record. He also came from behind to vanquish his fellow countryman Nicki in heat 17. Apart from that it was the visiting riders who rushed, mostly to the bank with payment for race points that in the ordinary course of events their bank manager wouldn't have seen. Or, possibly not, if Waggy's subsequent bankruptcy left some of the Silver Machine riders as high and dry as it did some other creditors.

Old habits died hard for Nicki, who attracts controversy like a magnet attracts iron filings in a science lesson. In this instance, it was the turn of Sebastian Ulamek to sample the delights of the first bend air fence courtesy of an introduction from Nicki, who often appears to act as an unofficial and unpaid representative of the Air Tek product demonstration team. It was a late season plunge into the rubber that didn't make Ulamek feel that joyous, and this dismal end to the season left the large home crowd equally subdued. This performance more or less confirmed the first trophyless season for the Pirates since 2000.

Jon Cook's concern about Davey Watt proved prescient, since his "form is a great cause of concern in this competition – maybe it is one competition too many", although low scores from Deano and Mooro didn't help prospects for the final leg at Sandy Lane either, since the Eagles would trail the home side by four vital points.

26th October Poole v. Oxford v. Eastbourne (Craven Shield Final 2nd Leg) 35–39–34

Robbed at the Last

27th October
The hottest October day since weather records began will be the official end of a long season for Eastbourne. The Eagles will be one corner of the triangle that makes up the third leg of the Craven Shield Final at Sandy Lane. It's the last chance for any silverware for the Oxford Silver Machine, the Poole Pirates and, of course, the Eagles. The idea of a triangular tournament didn't initially set my imagination on fire, when the idea was first mooted but now that we're down to the final meeting of the season there's genuine excitement generated by this format (three teams, six riders and eighteen races) and the intense interest in the *denouement* of the Craven Shield that this unusual concept inspires. The excitement is particularly felt in the Oxford and Eastbourne camps since their aggregate scores of 79 and 75 respectively to Poole's 62 would lead you to conclude that only they have a realistic chance to lift the trophy. For economic reasons, many promoters detest three and four team tournaments as away fixtures, for which they get no gate receipts, necessarily outweigh home fixtures.

Oxford start their home leg at Sandy Lane as firm favourites with the crowd, in the press and on the speedway forums. This will be Eastbourne's fourth visit of the 2005 season and past performance would appear to indicate that the likely margin of an Oxford victory will be around eight points; since previous Elite League scores were 50-41, 49-41 and in the earlier Craven Shield qualifying leg with Belle Vue the odd-looking score 42-34-32. However, the unique factor of this format and the continued presence of the Pirates means that they, as a team, will essentially be either the spoilers or the 'king makers' this evening. Suspicions abound that they would love to play a key part in depriving their local south coast rivals of any chance to gain a trophy, if they possibly can. Whatever the likely outcome, this meeting has fired the collective imaginations of all three teams' supporters as well as a large number of other 'neutrals' who have flocked to Blackbird Leys to witness one of the very last speedway fixtures of the 2005 season. There is also the additional bonus that Oxford's remaining Elite League fixture against Wolverhampton will immediately follow the Craven Shield final.

The narrow roads around the stadium teem with people and the traffic is gridlocked on the residential streets that surround the Sandy Lane stadium. It's a beautiful evening, still amazingly hot for October and, as I join the substantial queue of fans that patiently wait for the gates to open, the sky glows with a fantastic red sunset.

There have been a number of rumours that this will be Nigel Wagstaff's last meeting in charge of Oxford. These have swirled for the last few months and the talk among the Oxford fans in the queue is of practically no other topic. The consensus appears to be that he will definitely leave and the candidate that they hope will take over the club is King's Lynn promoter Keith 'Buster' Chapman, a successful promoter with a proven track record. There is a school of thought, well represented within this queue, which believes that Nigel chopped and changed the squad so often this season that it deprived the team of any real chance to bond and meld together. Some of these team changes were forced upon Oxford by injury and the rest by the capriciousness and pursuit of success by Waggy. Whatever the reasons, the backlog of fixtures and the regular racing for a comparatively stable squad during the last month of the season has seen the Silver Machine become, arguably, the form team of the moment. This improvement in form, allied to the fact that the Craven Shield format requires that you have only six riders, gives the Silver Machine comparative in depth strength and renewed confidence. The talk is definitely optimistic, as we surge forward towards the open gates, with many of the opinion that "it would be nice to get a bit of silverware" and that "the team has come good at the end". They would be prepared to forgive Nigel Wagstaff many things if, as looks likely, the team emerges with a trophy at the season's end. They still complain loudly about his vanity; indicative of this narcissism is the fact that the Oxford speedway match programme has a photo of their promoter on the cover. They are the only club to have such a picture, never mind that this image is given greater prominence than the actual riders! The grumblers in the queue continue to loudly catalogue his endless team changes and even give unsubstantiated credence to the rumours that a high number of unpaid bills have soured relations with riders and suppliers alike.

Inside the stadium on the packed terraces, all these complaints and quibbles are put aside, while the home side luxuriates in the mantle of pre-meeting favourites and the fans bask in their newfound confidence in the team and its chances of success. Waggy's comments in the match programme do nothing to dispel the 'end of an era' atmosphere of this fixture, particularly as the majority of his 'Engine Room' column consists of an extensive list of thank-yous to everyone ever connected to the Oxford Silver Machine. It's a list so fulsome that it appears to go way beyond the normal bounds of these end of season round ups. But, perhaps, it is also an indicator of the complexity and level of help required to run a modern speedway club. Waggy hopes for a win tonight ("we have proved what we're about"), but also, in philosophical fashion, takes the chance to answer or dig at some critics of his approach to the team this season. "It has been said on many occasions that the team this season has seen many changes and numerous personnel. This had nothing to do with me not knowing the best formula, but in fact the complete opposite".

The past is definitely a foreign country here this evening and there's an enthusiastic buzz around the stadium as the first heat pits the Silver Machine against the Eagles. One of the methodological aspects of this three-team format is that each team depends upon their opponents' success or failure against each other on the track, while they remain as spectators in the pits. Whether this is a real delight or serious flaw often depends upon how likely your team are to win. There is also, of course, the chance for your team to influence the outcome through their own activities. Oxford appear to severely dent the Eagles chance of success on the night with a resounding first heat 5-1 victory after Shieldsy falls and Deano trails in third, despite the expertise you'd expect him to show as a result from the three seasons he spent here years ago. This race result takes the aggregate difference in their scores to an apparently insurmountable eight points. However, the Eagles still have their talismanic Nicki Pedersen to ride as well as the always wholeheartedly competitive Mark Loram, in the squad as a guest replacement for the injured David Norris. Both riders would prove to be crucial, in different ways, to the overall result.

The next heat has the Eagles gain a heat advantage when Nicki P wins but, more helpfully, Pirate Grzegorz Walasek has an engine failure. It's a mechanical difficulty that's not appreciated by the partisan Oxford crowd that surrounds me. Some of the politer comments made to the unlucky Polish rider are along the lines of "Walasek you're rubbish". The anxious mood of the home crowd isn't then helped by a drawn heat with Poole, which is immediately followed by a 5-1 reverse against the Eagles pair of Davey Watt and Mark Loram. It's a surprise on many fronts, since Watty's star has waned sharply in recent months, particularly since his injury and the blown 'favourite' engine took the gloss off his early season exceptional form. Watt's win delights the Eagles fans in similar measure to how Billy Hamill's last place punctures the confident mood of the Sandy Lane faithful. It's a level of concern that's not assuaged by another good Eagles win in the next race against Poole.

They say form is temporary but class is permanent and the next head-to-head encounter between the rivals for the crown pits the Silver Machine's Billy Hamill against Nicki to whom he narrowly loses. However, the significant factor in this race is the controversial decision of the referee Dale Entwhistle to award third place to Henka Gustafsson over Andrew Moore in a neck-and-neck finish on the line. Many Oxford fans appear to feel, as I do, that Mooro had just about shaded his opponent by a fraction of tread on the line. To learn that the referee sees it so differently that he even failed to award a tied heat disappointed me to the same understated extent that it delighted the large Oxford contingent near the finish line. It was to prove a vital decision in the context of the whole meeting, but had the immediate benefit that it allowed Oxford to regain some momentum, after a series of poor heats.

This was to be the first of many heats when the possibility of victory slipped from the Eagles' grasp for a wide variety of small but important reasons. Heat 10 was one of those heats that ran the gamut of emotions for both sets of supporters, when at first the initial race leader Greg Hancock was overtaken on the first lap by a resurgent Davey Watt. This happened almost at the same moment as Mark Loram decided to dramatically overtake both Oxford riders with a quick burst on bend 3. With Oxford apparently headed for disaster, unfortunately Loram then fell. Although he remounted the decisive Eagles advantage was lost. This stroke of luck stirred Hancock who gave strong chase to Watty and very nearly caught him on the finish line. Worse was to follow in the next heat when Poole's Bjarne Pedersen again won imperiously, but rather than gain a consecutive drawn heat by occupying the minor places with his junior partner, unfortunately Deano suffered an engine failure. So, a last place gifted Glen Phillips his only point of the night and left the Eagles to rue yet another missed opportunity to stretch their aggregate lead over the home side. Events didn't improve for the Eagles when Billy Janniro, as a guest rider for Poole, chose heat 14 for his only win of the night against the strong Eagles pair of Watt and Loram.

Prospects for the Eagles are raised in their penultimate race when a heat advantage won by the combination of Adam Shields in first place and Deano in third secures an overall aggregate tie. Since separate heats remain for both teams against Poole, Eastbourne and Oxford hold the final destiny of the trophy whereabouts within their own hands. But the intense competition between fellow countrymen that appears to afflict the two Pedersens, Nicki and Bjarne, undoes the Eagles. With no disrespect to Edward Kennett's replacement Glen Phillips, you can predict that it's highly unlikely that he will trouble the score chart, so all that's really needed is a race victory for the undefeated Nicki. Unfortunately, it's Bjarne who wins to complete his maximum and thereby shifts attention to the last race of the night where Oxford will still need a race advantage to win the Craven Shield on aggregate. There was never any doubt that Hamill would win, given that his form had improved throughout the evening, and a third place for Gustafsson ahead of the very disappointing Walasek is enough to spark ecstatic celebrations among the crowd. But even more so among the Oxford riders, mechanics and track staff who rush onto the track to congratulate Hamill, but conspicuously don't give him the bumps in deference to his severe early season injuries. Eastbourne find themselves missing out by a single point on aggregate

Oxford crowd go wild at Sandy Lane. © Jeff Scott

OSM team and trophy pose with Waggy. © Jeff Scott

Greg Hancock with trademark smile and the Craven Shield © Jeff Scott

and Oxford, after their season seemed for so long destined to ebb in a whimper, ends with a conclusive bang to cap off the Wagstaff era at the helm. A brief review of the race card shows that Oxford have won through on the night with a consistent all-round team performance without any exceptional heroics from any one particular rider. It has been their ability to gel as a team in the last month of the season, as opposed to every other month beforehand, which has enabled them to triumph.

Joy is unalloyed for the victors and their fans, who quickly embark on one of those laps of honour that so typifies all that is good about speedway. They parade the Craven Shield on a slow meander round the circuit on the tarpaulin-covered dog track. They progress extremely slowly as they pose for photos, as a team and individually, with apparently every Oxford fan in the stadium – both officially for the *Speedway Star* coverage and as personal mementos for the Oxford faithful. They also sign numerous autographs, get hugged by fans that lean awkwardly over the dog track wall and genuinely appear delighted. Waggy, never a man to publicly show false modesty, celebrates in a manner that suggests that he won the cup and definitely appears to view this triumph as a final vindication of his unique approach to team building and his own version of the "cult of personality" in speedway promotion. It even takes some time before the riders can wrest the Craven Shield from his grasp, which then allows Waggy to end his promotional career at Oxford in an orgy of handshakes and mutual congratulation. The normally placid and taciturn Billy Hamill is caught up in the emotion of the moment and repeatedly shouts "we've given you value for money!" as though a careful balance of economy with results, rather than brilliance, was the ultimate performance wish of speedway fans everywhere but especially the fans of the Oxforf based Silver Machine. By the start line the team pose for yet more photos for the aforementioned *Speedway Star* as well as the *Oxford Mail.* They do this in a slightly stagey almost wooden manner that completely lacks spontaneity before they continue again with spontaneously greeting the crowd in more authentic fashion. No bottles of champagne or sparkling wine are lashed about the place because they still have the anti-climactic and sobering task of an Elite League fixture to race against Wolves. It's a late season fixture that typifies the slightly shambolic nature of the administration and organisation of the sport in this country, since they will race a league fixture, *even though the league champions were determined weeks ago through the televised play-off formula.* At least, there's the consolation that all the league fixtures have actually been completed, which is something that can't always be said about all recent seasons.

Also watching in the jubilant crowd, is the SCB referee Chris Gay who has attended as a long-time fan of speedway, in order to get his last fix of the sport before the end of the season ("I just wanted to see another meeting this season"). When he's not officiating he travels to as many meetings as possible from his home in Southend, particularly to his local speedway track Arena Essex, though his favourite tracks of recent years, where he has many memories of great meetings have been Trelawny and Peterborough. Well over a decade ago, he fell into refereeing after he answered an advert in the *Speedway Star.* Chris can understand why some people claim that all officials should be ex-riders, but he believes that "while they can possibly understand racing incidents better" there's a lot more to the role than meets the eye or is understood by most fans'. There are two major components of the referee's job – on the one hand there is the quality control and paperwork aspect with six forms per meeting, while on the other there is the human relations management role that requires quite advanced diplomacy skills if the job is to be done correctly. These requirements must be allied with the other vital tenets of safety and fairness. The application of these skills varies from place to place since "at the Elite League level you have to keep an experienced eye out for the little things, whereas at other levels you're supervising things more". If there's a problem in the delicate eco-system that is the closed world of British speedway, he believes that it is "that some teams just want to win at all costs". He enjoys going to Eastbourne "the scene of lots of exciting meetings – Bob Dugard does prepare a good track – and I like Matt Ford at Poole, he's a real promoter".

Chris believes that the appeal of the sport for the fan lies in the fact that "you can see everything – it happens in short bursts – also you can go as deep as you want to in your understanding of tactics, rules and stats – a sort of team management on the terraces if you like – or you can just watch on the surface. It's up to you!" If Chris could improve one thing within the sport it would be "track preparation – if you can get lots of overtaking, you then get a product that people will always come back to see again and again. Very few things in life will top a good race meeting, whereas no overtaking generally means no excitement, which also comes down to the track shape but it's no good if it's all decided on bend 1".

With that Chris walks towards the back straight to watch the Oxford riders on their victory parade as an interested but impartial observer – since he's allowed to go to any British fixture as the proud owner of an SCB official's badge – whereas I'm left with the jubilant Oxford fans.

The subsequent Elite League encounter with the Wolves results in another win for Oxford 47-43, which finally lifts them from the bottom of the Elite League table, where they have remained rooted all throughout the season, and thereby condemns Arena Essex to dwell there instead for the rest of posterity. It's a win based around another great performance by Greg Hancock, ably supported by the rest of the team, particularly Chris Mills who rides with a degree of determination and skill that belies his experience at this level.

My 2005 season officially ends at precisely 22.37 in late October 2005.

27th October Oxford v. Eastbourne v. Poole (Craven Shield Final 3rd leg) 36-39-33

---

[1] See chapter 31 in my book *Showered in Shale* where I follow referee Chris Durno throughout his duties to gain a real insight into the wide-ranging duties and work of a SCB official as well as the numerous demands placed on them on a typical race night.

Tripping the Light Fantastic and Repartee at the Eagles Dinner Dance

28th October

After a journey through an awful night of driving rain and wind, I find myself at the Langney Sports Club in Eastbourne, home of Eastbourne Borough Football Club and the location for tonight's official 'End of Season Dinner and Dance'. The programme bills this as an unmissable event and "the social occasion of the year". The adverts have also strongly featured the location, the "Disco courtesy of Elite Discos" and lovingly lingered over the details of the three-course menu. There is even a "vegetarian option" that replaces the prawn cocktail, topside beef and raspberry pavlova courses, with the assumption that the sport might nowadays attract such non-carnivores. The venue is popular with the fans and the club's management because it's more in keeping with the goals and ethos of the club. A few years ago, after Terry Russell purchased the promotional rights for the Eagles, he initiated a move to stage the event at the much more upscale Grand Hotel in Eastbourne. The need for dinner jackets and posh evening attire, the expense of the tickets, plus the sheer amount of cutlery and the stuffy formality of the night meant that this became a poorly attended, unpopular and failed experiment in social climbing that was quickly abandoned. It also failed to break even, for obvious reasons.

Even though tonight's meal and dance will be held somewhere much more down to earth, I'm still quite nervous as I enter the rain-lashed car park. Mostly because I'm sure that I'll hardly know anyone at the event never mind at the table that I've been randomly assigned to for the evening. When I looked earlier at the seating plan listed on the Eagles official website, it's pretty clear that with the majority of the seating plans for the 13 tables of the event that everyone's family and friends appear to stick together. There is an undoubted hierarchy within the many large groups who I imagine all know each other, in fact have known each other for years, and have naturally enough chosen to sit together. Nonetheless, it's a unique event and typifies the community-based and approachable nature of the sport. What other sport lets you sit down in the same room as your heroes, share the same food (on different plates), and have the chance to informally socialise with them? This assumes, of course, that your shyness doesn't restrain you or that you aren't intimidated by the familiarity they have with each other that you could politely interpret as: 'please don't interrupt me; I'm enjoying myself with my friends'. As I trawl through the various Internet speedway forums, it's clear that some of the more zealous and dedicated fans travel from provincial town to provincial town and participate in as many club's dinner dances, gala evenings, discos and awards nights as they can manage. It appears that there's quite a party circuit for those obsessional enough or 'in the know' among the more avid members of the speedway community and Internet bulletin board *cognoscenti*.

I'm not quite sure what to expect when I walk through the double doors of the Sports Club, which from the outside looks like a village hall or scout hut. In order to try to blend in more effectively, I checked with Eastbourne's promoter and co-team manager, Jon Cook, to learn exactly what he understood to mean by the 'smart casual' dress code requirement. I'd found when I'd previously worked with some particularly styleless Americans that interpretations of what constitutes 'smart casual' often differs tremendously from person to person and event to event, often with very embarrassing results. Jon explained I should "wear the sort of clothes you'd wear if you went to a nightclub" before he quickly adds the afterthought "that's if you *still* go to nightclubs". Because it's an event when Deano, the Eastbourne captain and self-proclaimed all-round party-animal cum babe-magnet will also attend, I expect that the unsaid qualifying phrase of "on the pull" would be useful to keep in mind. I considered all these things as I carefully chose my clothes for the evening.

It's said that a camel is a race horse designed by committee and, when I enter through the doors at 7.30 for 8 p.m., a quick glance round immediately gives me second thoughts about my final choice of garments. The riders themselves can turn up in whatever suits them or that they feel comfortable in for the evening. They're the stars of the show, have a unique dress sense even for their age group, and mostly seem to feel comfortable in their own skins. I've come, it appears, dressed with the sort of casualness and grace that you'd expect Prince Charles to bring to such an event; basically, stiffly formal and out of sync with pretty well everyone else there. Even the old buffers who I would expect to have come dressed in what could be termed 'bank manager casual' – by wearing at least a jacket and dress shirt – haven't apparently chosen to do so. Despite my paranoia, awkwardness and self-consciousness, no one else notices or really cares what I wear.

Some of the riders present show greater vanity and take more care of their appearance than others. There's Deano, of course, who – since he's surrounded by women in short skirts who also reveal considerable *décolletage* is definitely already in his element – wears a tight-fitting top to emphasise his comparatively well-preserved physique. It's a style that "works" well for him. Davey Watt is dressed dapperly but casually in a manner that says, "I'm here with the missus". David 'Floppy' Norris, who smokes roll ups and chats animatedly with his mechanic Chris 'Geernob' Geer, is well turned out in a white shirt with some small patterned patches on it, set off with some jeans with what can only be described as having uniquely distinctive design features. I can't imagine that he'd even consider dressing in a run of the mill, predictable fashion, but his attire appears to say he always wants to be slightly different and well observed. Andrew Moore seems unencumbered by any hint of vanity in his outlook on life and dress, when he eventually turns up late, in what he claims are his "nightclubbing clothes" for his trip out on the town in Brighton later tonight. Even I can see that they must do such things differently where he lives.

Following on from my earlier season accidental encounter with Nicki Pedersen by the sink in the loos at Arlington, tonight I meet Davey Watt in the Langney Sports Centre gents' toilets. I learn that he will return home to Australia in November "for some decent weather and to relax". He confirms that he's delighted that the season has finally finished "you can believe how glad I am that it's over!" Mainly because, after initial promise, it's been a season of some misfortune and miscalculation for Watty. He blew up his number 1 and fastest engine, got injured, and then compounded that problem by resuming riding before he'd properly recovered. He's here tonight with his fiancée, "she's a bit nervous as it's the first time she's ever left the baby at home, I'm okay with it as I go to Sweden every week but she's not really happy at all". By the time I return to my allotted table, there's only one place left. I'm introduced to everyone else in efficiently friendly fashion and it appears that practically everyone comes from Hailsham, hometown to the Eagles' most famous son – Floppy. The ladies seated to my left are all mad keen fans who stand on the Hailsham bend (the third corner of the track) every week. They reckon it's the best place to watch from as "we only get covered in dust when Crumpie rides". Their sons all want to be speedway riders and are all members of the Junior Track at Eastbourne, that's run by Debbie Heath. It's been a very tragic year for the club and Debbie given the widely lamented death of her highly respected husband, Steve Heath. "It hit us all very hard" they agree somewhat disconsolately - suddenly sombre at the recollection of his absence this year, but they say Debbie has carried on running the junior track since his death. With hushed voices they point her out, over at the far side of the room as she wears a brave face and tries to get on with her life. It was a loss that deeply affected many people at the club who'd met, worked or trained with him. At the next Eagles meeting after Steve's death, the ladies confirm that "the riders had tears in their eyes" and Floppy dedicated his next race win to Steve's memory. They all think very highly of Floppy, who's out of earshot but at the table next to us with his father ("always a kind and polite man") and the rest of his family. Floppy is especially well liked because "he's great with the kids" at the junior track. Many of the "experienced boys are good with the kids; they're so friendly with help and advice", but Floppy stands out because he "always finds the time and gives a kind word to everyone". They hope that their own boys will eventually follow in the tyre tracks of the professional riders, after they successfully graduate from the junior track and will aim to emulate Floppy. They're understandably keen that their boys (Chris Granville, aged 15, and 'Baby Lindback' aged 7) get all the experience, practice, and encouragement that they possibly can. Chris's mum stresses that he has been "specifically mentioned on the Eagles website as a star of the future" and it seems that "everyone knows Little Lindback" according to his equally proud step-mum.

On my right is another proud mother, Janet Chappell from Crawley, whom I've often seen with her daughters, Lorraine and Karen, at various Eagles meetings throughout the season. Her daughters always seem to camp out in or by the pits at all the home meetings and quite a number of the away ones. Her 18-year-old gothic-looking daughter, Karen, isn't here tonight but has apparently just been appointed by promoter Ronnie Russell as official track photographer for Arena Essex starting next season[1]. The appointment came after Karen cheekily showed her photographic portfolio to Ronnie, which must be impressive, if the sheer volume of shots I've seen her taking this season is anything to judge by! According to her mother, pride of place in Karen's collection goes to her image of "half a wheel touching the tapes" which was the winner in the recent 'Essence of Speedway' photography competition. Though I'd never heard of this award, it was a contest that attracted numerous entries, although each photographer was restricted to "only three photos". Karen's work was judged by the legendary Mike Patrick to be "one of the top six". I have already learned from Karen previously – ironically at Arena Essex – that her day job at Jessop's helps her to keep the costs down on what is a very expensive hobby that could be seen to border on

---

[1] I doubt this information as soon as I hear it as the legendary Alf Weedon holds this position and, even though he's 85, I hadn't heard that he was retiring. A trip to the Arena Essex Raceway and a brief glance in any of the 2006 match programmes quickly shows that Janet's pride in her daughter's achievement is well placed. Karen is, in fact, one of seven track photographers employed there!

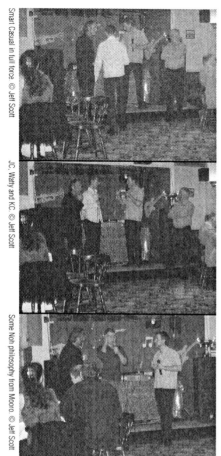

Smart Casual in full force © Jeff Scott

JC, Wally and KC © Jeff Scott

Some Noh philosophy from Mooro © Jeff Scott

the obsessive. The pride of her mother as she tells this tale is written all over her face and is shared by her equally fanatical speedway-loving sister, Lorraine. They travel to as many meetings as they can and attach great value to the fact that the "riders happily mix with the fans, practically everywhere". Before I can discover more, our talk is cut short by a severe panic over a lost mobile that eventually turns out to be a false alarm.

The food arrives quickly in very large portions. It's wholesome and homely grub, though the prawn cocktail is avoided by many of the ladies on my table on account of the "too spicy" rose marie sauce. My table has its own kitty for purchasing alcohol and is handily placed near to the bar. Most of the ladies will not drive tonight and, after they've established that they all actually drink wine, start to drink their alcoholic beverage of choice with gusto. The talk of my table is how much everyone anticipates hearing from each of the riders speak individually after the meal, some of whom are reputedly "hilarious". I'm told that the evening's comments are made all the more enjoyable by the witty repartee of the joint comperes: the inimitable Kevin 'KC' Coombes and his droll and often caustic sidekick for the evening Jon 'JC' Cook. By all accounts they're quite a combination as dual 'Masters of Ceremony', indeed "unforgettable" is a word that's been bandied about along with others like "just so funny".

With expectations at fever pitch, and with no need to dim the already subdued lights, just after coffee has been served MC's KC & JC take to the microphones on the small dance floor area in front of the slightly raised stage already filled with disco equipment. All eyes are on the comperes, aside from the slight distraction of the imitation flame effect lights of the disco, which manage to echo those once state-of-the-art electric fires with the under-lit plastic moulded coal your OAP neighbours had during the 1970s. The anticipation grows. From that point on, there's never any doubt in the audience's mind that KC finds himself funny, plus we learn that each of the riders (though "Nicki Pedersen +1" that appeared on the club's seating plan issued on the official website is sadly absent) will each be invited up to be interviewed and exchange witty repartee.

KC optimistically tries to enthuse the crowd with the promise of visions of Floppy as he struts his stuff on the dance floor later. Then JC quickly reviews the circumstances and the "narrowest of margins" that saw Eastbourne deprived of "a trophy" (in this case the Craven Shield) the night before at Oxford. He sums the last meeting of the season up succinctly as he mentions in turn the various factors that contributed to the Eagles just not quite making sure of victory. JC picks out, "Dean's EF, Loram falling on his *derrière*, and then the Gustafsson–Moore mistake where the ref somehow couldn't tell them apart!" JC views the last evening at Oxford as symbolic of the whole season, "we probably weren't quite good enough in the end but - and it's a big but - with a fully fit team I'm sure we'd have had some honours". He goes on to compliment the staff and mine host at the Langney Sports Centre "where the plates get bigger and the food even more filling, much better than 'The Grand' where we had so many knives and forks we didn't know what to do with them!" JC then praises John Miles the team sponsor and Les for "producing the best programme[2] in the

[2] It is worth pausing to acknowledge the contribution of the club's Press Officer, Kevin Ling, who supplies much of the copy for the programme and the match reports for the official website. Without his dedication and effort, along that of Programme Editor Mick Corby, along with many others who also contribute material, no matter how sublime the skills in layout, design, format etc are at the printers, then the 2005 programme couldn't have won this prestigious award for "best programme". Harrods would still be an impressive shop without any goods inside it, but with them it can really shine.

League" before he notes approvingly, "fully sponsored as well!" It's an obsession peculiar to speedway, the compulsive focus on the relative quality of your team's programme in comparison to your rivals. Quite why is all a bit of mystery to me, other than maybe all the concentration required to constantly fill out your race card during a meeting leads fans across the country to develop a strong attachment for their particular version of the thing over time? JC welcomes Edward Kennett to tonight's proceedings, clearly delighted to have him there despite the fact that he rode for the "enemy" in the form of Poole this season. JC notes, "it's nice to see he's recovered from his illness", which I understood as an allusion to his riding this season at Poole. JC then gets the first raucous laugh of the evening when he repeats a quite clever and topical speedway in-joke. "Edward was on the phone when he was eating, he said he was calling Matt Ford to have his plate measured". They say that if you have to explain a joke, it can't have been that good in the first place, so I'll not bother to do so and just imagine you have already laughed like I did.

First up on stage for his turn on the mike is co-team manager, Trevor Geer, introduced by JC as "a man of many words, he means well though I always have to fill his programme out for him; sadly we won't be able to get him off the mike with his boring stories". Trevor then chooses his rather eccentric highlight of the season, "last night was brilliant – I wasn't there as I was working late in the office!" He then briefly wanders down memory lane, "we had good teams back in the 70s, but this one gets on just as well together". Trevor characterises David as "one of the oldest ones here" and Deano as similar to himself in that he's "a man of many words".

KC flourishes the microphone with casual insouciance but professional élan in a manner that says, "this is the tool of my trade and look how comfortable I am with it", as he invites up "the boys who have thrilled us from March to last night". Davey Watt, "very candid usually" according to KC in his preamble, is the first of the riders to speak. Continuing from where he left off when I spoke with him in the toilets, he reiterates his theme that "I'm so pleased it's over, I didn't care any more and I'd just had enough of riding".

This is too honest, even for KC with his renowned love of candour, who interjects and immediately reveals the true fan with a keen eye for detail and a tendency to anarokishness that he really is, "you're nuts; that fourth bend is yours".

Not quite sure of the appropriate response, Davey mumbles "well, thank you" before he composes himself for more brutal honesty. "My crash did a bit too much damage, though early on I was beating all the big guys; it confused me a bit and I didn't quite know what to do next? Also at the start of the year, I didn't get on well with Deano – I hated him! – we had a few bust ups but now we get on great".

He thanks JC "for giving me a job" and Trevor "for the three meetings he's attended this year". Almost believably Davey publicly hopes that he'll be invited back next year though "I tapered off a lot at the end which was unfortunate. I've been tired and sore, blah blah. If I bitch and moan no-one will care". With that he returns to his fiancée at the nearby table while KC turns to JC saying "2006?" which, tellingly, gets no reply.

Instead, JC smoothly shares the MC duties and says "I'd like to invite up my favourite rider – no it's not you, Deano. He was truly inspiring last year and next year, he's a mate of mine, David Norris". Floppy immediately launches into song with a rendition of 'My Way' that starts with the verse "and now the end is near and I face the final curtain" before he builds to a finale of "I did it my way". It's a performance more suited to the privacy of the shower than the Dinner Dance but the chutzpa to attempt such a bravura display says it all about him really. Floppy has perfected the shield of a public persona that is always pointed and acerbic, though it has to be said that he is happy to treads over the fine line that separates the caustically sarcastic from the rudely belligerent. The consensus tonight and around Eastbourne definitely falls on 'the funny guy with a great sarcastic sense of humour' side of the equation, and those who hold other opinions of Floppy's humour as 'not quite getting it'. I personally enjoy the charade he's perfected of appearing brittle and hypersensitive to criticism and his bravado in self-consciously affecting not to give a stuff. Tonight, we're treated to the quick-fire wit of the affectionate and rebellious Floppy. Confident in this company and in the love of the people that surround him, Floppy gives full reign to his grumpy and terse alter ego, though he still knows that the audience, his family, and friends know him for who he is, not merely for this persona or his considerable speedway experience and achievements. Luckily we don't get the chance to beatify him or have Woody Allen sign him up for his next movie. Instead, in response to KC's trademark gentle "tell us about your season" question, we get treated to the following:

[Floppy]   "Swindon – I just fell off and you know the rest"
[KC]   "And?"
[Floppy disdainfully] "You pay my wages, that's why you can get away with it or you'd be out on your ear! We didn't win nuffin' so that's it… 2006 get fit. My favourite colour is blue and for Christmas I want a tree."

[KC] "Isn't that irritation sweet?"
[Floppy] "Rider of the year is Nicki Pedersen – I'm under contract. You only have one more question."
[KC rather nervously] "Um, I love it, fantastic!"
[Floppy] "With the team something was missing – I don't know what it was…"

And then with that he promptly departs the slightly raised dance floor back to his table, completely done with the KC interview.

JC then announces, "next is someone who's been far more of a prolific scorer than expected [brief pause for comic effect] – sit down, Deano – and has been fashionably late for two of these dos so far: Andrew Moore". JC continues, "In the pits you always have Nicki stretching, David doing windmills with his arms, and Andrew snoring in a chair".

Apparently adopting the *Noh* philosophy of life and drama[3], even at this relaxed event, Andrew totally refuses to mystify his "work" or accept his exalted "speedway rider" status.

"I really can't get excited about speedway, it's four laps, tapes up, it's not exciting". This is spoken in a quiet but bluff, slightly indeterminate regional accent, part Yorkshire, part Lincolnshire perhaps, that provokes Floppy to yell, "Where's your interpreter?" Honestly straightforward throughout, Andrew categorically asserts that he wants to remain in the Elite League rather than ever try his luck again in the Premier League. He sums his season up in the briefest fashion, "I liked some of it and I just want to come back", despite a weekly journey to Eastbourne that is arduous and takes five hours in each direction. He welcomes the "unreal support" from the fans, though he admits, "some of the emails aren't so nice, but at least it's not hate mail".

KC tries to elicit some further information by asking, "What did you think of last night's meeting?" Nonetheless it baffles Andrew: "last night, where were we? Um, don't ask me any technical questions – scores, standings, averages – I just don't know!" he passes on a "big thanks" and a bunch of flowers to the club physio Jayne and praises the unstinting support of her partner and his mechanic Ashley "who's been absolutely fantastic and never asked for anything". He praises Turner Engineering for giving him somewhere to stay before KC reveals that Andrew has to work during each winter to make ends meet after his packed summer of speedway meetings. He's off to spend the winter as a cake packer for Mr Kipling of the 'exceedingly good cakes' fame, but not before he's had a night on the town with his mates in Brighton.

At this point, while Mr Kipling might create delightful comestibles we've been pretty crap about something – namely the Eagles other reserve rider for most of the season, Steen Jensen. Did we think to invite him? Or make the point that we really wanted him to be here? It is suddenly very noticeable that we're missing two Danes tonight – Nicki, obviously, but also Steen who, by rights, we really should have adopted and taken into our hearts, as a gallant loser or inveterate trailer behind in races, much more than we have since he so clearly embodies so many English values, especially the admiration of the perpetual failure bits that

[3] The term *Noh* itself is a Buddhist term, which refers to the mental bond between the performers and the audience.

we often as a nation traditionally pride ourselves on. It would, also, have been the Eastbourne way. Though Steen looks the part, is acclaimed as "our Arena track specialist", means well, promised much and has made sacrifices – often just to desperately try and adapt to a strange life in a strange country living in a caravan on the Isle of Wight – something has gone fatally awry. For some unfathomable reason he just hasn't cut the mustard and we've abandoned him to his fate. I feel bad for sometimes taking the mickey in this book (sorry, Steen) now that I realise that he's not here. Maybe he's off enjoying himself properly somewhere back home rather than feeling rejected by our insularity. Or, maybe he doesn't feel rejected but disappointed in himself. Strangely, he's so much of a consistent loser, we could have celebrated and gloried in this fact more, but somehow we were embarrassed enough, both as a club and as the fans, to sometimes shun him. Even at the Dinner Dance, if we'd laughed at him here it might have made it alright again, even though we know he won't become the star speedway rider he'd aspire to be. Hmm. It doesn't make you all warm and fluffy to recall on this warmest and fluffiest of Eagles nights. Wasn't it Cliff Richard that remarked "these miss-you nights are the longest"? He did, actually, but it has no relation to what I'm talking about with regards to Steen's treatment, so it's lucky that everyone was awash with alcohol, laughter and that the only real looker in the team was about to take the stage.

Next up is Deano, whom JC describes as "having a unique way of keeping everyone happy". With heavy irony, Deano not so obliquely refers to his chequered past, particularly in Thurrock – though it was only chequered in terms of his relationship with Ronnie Russell and the Arena fans rather than seeing the actual flag waved that often for first place – a one year spell at Arena Essex ("a superb club") last season before he returned to the Eagles fold (or perch?) this season.

The banter went as follows. KC with his cut-glass Sussex County accent and Deano wiv 'is Nyyice Lundun one:
[Deano]   "E got rid of me after we'd done a deal, I was out the door so I won't go into that".
[KC]   "You exceeded expectations as team captain."
[Deano]   "I dunno, obviously I was better than David. To be honest I don't really give a monkey's who knocks me. I'm here to do a job, well, Colin's done all the work, to be honest, I've done shit all."
[Floppy interrupting] "Who's slated you?"
[Deano]   "You was the one that told me about it, Hackett or summat? To be honest there's been a fair few of them. I put a bit more effort into it, not a lot, mind. I can't help it but I did try more! People say 'he's a good second string' though I wanna do better. I gotta fank PT for doing all the drivin' when I was a little bit drunk on the way home – which was only once this year… the most pleasing thing of the year was when his [Davey Watt's] engine blew up, it was well over size; it was so big I was gunna pay for an inspection myself, but then he had to join the rest of us on a normal engine after all."

Deano then ranges widely in his speech. He alleges JC wears hair lacquer to hide his greying locks, and that he can't wait for a real event of celebration as he has "a big party tomorrow night" but refuses to divulge the location as it's "secret" and "I'm really going to let my hair down". The audience boggles at the licentious depravity that will be a party *chez* Barker or a *soirée* organised under the guidance of a Deano unencumbered by the need to remain on the straight and narrow like he will do tonight and has had to do during the season!

As if it wasn't an already unenviable task to follow Deano, the next rider up personifies an unemotional and taciturn approach to life as well as to Dinner Dance speeches. The MCs have no choice but to openly acknowledge the possible boredom or blandness issue as JC warns "hold onto your hats, he'll be as exciting as normal" and KC more elegantly notes, "he lets his racing do the talking". It's only a shame that the bike doesn't get up and do the honours instead. Adam Shields immediately concedes the season "had its moments" before he startlingly reveals to a stunned audience the insight that, "I'm racing a speedway bike for a living". Not that he's without a hint of a very dry sense of humour."I've been on the track more than I've stayed on the bike, so should have had more injuries than I've had". Adam intends to return home to Australia, to recharge his batteries, and to come back refreshed for an even better season next season. KC, as he has done intermittently throughout the season at Arlington, doesn't hesitate to trot out something we all already know, namely that Adam is "the only speedway rider with his own speedway track in the garden". While we once again all boggle our minds and try to imagine the size of the garden or the track, never mind, pondering if should still be technically called a "garden", JC announces the 'Rider of the Season'. Unsurprisingly, the award goes to Nicki who JC notes, "is one of the best three riders in the world; he's only dropped a few points and is becoming a legend at Eastbourne – it's been an honour and a privilege to see someone like him!" Not that we do see him as he's back home in Denmark. JC had already eliminated all possible suspense over this award for the Pedersen household and thereby obviated the need for a satellite link up to the Langney Sports Centre complex since he presented Nicki with the trophy the previous night, when he gave him a lift to Gatwick Airport. We're not told the exact details of the presentation, whether this was presented in a moving kerbside ceremony at Gatwick North or South Terminal or even if there's a trophy! Instead, JC reminds everyone that there's "plenty of dancing and drinking to be done" before he alludes to a similar Dinner Dance event also being held tonight but this time in King's Lynn "where they're all sitting round deciding how to divide the carrot!" The presentations close with JC in upbeat mood: "This is the team that should have won something this season and next season we'll make sure we do!"

With that it's a signal for the dancing to start, as some gamine ladies take to the floor and pretty well everyone else crowds to the bar for more drinks. The riders mingle with the fans. Davey Watt is surrounded with friends and admirers while Floppy and Deano chat together at the bar. Deano's friend, Scott something or other, who legendarily went out with Jordan in the dim and distant mists of time[4], holds forth at the bar. There's quite a gaggle of pleasantly attractive, animatedly laughing young ladies in tiny dresses and more notable *décolletage*, including one with an astonishingly short skirt and big hair. Mooro and Geernob are deep in conversation, apparently oblivious to the raucous laughter and banter that surrounds them.[5] I chat with the charming Ashley, a real enthusiast for people and motorcycling about the season just past. He's a great believer in the spirit of motorcycling, having competed for 20 years himself in many different motorcycle disciplines to that of speedway. He lays great store by the ethos of "people doing things because they love bikes" and relishes the camaraderie among motorcyclists everywhere. He's come to Eastbourne speedway as "an outsider" and is eager to highlight that there's much more to Deano that he affects to pretend or that his reputation would have you believe. "Though before I never rated Deano, I've watched him in the pits all season and just having him in the team and about the place is worth at least five points a meeting". He's the "real deal" and has been strongly infected by the spirit of motorcycling Ashley loves, "he's one of those trying to do things, sometimes crazy things, but he's something special".

Just as I leave the club, a crowd of ageing men gossip in the toilets while outside in the corridor Floppy and Deano pay very close attention to some ladies there with them. No doubt, Deano's still trying to play to the crowd with the things they expect or for which he's renowned, but as the entrance doors swing shut I hear Floppy plaintively say: "But I think you look really attractive, too!"

---

[4] And apparently also Jodie Marsh, quite a combination by any measurable standard and a testament to his persuasiveness, charm and, probably, his wallet. The *News of the World* habitually refers to him as "millionaire's son Scott Sullivan". I had heard on the grapevine that Deano was once sponsored by Jordan and was even mentioned by her in her book written under her real name, Katie Price, called *Being Jordan: My Autobiography*. Trying to read this in WH Smith's proved fruitless and so, in the interests of research, I bought the book. Mentions of Deano in this book are, I believe, an urban myth since I haven't found any, although there isn't an index to be absolutely sure. I haven't had the inclination to look into the story that Deano was often pictured in the background in Australia when Scott went out there to be publicly dumped for Peter Andre after the 2003 version of *I'm a Celebrity, Get Me Out Of Here!* Scott comes across well in the book though for the exact details you'll have to go to WH Smith's and read chapter 33 'Lover Boy'. We all have our brushes with fame or, in this case, Jordan. I sometimes see her at Tesco's. She used to live upstairs in the same building I did at Lawrence Moorings in Sawbridgeworth when she went out with Warren aka her Gladiator Ace. It is now a town made famous by the Beckhams. Ace never looked happy, particularly whenever I saw them together. They had a big dog and big cars to match as well as a ghastly looking sports car that sounded throatier than it looked.

[5] When I spoke with Geernob a few days later at the *Brighton Bonanza*, he sincerely praised many of the people that he worked with. He holds Floppy, Nicki, Joonas Kylmakorpi, Jon Cook, Mark Loram and Deano, who he lived with when we spoke. Geernob mused, "Deano, I live with him so I know, that if he got it right in his head, if he really believed, he'd be brilliant – he's great now for his age with a seven average at 35 years old and still regularly pulling 19 year olds!" Maybe if the powers that be in the sport were to adopt the theme of this comment as slogan ('*Become a speedway rider and pull a 19 year old every year of your life until you're 40 or retire*'?) there would be many more youngsters only to keen to try out for a long career in speedway, but would do so in preference to practically ever other career option!

Looking back on the season with the benefit of hindsight is a luxury we can never have when caught up in the maelstrom of the campaign. The *Speedway Star* luxuriates every winter in a detailed summary of every league club's recent campaign. The regular reporter on the Eagles, gifted writer and expert summariser, Paul Watson, covered all the events and alluded to all the machinations and minutiae in his usual trademark style honed over 40 years as a journalist. Throughout the season he provided numerous insights that I have included in some of the preceding reports and after the season had finished, he caught Jon Cook in an expansive and descriptive mood. Some of Jon's reported quotes and thoughts on the performance of the riders and the club overall adds further depth and insight to my own account in this book.

The season started with a team that the management expected to challenge for honours. As ever with the Eagles, there was a great measure of stability as Nicki, Floppy, Shieldsy and Mooro all returned. Deano came back from his sabbatical year at Arena, the club landed their long-term target Watty, while Adam Allott and a 'great prospect for the future' Steen Jensen were to share the other (reserve) slot in the team.

Looking back on the 2005 campaign, Mooro was to be our only ever-present rider. It seemed every other rider, at some point, had their own issues to fight. With some understatement Jon Cook noted after the season had finished, "when you review where we were then to where we are now, the plan did not go particularly well".

The injury to Floppy has been well documented. "David gave it his best and tried to get through a very nasty injury. He did what he thought was best for the team and what I thought was best. Perhaps we are both guilty of caring too much for the Eagles. If we had looked at it a little bit more objectively we would not have tried so many comebacks. I don't criticise him and he doesn't criticise me. We did what we thought was the best."

Another rider to have his season interrupted by injury was Shieldsy, who otherwise would have enjoyed another year of marked improvement on the track. "Against a backdrop of injuries for an unspecified length of time it was so fantastic from a promoter's perspective to speak to a rider who was so determined to get back absolutely as quickly as he could. From a team perspective to see someone go to that extreme and those lengths to ride through the pain barrier [at Peterborough] was a real season highlight. And to see someone that had struggled so badly and been a pale shadow of the rider we had known to come back and do that was a season high for me. Adam really does his talking on the track; he is a quiet lad and very likeable".

Everything that could be said has been said about Nicki, and Jon left it at that. Despite the calls placed on his time by his Grand Prix commitments, he was still a talismanic and committed team member who was really missed when the club struggled to adequately replace him, though Mark Loram often performed well, when fixtures clashed with the GP.

Deano showed the Arena fans what they were missing, "I think he was second highest bonus points scorer in the Elite League and that affects his average. I think his average this year is much the same as last year at Arena but I think if you take the bonus points into consideration he outscored his Arena average by over a point. It shows he is back in the right direction. He took the captaincy over with a smile on his face and that transferred to other members of the team and to the terraces".

Events at Monmore Green got mentioned in an aside, "we had the incident at Wolverhampton which resulted in some of their security staff being banned from speedway" before they were placed back under the carpet. The results of the subsequent SCB investigation into that meeting wasn't alluded to at all, while Steen's place and contribution to the team during the 2005 season were completely airbrushed from history. Even the ever-diplomatic Paul Watson only notes "Jensen wasn't on the pace" and JC, very noticeably, went on to offer in-

depth comments on everyone else who occupied the No. 7 berth – Adam Allott, Richard Hall, Ulrich Ostergaard, Oliver Allen, Trevor Harding, Joel Parsons, Cameron Woodward and Troy Batchelor. Basically everyone who wore an Eagles race jacket except Steen. There was no doubting this was, along with other injuries to the team that are part and parcel of the sport, our Achilles' heel. Often it appeared that the club must have run over a black cat or had hung an albatross around its own neck. JC wryly noted that injuries afflicted riders so much that, "if you are a young Australian and Eastbourne phone you and say 'do you want to appear as our No 7', you have to turn it down as quickly as you can". Overall, you couldn't imagine the run of misfortune endured by the many men who rode in this position for Eastbourne.

The club patiently persevered with Mooro after a poor start, when he struggled to regain the promising form he demonstrated the previous year before his bad leg injury. "Two months into the season my phone was ringing off the wall with Premier League promoters asking when he would be available, assuming we would not be sticking by him. There was never a doubt in my mind that we would be sticking with him. We had made a plan and to be fair to Andrew he never once questioned whether he was in the right league".

Davey Watt started the season as the best reserve rider in the Elite League and was, for a couple of months, arguably one of the best to have anywhere in any team, if based on his initial high-scoring displays. "His season was simply stunning; some incredible performances when he was down at reserve. Double figure scores were expected of him after the first month or so. He never let us down. Even when he moved into the main body of the team, he kept that going until he was the innocent victim of a crash at home against Oxford when he was hit from behind and that put him out for a while." This injury along with his blown "number one" engine meant that from then on he struggled to regain his earlier superlative form, though he did enjoy a resurgence and his own Indian summer in August. Jon noted in a matter of fact but subtly coded fashion, "it was only when September came that his form tailed off. That was a great shame for Davey because in the last two months he didn't do himself justice and it has undermined him from the fans' perspective; in speedway memory is short. Over the course of the year he has had a season to be proud of. It was a shame he did not carry through right to the end. It was a long season and I think Davey felt that more than most. But to go from a three-point rider to the Australian World Cup team inside four months was a fantastic achievement".

Before the season started the club would have probably accepted our nearly but just not quite achievements:
Air Tek Challenge – won!
Knockout Cup – lost in final
Elite League – lost in semi-final play off
Craven Shield – second in final
South Coast Trophy – won!

Jon reflects on our "nearly season" positively. It not only provides a good base for the next season's campaign (!), but without any silverware for the trophy cabinet, JC noted, "you would say we didn't have a very good season. But I think we had a pretty stunning season. We were in everything until the very last race of the season. To even qualify for the play-offs was a major achievement and that was an achievement six other teams did not make. We made the cup final and in the second leg at Belle Vue, against the best team in the land, man-for-man, we gave them a scare and, of course, the Craven Shield went to the very last race".

To understand the next bit you need to well trained at the University of Speedway to fully grasp the complex use of the terminology. "Summing up, I would say it was a *nearly* season. We were nearly good enough, but we were not quite good enough. Mainly because we had an injury to a ten-point rider which made him a seven-point rider when he was able to ride and his allowed rider replacement was generally as good as a seven-point rider. We had three points missing there and we had a third heat leader [Shields] who, over the course of the season, didn't do the job, although he did towards the end of the year. We had a team that as a whole could have performed a little bit better than they did, but still rode to a standard that would have been acceptable to most other teams in the league".

Some Brief Statistics and Random Facts

MICHAEL DONAGHY
"The machinery of grace is always simple"

Nicki Pedersen
31 matches, 160 rides, 7 maximums, 5 bonus points, 110 heat wins, 3 lasts and 4 exclusions for a 10.30 average

David Michael Norris
25 matches, 112 rides, 2 paid maximums, 12 bonus points, 34 wins, 13 lasts and 2 exclusions for a 7.75 average

David John Watt
39 matches, 211 rides, 1 maximum, 37 bonus points, 57 wins, 40 lasts, 3 exclusions for a 7.22 average

Adam Matthew Shields
38 matches, 189 rides, 32 bonus points, 49 wins, 31 lasts, 5 exclusions for a 7.11 average

Dean Barker
40 matches, 183 rides, 59 bonus points, 17 wins, 33 lasts, 2 exclusions for a 6.45 average

Andrew David Moore
43 matches, 191 rides, 40 bonus points, 17 wins, 78 lasts, 2 exclusions for a 4.65 average

Steen Jensen
14 matches, 50 rides, 32 points (including 5 bonus points), 2 wins, 5 seconds, 11 thirds, 31 lasts for a 2.56 average

Jon Cook
No matches, two rides, numerous ribald comments from Kevin 'KC' Coombes

Afterword

Well, there you are. That wasn't so bad. You have finished the end of the companion book to *Showered in Shale*. If this was a cartoon character, this book is much more Benny to the previous one's Top Cat. Both were researched at the same time, but after that, the real trick is to write these things down. They have ended up being different books, both from the same family but with their own distinct, quirky, and unique personalities. In my ideal world, I would have published this book earlier, but then, as I'm not a machine, managing a book's writing and production requires a lot of effort, coordination, and much help from others. So while some information here has inevitably become dated and all these fixtures now happened some while ago, I think there's still a certain benefit and pleasure to recall what I saw, thought, read in the *Speedway Star* or online and heard that season that endures far beyond the winter months immediately afterwards. In fact, with my pretentious hat on, I like to think that this book has value as a personal history and part of the social historical record.

Laying aside my pretentious hat, I must stress again that I have the utmost respect for any rider of any team who risks life and limb for the purposes of our entertainment at the speedway track. They are all "handlebar heroes". Having watched them so often, this obviously applies to the many characters that make up the Eagles team in 2005 and the future!

Following any team in any sport is fraught with elation and sloughs of despond if you are a fan. People like to occasionally complain but mostly, still pathologically return for some more services in their chosen temple of worship. Based in Brighton, it has been a delight to adopt and follow my local team, the Eastbourne Eagles. I am fortunate indeed. My account of them and the 2005 season is necessarily personal, partial and subjective. Impressions often take the place of 'facts'. Obviously all mistakes remain my own. My intention hasn't been to upset anyone at Eastbourne speedway or elsewhere with what, after all, is something that fundamentally is intended only for light relief. If you have any comments, of either persuasion, please get in touch via my website on www.methanolpress.com

This isn't the last of my speedway endeavours as, apart from my Blog on my website, there will also be a book of photographs on the launch pad shortly.

Every effort has been made to get in touch with all copyright holders and many people featured in the photos in this book but, again, I would be delighted to hear from you to make the appropriate credits or acknowledgements.

I mentioned earlier that I have been overwhelmed with help, advice and kindness as I researched my books. I hesitate to name everyone as, inevitably, I will make a mistake and miss someone off that I'm extremely grateful to. So, with apologies for those I do manage to miss out I would like to thank the following people for their help, advice or thoughts on this book, notably: Peter Adams, John Barber, Nick Barber, Dean Barker, Robert Bamford, Kevin 'KC' Coombes, Martin Dadswell, Gordie Day, Steve and Debbie Dixon, Kevin Donovan, Dave Fairbrother, Chris 'Geernob' Geer, Trevor Geer, Mick Gregory, Andy Griggs, Tim Hamblin, Dave Hoggart, John Louis, Ian Maclean, Neil Machin, Colin Pratt, Dave 'The Rat' Rattenberry, Ronnie Russell, Trevor Swales, Peter Toogood, Ian Thomas, Chris Van Stratton, Neil Watson, Paul Watson, Nigel Wagstaff, Alf Weedon, Michael Whawell and Tom Woolhead.

There are, of course, the always welcoming group of Eagles fans it's a real pleasure to stand with by board number 51 at Arlington – the Hazeldens (John, Judy, Mark, Karen, Billy and Jordan), the Rices (also keen Elvis fans, Dave and Margaret) and Jane Rogers – who're always committed to the Eastbourne cause and a rich source of comment, analysis and gossip.

To pick out anyone in particular would be invidious. However, I again owe so many 'thank you's' that it would be ungrateful not to do so. The book wouldn't look as lovely as it does without Rachael Adams's brilliant design and artistic skills, along with her persistence as well as her intransigence. There would be many more errors than there still are without the diligence, questioning and proofreading of

Caroline Tidmarsh. I am also indebted to the proofreading, advice and encouragement I have received from the always watchful Billy Jenkins, who has dedicatedly read this with enthusiasm and his perceptive 'speedway eye'. Among other things, Graham Russel has shown tremendous pedantry and knowledge to wrangle with my words and put them into some sort of sense. Before Graham even got to manfully struggle with the manuscript, the gifted but still playful Michael Payne had suffered tremendously as my editor, critic and mentor, so without him there would be no book, never mind an even vaguely coherent one. Steve Dixon and Jules Martin have been my kind but skilled photographic advisers and provide the stunning photographs on the cover of this book. I have been grateful for the advice and enthusiasm of the always enthusiastic and friendly 'Scary' Sheila Le-Sage. I am also particularly grateful to Jon Cook who has been consistently supportive and who read the various versions of the book thoroughly, with a skill that wouldn't disgrace a literary critic. Once more I have received help from the kindly, conscientious and informative SCB Referee, Chris Durno, as well as some advice from his colleague on the buttons the quiet, modest but always perceptive Chris Gay.

Anne Brodrick has encouraged me for years to write and has shown much perspicacity in many things. Even more insightful, my true friend Sue Young has encouraged me often in so many endeavours and really saved me when I needed that most – for which she has my eternal gratitude. Of course, without the love and guidance of my parents – Mary and Alan – none of this book or so many other things would have been possible. I would never have become a speedway fan without the kind help of Newcastle supporter, George Grant. He faithfully, all those years ago - as regular as clockwork - took me some distance in his car to Smallmead every Monday night, particularly impressive when he didn't even really know me or my family (he was the husband of a friend of my mum's friend). A very kind gesture that, in one action, typifies speedway and the people you find there. Last but not least, you can never have too many teachers and I was lucky enough to be inspired to write by a truly great teacher, poet, musician and funny bloke – Michael Donaghy. (It would have doubtless already have amused Michael many times before in the past that the spell check insists his name is Dinghy. Then, thinking about it, though no longer alive, he has helped me get from one place to another much more positive one with the help of my writing.) A book on any subject would have satisfied an element of Michael's perpetual curiosity! And it turns out not to be a book of poetry but yet another speedway one. He was sadly taken away from this life prematurely but not before he had touched so many different people.

By the way, if you enjoyed this book and haven't read *Showered in Shale* yet, please don't hesitate to treat yourself.

Finally, if you go to speedway already, why not make it a point to take even more friends this year, and if you haven't been for a while or have never been, now's as good a time as any to start!

This season in the slipstream of the Eagles promised so much, delivered lots – some of it unexpected – but it was never dull; but then that's Arlington and that's definitely speedway!

Thank you for getting this far.

2nd October 2006
Brighton

Acknowledgements

Books and magazines
I have quoted with kind permission from the following sources:

Speedway Star (2005) For subscriptions call 0208 335 1113
Dances Learned Last Night - Poems 1975 -1995 by Michael Donaghy (Picador, 2000)

I also enjoyed these books:
Wheels and Deals by Ian Thomas (Pinegen, 2005) For orders call 0208 335 1113
10th yer Baws! By Gary Lough (2004) For orders call 07718 909343
A Ref's Tale by Dave Osborne (2005) <ozzymike0412@hotmail.com>

Photographers
Steve Dixon <www.stevedixonphotography.co.uk>
Julie Martin <www.juliemartinphotography.co.uk>

Designer
Rachael Adams <www.scrutineer.co.uk>

2005 Fixtures Covered in this Book

16th March	Arena v Eastbourne (AT Challenge) 53-37
19th March	Eastbourne v Arena (AT Challenge) 57-36
25th March	Poole v Eastbourne (ELA) 50-44
30th March	Peterborough v Eastbourne (ELA) postponed
25th March	Eastbourne v. Poole (ELA) 44-46
2nd April	Eastbourne v Peterborough (ELA) 51-40
7th April	Oxford v Eastbourne (ELA) postponed
9th April	Eastbourne v Oxford (ELA) 55-39
16th April	Eastbourne v. Ipswich (ELA) 48-45
21st April	Ipswich v Eastbourne (ELA) 41-50
28th April	Swindon v Eastbourne (ELA) 48-44
2nd May	Wolves v Eastbourne (ELA) 46-47
7th May	Eastbourne v Swindon (ELA) 56-40
13th May	Peterborough v Eastbourne (KO Cup) 56-37
16th May	Eastbourne v Ipswich (ELB) 1-5 abandoned
21st May	Eastbourne v Peterborough (KO Cup) 59-36
23rd May	Coventry v Eastbourne (ELA) 52-41
25th May	Arena Essex v Eastbourne (ELA) 43-47
4th June	Eastbourne v Poole (ELB) 46-44
18th June	Eastbourne v Arena Essex (ELA) 52-42
22nd June	Poole v Eastbourne (ELB) 50-40
23rd June	Ipswich v Eastbourne (ELB) 55-38
27th June	Eastbourne v Belle Vue (ELA) 53-37
29th June	Peterborough v Eastbourne (ELA) postponed rain
1st July	Coventry v Eastbourne (ELB) 14-4 (abandoned)
2nd July	Eastbourne v Coventry (ELA) 42-51
4th July	Peterborough v Eastbourne (ELA) postponed rain
11th July	Eastbourne v Peterborough (ELB) 48-42
16th July	Eastbourne v Oxford (ELB) 57-35
18th July	Wolverhampton v Eastbourne (ELB) 49-41
23rd July	Eastbourne v Arena (KO Cup) 55-40
30th July	Eastbourne v Swindon (ELB) 55-39
8th August	Eastbourne v Ipswich (ELB) 58-38
12th August	Eastbourne v Wolves (ELB) 49-41
20th August	Eastbourne v Belle Vue (ELB) 46-43
22nd August	Belle Vue v Eastbourne (ELB) 59-35
25th August	Oxford v Eastbourne (ELA) 50-41

27th August	Eastbourne v Arena (ELB) 56-37
1st September	Peterborough v Eastbourne (ELA) 62-31
1st September	Peterborough v Eastbourne (ELB) 52-43
3rd September	Eastbourne v Coventry (ELB) 43-46
5th September	Oxford v Eastbourne (ELB) 49-41
7th September	Arena v Eastbourne (ELB) 43-47
8th September	Coventry v Eastbourne (ELB) 58-37
12th September	Belle Vue v Eastbourne EL Play Off Semi Final) 53-40
21st September	Arena Essex v Eastbourne (KO Cup) 52-41
24th September	Eastbourne v Poole (Challenge) 2-1 (or 52-40 in old money)
1st October	Eastbourne v Belle Vue (KO Cup Final, 1st Leg) 46-44
3rd October	Belle Vue v Eastbourne (KO Cup Final, 2nd Leg) 53-37
8th October	Eastbourne v Belle Vue v Oxford (Craven Shield Semi-Final, 1st Leg) 37-26-27
13th October	Oxford v Eastbourne v Belle Vue (Craven Shield Semi-Final, 2nd Leg) 42-34-32
17th October	Belle Vue v Eastbourne v Oxford(Craven Shield Semi-Final, 3rd Leg) 34-36-38 (aggregate 92-107-107)
22nd October	Eastbourne v Poole v Oxford (Craven Shield Final 1st Leg) 41-27-40
26th October	Poole v Oxford v Eastbourne (Craven Shield Final 2nd Leg) 35-39-34
27th October	Oxford v Eastbourne v Poole (Craven shield Final 3rd leg) 36-39-33 (aggregate 115-114-95)
28th October	Dinner Dance

Also Available from Methanol Press

Showered in Shale

One man's circuitous journey throughout the country in pursuit of an obsession – British Speedway

508 pages, 409 photos Paperback £20
Jeff Scott

Showered in Shale is a quirky book, it's different and off-the-wall... it should find its way onto any true speedway fan's book shelf.
Brian Burford, Speedway Star

What I regard as one of the most fascinating books I have come across since I saw my first speedway meeting at New Cross in 1946. It doesn't need fact files, historical facts and biographies to make it buzz.
John Hyam, South London Press

A fascinating book that holds up an illuminating mirror to both the sport and the community as a whole... simultaneously laugh out loud funny and hugely respectful. Highly recommended.
Tim Hamblin, Wolverhampton Express & Star

Scott's Homeric quest is to visit every track in the UK in one season and observe (and he certainly is a comprehensive recorder of the minutiae). The 'heroes' of the book and the medium through which the stories are told are third parties: the great, good and mostly spectacularly ordinary folk of British Speedway... you may like Jeff Scott's book or maybe not: you certainly shouldn't ignore it!
Derek Barclay, Keeping Track column

This book provides a unique behind the scenes look at the 2005 speedway season. The author travelled 10,000 miles, attended 70 meetings, & watched over 1,100 races. He has selected key meetings from his odyssey and created a fascinating speedway travelogue consisting of a cornucopia of historical, technical, sometimes whimsical information and impressions.
- Coverage of 30 British League tracks
- Quirky stories galore, the odd rant and captivating photos
- Plus exclusive interviews with: promoters, managers, riders, obsessive collectors, a vicar, photographers, referees, start girls &, most importantly, fans & aficionados of speedway!

£20 at all good track shops, order via paypal at www.methanolpress.com or send £24 cheque to cover P&P made payable to *J Scott* at Methanol Press, 2 Tidy Street, Brighton BN1 4EL

Printed in the United Kingdom
by Lightning Source UK Ltd.
116270UKS00001B/24